GREAT FORTUNE DREAM

Caitlin Press Inc.
8100 Alderwood Road, Halfmoon Bay, BC,
V0N 1Y1
www.caitlin-press.com

Text and cover design by Vici Johnstone
Edited by Catherine Edwards and Kathleen Fraser
Printed in Canada

Caitlin Press Inc. acknowledges financial support from the Government of Canada and the Canada Council for the Arts, and from the Province of British Columbia through the British Columbia Arts Council and the Book Publisher's Tax Credit. We would also like to thank The Peoples Publishing House of Beijing, China, for their generous support.

Canada Council for the Arts   Conseil des Arts du Canada   BRITISH COLUMBIA ARTS COUNCIL   经典中国国际出版工程

Library and Archives Canada Cataloguing in Publication

Lai, David Chuenyan, 1937-, author
    Great fortune dream : the struggles and triumphs of Chinese settlers in Canada, 1858-1966 / David Chuenyan Lai, Guo Ding.

Includes bibliographical references and index.

ISBN 978-1-987915-03-7 (paperback)

    1. Chinese—Canada—History. 2. Chinese Canadians—History. 3. Chinese—Canada—Social conditions. 4. Chinese Canadians—Social conditions. 5. Chinese—Government policy—Canada. 6. Canada—Emigration and immigration—Government policy. 7. Race discrimination—Canada. 8. Canada—Race relations. I. Guo, Ding, author II. Title.

FC106.C5C67 2015   971'.004951   C2015-904044-2

GREAT FORTUNE DREAM

THE STRUGGLES AND TRIUMPHS OF CHINESE SETTLERS IN CANADA, 1858–1966

DAVID CHUENYAN LAI
and
GUO DING

CAITLIN PRESS

*Dedicated to all Canadians whose
stories have not yet been told.*

Miss Koo-Yu-Ching dances to a Chinese orchestra, 1938. City of Vancouver Archives,
Port P824.

CONTENTS

ACKNOWLEDGEMENTS

The authors wish to thank Sarah Tang, MA, Beijing Foreign Studies University, and Liang He, MA, University of Warwick, for their initial translation of the Chinese text. Both of them are experienced translators. The authors also wish to extend their gratitude to Jia (Bobbie) Bao Heng for her hard work in reducing the Chinese volume, and proofreading and improving the initial rough translation. The authors also wish to thank the many Chinese community leaders who agreed to be interviewed and who provided research materials for the book. Thanks are also extended to the People's Publishing House, Beijing, who provided financial support for the translation through the Classic Chinese International Publication Program. Last but not the least, the two authors wish to deeply thank Vici Johnstone, Catherine Edwards, and Jia (Bobbie) Bao Heng for spending a great deal of time and effort even during the holiday season to complete this volume in time for spring 2016 publication.

David Chuenyan Lai
Guo Ding

PREFACE

❧

The history of Chinese immigration to Canada can be divided into two periods. From 1858 to 1966, the Chinese entering Canada experienced discrimination and segregation. After 1967, federal immigration policy shifted, allowing Chinese immigrants to enter Canada on the same basis as other immigrants. Canada also adopted its current policy of multiculturalism, responding to changing attitudes towards Asian immigrants, and enabling the Chinese to become integrated into the mainstream of Canadian society. This volume covers the first part of the Chinese experience in Canada.

This story of the Chinese in Canada reflects on and challenges the discrimination and negative stereotypes that plagued Chinese communities in Canada before 1967. The recent research into peoples' migration that inspired this book reassesses the policies and attitudes adopted by the host country, Canada, according to contemporary standards, contributing to a more profound analysis of the experiences of migrant people than has been the case in past historical studies. It is an interdisciplinary study that draws on history, geography, anthropology, and statistics to paint a comprehensive picture of Chinese experiences within mainstream Canadian society in the past, and to allow today's readers to appreciate the historically significant and valuable contributions the overseas Chinese made to the development of Canada. Interviews with the descendants of Chinese immigrants and both Chinese and English-language archival materials supplement and bring to life the experiences of the Chinese in this country.

A note here about the romanization of Chinese words: if there is an English romanization commonly in use, we have used that. If there is no widely accepted romanization, we have used the Pinyin system, which is in common use today. An example can be seen in the name of one of the authors. Lai Chuenyan is in common use, whereas the Pinyin system would romanize his name as Li Quanen. Since the latter has not been used in any of his publications, we used the commonly used romanization.

The book, originally written in Chinese by Dr. David Chuenyan Lai, Dingguo, and Jia Bao Heng, was published in 2013 by the People's Publishing House in Beijing. The present volume is an English translation of the abridged Chinese volume by David Chuenyan Lai and Dingguo, adapted for a Canadian readership.

Street vendors on Fisgard Street in Victoria, BC, 1898. City of Vancouver Archives, Str P351.1.

THE CHINESE JOURNEY

The Chinese people today represent the largest ethnic group in the world. The Chinese are also among the largest groups of migrants. In the early years of the twenty-first century, it is estimated that there are between forty-five and sixty million ethnic Chinese people living in 150 countries outside of China, Taiwan, Hong Kong, and Macau.[†] Although Chinese emigration to the outside world dates back more than two thousand years, it was only in the middle of the nineteenth century that mass migration of the Chinese began. This mass migration in the years from about 1850 to 1950 has come to be known as the Chinese diaspora—the dispersion of the Chinese from their homeland. Some of these migrating Chinese came to Canada; in 1961, there were fifty-eight thousand Chinese people living in Canada, and today more than 1.5 million people with Chinese ancestry make Canada their home.

After the nineteenth-century Opium Wars between Britain and China ended, the Chinese began to emigrate in large groups to North America, at first to San Francisco to take part in the California gold rush and later to Canada's west coast when gold was also discovered in British Columbia.[‡] Most of the Chinese who migrated to Canada came from Siyi (the Four Counties of Taishan, Xinhui, Kaiping, and Enping) and Sanyi (the Three Counties of Nanhai, Panyu, and Shunde) in the Zhujiang Delta (Pearl River Delta) in Guangdong Province. At this time, Hong Kong and Canton (Guangzhou) were the two cities with the strongest British presence. People in these cities learned about North America, and the rural people of the Pearl River Delta in turn learned about it from these city people. A chain migration process led to people from all the counties on the delta emigrating to North America.

[†] It is difficult to determine the exact number of overseas Chinese around the world. Estimates vary from forty-five to sixty million people. Many people with Chinese ancestry who have been naturalized in their country of residence are not recorded as Chinese, but are still considered to be overseas Chinese by the Overseas Chinese Bureau in Taiwan. In addition, undocumented Chinese immigrants may not be recorded in population statistics.

[‡] The first Opium War occurred between 1839 and 1842 and resulted in China ceding the island of Hong Kong to Britain and establishing treaty ports on mainland China to facilitate trade. The second Opium War from 1856 to 1860 was concerned with legalizing the opium trade, which Britain favoured. France was also involved in the second war.

A complex array of internal and external political, economic, societal, and historical factors caused Chinese emigration. In the Pearl River Delta region, there was simply not enough arable land to support the growing population. In the early years of Qing Dynasty rule—the Qing or Manchu Dynasty ruled China from 1644 to 1912—a thriving economy in both Sanyi and Siyi was sustained by such industries as iron smelting, textiles, sugar refining, silk reeling, and export porcelain manufacture. By the middle of the nineteenth century, the populations in Sanyi and Siyi had increased tremendously but the arable land, monopolized by a few landlords, was relatively scarce. Though Taishan County, for example, had an area of 4,600 square kilometres, only 400 square kilometres were arable. The county had a population of 500,000—meaning that 1,250 persons had to survive on food grown on just one square kilometre of arable land. In poor growing seasons, many people faced starvation.

Guangdong Province also suffered economically in the period that followed China's defeat in the two Opium Wars. At the time, rural people used copper coins, but silver was used in cities and for foreign trade. After the wars, copper currency was devalued and silver currency appreciated, greatly damaging the rural economy. Many craftspeople and merchants were pushed towards bankruptcy, and peasants working on the land became even more impoverished. In addition, with five ports forced by treaty to open for international trade, trade gradually increased in the port cities of Shanghai and Hong Kong, further weakening Guangzhou's economy.

An influx of foreign merchandise through these treaty ports caused traditional handicraft industries in the Pearl River Delta region to crumble. Many workers in the textile industry lost their jobs because of the newly available machine-made foreign cloth. The iron-smelting, steel, and oil-pressing industries were also negatively affected. Since the southeastern coastal region already had a dense population yet insufficient land, the decline of traditional industries meant a growing number of workers had to struggle harder to survive. Heavy taxation by the Manchu government was yet another burden that increased after the Opium Wars. Social conflicts intensified and poverty spread.

Invasion by British forces and exploitation by the Manchu government intensified conflicts in the Pearl River Delta region. Members of the Heaven and Earth Society started an uprising (also known as the Red Turban Revolt) in Guangdong Province against the Manchu government in 1854–56, which was jointly suppressed by the Manchu government and Western forces. The ensuing annihilation of insurgents forced large numbers of villagers from Guangdong and Fujian provinces to flee to Hong Kong, Macau, and Southeast Asia, causing a wave of Chinese emigration in the late 1850s. Furthermore, the Punti people, local residents of Guangdong Province, occupied the

Chinese miners washing for gold near North Bend, BC. City of Vancouver Archives, CVA 1376-375.24.

fertile land of the river deltas and lower plains whereas the Hakka people, who migrated to Guangdong Province from northern China, had to cultivate land on the less-fertile mountain slopes of the upstream parts of the rivers. The Punti people complained that the Hakka people used the upstream waters, leaving little water to flow down to the plains to water their crops. As a result, the two groups fought with each other for fourteen years. The Manchu government was unable to stop this civil conflict. By the 1860s, the economy in the Pearl River Delta region was on the brink of collapse. In order to survive, people from Sanyi and Siyi had to leave for other places to eke out a living.

When gold was found in California and later in Canada, a few Chinese individuals made great fortunes in the gold rushes and returned home as wealthy people. Many of the villagers in the Pearl River Delta who lived in very harsh subsistence conditions were inspired by this perceived opportunity to free themselves from poverty—and thousands of young men from Guangdong and Fujian provinces began to uproot themselves to make the trans-Pacific voyage to pursue their "great fortune dream" in Canada.

Part I

The Era of Free Entry, 1858–84

Ah Hoo was one of the first Chinese miners to go to the Omineca gold fields at the beginning of the gold rush in 1871. Courtesy of the Royal BC Museum and Archives, image I-58199.

An unidentified Chinese cook at Skeena River. City of Vancouver Archives, M-3-38.1.

Two Waves of Early Chinese Immigration

❦

The first Chinese to come to Canada arrived in the late eighteenth century. During the 1780s, European and American traders on the west coast of Canada engaged in trade with Chinese merchants in China to satisfy the demand there for luxury items such as sea otter fur. According to Captain John Meares's journal, the first Chinese people arrived on the western coast of Canada in the late eighteenth century. Captain Meares employed 120 Chinese blacksmiths and carpenters from Macau in 1788 and 1789 and brought them to Nootka Sound on Vancouver Island, where they helped build a fur-trading fort and the forty-ton *North West America*—the first ship of European design built on Canada's west coast. These Chinese labourers were not immigrants; rather, they were contracted artisans who expected to return to their homes in China when the work was finished. Chinese immigration to the west coast of Canada commenced almost a century later, in the mid-nineteenth century.

The Fraser River gold rush marked the first wave of early Chinese immigration to British Columbia, beginning in 1858. A second wave began in the early 1880s, when hundreds of Chinese labourers were recruited to help build the Canadian Pacific Railway that would connect the new province of British Columbia to the rest of Canada. Chinese gold miners and railway workers both made great contributions to the development of the frontier region of western Canada, and many gold-mining sites and the Canadian Pacific Railway line itself symbolize Chinese contributions to this nation.

Early Chinese Arrivals

The first Chinese people to emigrate to North America travelled to California during the gold rush there. Between 1848 and 1852, approximately twenty-five thousand immigrants from South China sailed across the Pacific Ocean to California in search of gold. After the gold rush there ended, many of the Chinese settled in San Francisco and Sacramento. Between 1855 and 1857, a team of California prospectors travelled north into Canada searching for more gold. In autumn 1857, they discovered it on sandbars in the

Fraser River near Fort Hope and Yale, two fur-trading posts that were established by the Hudson's Bay Company in 1848. News of their discovery immediately attracted an influx of people from near and far, marking the beginning of the Fraser River gold rush. The British government promptly established the colony of British Columbia on the mainland—the colony of Vancouver Island had been established a few years earlier—and began issuing licences to gold seekers.

Chinese merchants in San Francisco heard news of the discovery and sent a Chinese man, Ah Hong, to the lower Fraser River valley to investigate. Ah Hong returned to San Francisco in May 1858, confirming that gold had been discovered. These Chinese merchants in San Francisco immediately sent labourers by ship from California to British Columbia to look for gold. Very soon after, a large number of Chinese from the Pearl River Delta in Guangdong Province in China began the first wave of Chinese immigration to the British colonies of Vancouver Island and British Columbia, travelling via nearby Hong Kong, also a British colony at that time. The first group of 265 Chinese labourers (including one woman, the wife of a merchant) arrived in Victoria in April 1860 on a Norwegian boat.

The voyage across the Pacific was dangerous because of possible pirate attacks. The passengers were also often exploited by the ship's owner. He might promise one pound of rice per day for every four persons before embarking, but the rice would actually be shared by ten people once they were under way. If passengers had extra money, they could buy more rice from the ship's owner; those who were penniless suffered from hunger and often died of starvation. Not only that, the food they did have was mostly decayed and their diet was deficient in drinking water and fresh vegetables. The narrow cabins were filthy and poorly ventilated. Many people lost their lives on the long voyage to British Columbia.

Guangdong, located on China's southern coast, was the first Chinese province to open its port for trade with foreigners. Chinese people living in the Pearl River Delta therefore learned about the outside world earlier than residents of the interior mainland of China. Moreover, they had already developed a mature clan and county system with strong networks built on bonds of geography, family, and language. After some of the first emigrants returned with wealth to their home villages, they inspired more people from this region to make the hazardous trans-Pacific voyage to pursue their "great fortune dream" in western Canada.

The gold rush to the lower Fraser Valley in 1858 and 1859 was followed over the next few decades by a string of gold rushes at locations across British Columbia, of which the largest and most famous was the Cariboo gold rush of 1861–67. At the beginning of the gold rush period, most Chinese miners were sponsored by merchants who paid their way to British

Columbia. These miners repaid the merchants out of their wages. A smaller portion of these immigrants were supported by relatives or borrowed money from relatives to pay for their trip to British Columbia.

After landing in Victoria, those labourers who were supported by relatives or friends paid fifteen dollars to obtain what was called a free miner's certificate. Chinese labourers who had been recruited and sponsored by merchants would have to borrow money from them to buy the certificates and the clothing and equipment they needed. Loo Chuck Fan, Chang Tsoo, and other Chinese merchants from San Francisco housed the recruited labourers temporarily in wooden shacks on Cormorant Street in Victoria. After acquiring simple gold-panning tools, food, and clothing, the miners headed for the Fraser River and walked to the gold-mining sites. They dispersed in two main directions. One group ascended the Fraser River along the Cariboo Road and spread out across the northern frontier region; the other group followed the Dewdney Trail and spread out eastward to the Similkameen River, Rock Creek, and the Kootenay River.

Most of the Chinese gold seekers were young men, either unmarried or having left their wives and families in China. They worked long hours every day on the gold-bearing sandbars in the rivers. Sometimes, they had to remove rocks lying on top of the sand, which they piled neatly on top of each other. The other miners called the piles of rocks "Chinaman's walls" and they became significant landmarks identifying Chinese mining sites.

The gold-mining process was not slow, and individual sites were quickly exhausted. The first, non-Chinese gold seekers panned for gold in the sandbars and bottom flats along the lower Fraser Valley between Hope and Yale. As the gold in these sandbars came close to being exhausted, white miners abandoned their claims and moved upstream. The white miners did not wish the Chinese to prospect for gold ahead of them, so Chinese gold miners commonly followed in their wake and continued to mine the sandbars the white miners had abandoned. Chinese labourers started panning for gold at Hope, then moved along to Yale, and by 1860, many had moved up the Fraser River to Lillooet. Many also travelled along the Thompson River and dispersed to Kamloops on the upper Fraser River. Wherever gold was discovered, there were Chinese footprints—in Wells, Quesnelle Mouth, Quesnelle Forks, Lytton, and other mining towns.[†] Place names on the map of British Columbia today show where Chinese gold miners once lived: for

---

† During the gold rushes, Chinese miners discovered jade at many mining sites and they began to mine the mineral, a luxury item in China. At that time, the non-Chinese miners were ignorant of the value of jade and laughed at the Chinese for collecting the "green stones." The Chinese gold miners had serendipitously initiated the lucrative jade-mining industry in British Columbia.

example, the towns of Princeton, Lillooet, Robson, Osoyoos, Quesnel, and Port Alberni all have a China Creek.

Towards the end of the gold rush period, some Chinese miners in the Interior had saved enough money to buy mining companies owned by non-Chinese people. By 1875, there were more than thirty Chinese-owned gold-mining companies in the Cariboo. The four largest companies—Quong Lee, Dang Sing Dang, Sing Dang, and Loo Gee Wing—had an average annual yield of gold sand worth three hundred thousand dollars. In addition, a large gold mine called the Dancing Bill Co., which had previously been owned by non-Chinese people, was also taken over by overseas Chinese partners, and produced hundreds of thousands of dollars worth of gold in 1878.

Although most of the first Chinese immigrants came to Canada primarily to seek gold, there were also some who took up other occupations. The colonial government of British Columbia needed labourers to cut trails through the dense forests to develop the upper Fraser Valley. Since white people were fully engaged in the search for gold and had little interest in taking these back-breaking, low-paying jobs, the government came to rely on Chinese labourers to clear the dense bush and build trails and wagon roads. When the Douglas–Lillooet trail was widened in 1860, many Chinese labourers as well as First Nations people were employed. An undetermined number of these workers died of injuries or fell off the cliffs along the routes. Many Chinese workers were also employed to build the Dewdney Trail along the southern border of British Columbia from Hope to the Similkameen River.

Ken Yip, a Chinese Canadian, said that in the early 1870s, his grandfather, Ben Yip, came to British Columbia from Panyu County, Guangdong Province, at the age of sixteen and panned for gold in Wild Horse Creek at Fort Steele. Ben Yip's gold miner's certificate is still on display in the Fort Steele Museum. He was a free gold miner in a wild and isolated place that was very cold in winter, very unlike his warm home province in China. After a few years' hard work, he had managed to save some money. When Chinese labourers started building the railway in the Wild Horse Creek area, Ken's grandfather saw a new opportunity. He and a partner bought a farm there and grew vegetables to sell to the Chinese railway workers. Later, they opened a shop in the Wild Horse Creek Chinatown where they sold Chinese merchandise and dried food. They also ran a post office business handling mail for the Chinese railway labourers.

Other Chinese people found similar opportunities. In 1861, potatoes cost three cents a pound in Lillooet but were twenty-five cents in Quesnel in the upper Fraser River valley and as much as fifty cents a pound in the northern Cariboo region. Some Chinese people saw this as a business opportunity and began growing potatoes at Keithley Creek in the Cariboo—the beginning of Chinese agriculture on the northern frontier of the colony.

Chinese workers made a major contribution to the building of the Canadian Pacific Railway, but were subjected to extremely harsh living and working conditions. Courtesy of the Royal BC Museum and Archives, image D-07548.

Construction of the Canadian Pacific Railway

The Canadian Pacific Railway (CPR), which stretches from Montreal to Vancouver, consists of over 3,800 kilometres of track. Completed in 1885, it was once called "the crazy dream of Canada," although it came to play an important role in maintaining the stability and prosperity of the country. The construction of the railway was extremely difficult, though, and at that time seemed to be of little economic value, merely linking the small town of Victoria, with its two or three thousand residents, with the large cities of Toronto and Montreal in the east.

British Columbia joined Confederation and became a province in 1871. Ottawa promised to build a railway running from British Columbia across the Prairies to eastern Canada to enhance the commercial and trade connections between the east and west in Canada and also to prevent northward expansion by the United States. Building the railway was delayed because of the high cost of construction, conflicts among different political parties, and many other issues, including a dispute over the employment of Chinese labourers. The decision to invite contractors to bid on railway construction was delayed until 1878 when John A. Macdonald was re-elected prime minister. In 1880, the federal government signed a contract with the Canadian Pacific Railway Company, which comprised British, French, and American railway syndicates, and railway construction in BC commenced.

It was well known by then that Chinese labourers were cheap and highly efficient. However, lobbied by white labour organizations, BC politicians opposed the employment of Chinese labourers on railway construction. Noah Shakespeare, president of the Workingmen's Protective Association (later renamed the Anti-Chinese Association), organized a petition in 1879 that was submitted to the federal government, requesting that "Mongolian labour" not be used and that the Chinese be prevented from "pluck[ing] the labour plum from the Canadian Pacific fruit tree." Many members of the association felt that, unlike Chinese sojourners who might someday return to China, white settlers would move permanently to the province so that "empty houses will be filled, unoccupied lands tilled, new resources developed, old enterprises strengthened and new ones inaugurated." Shakespeare also stated that he would lobby against the construction of the transcontinental railway if Chinese workers were employed to build it.

At the end of December 1879, Andrew Onderdonk, an American railway builder, won the contract to build the railway between Emory's Bar near Yale and Savona's Ferry near Kamloops, BC. In April 1880, the now-renamed Anti-Chinese Association sent a delegation headed by Shakespeare to ask Onderdonk what type of labour he would use on the railway. He replied that he would use white labourers in British Columbia and French Canadians outside the province. If he could not obtain sufficient labour, he would, "with reluctance, engage Indians and Chinese."

Onderdonk had been a railway contractor in the United States for more than ten years and knew very well that Chinese labourers accepted low wages and were hard-working and reliable. He estimated that he would need at least ten thousand workers to build the railway but the entire population of British Columbia in 1880 was estimated to be only about thirty-five thousand. He felt that he had to look elsewhere for much of his labour force. To avoid complaints from the white workers in British Columbia, Onderdonk recruited white labourers from San Francisco. However, these workers proved to be the wrong choice for this hard work. Onderdonk was very disappointed in their performance and eventually he was forced to "reluctantly" hire Chinese labourers. By June 1880, 160 Chinese and 40 white labourers from San Francisco had arrived at Yale and started working on the railway there. White workers did the blasting work on tunnels and lumber work on bridges, and the Chinese levelled the hills and filled the ravines with the rubble.

Additional workers were needed, and Onderdonk could not get white workers for the low wages he paid. Accordingly, he asked Lee Tin Pui, a Chinese merchant in San Francisco, to help him recruit 1,500 Chinese labourers. Lee Tin Pui immediately formed a company known as the Luen Chong Company (the Lee Chuck Company in English) in Victoria with his friend Lee Tin Shut of Kwong Wah Yuen in San Francisco, Lee You Kun of Kwong On Lung, and Lee Yik Tak of Tai Yuen in Victoria. The new labour-recruiting company was not able to recruit enough Chinese labourers from among those who had previously worked for the South Pacific Railway in California and the North Pacific Railway in Oregon. Lee Tin Pui therefore travelled to Hong Kong to seek more workers. In spring 1881, he chartered two ships to bring about two thousand Chinese labourers from Hong Kong to Canada. Soon after their arrival in Victoria, he sent them to work on the line above Yale. In addition, two white-owned transport companies in Victoria, Stahlschmidt & Ward and Welch Rithet, assisted in moving labourers from Hong Kong to Canada. Later, Kwong On Wo, managed by Yip Sang (Yip Chun-tin), operated as a railway contracting company in Vancouver. This began the second wave of Chinese immigration to British Columbia.

Like the gold miners before them, Chinese railway labourers sailing from Hong Kong narrowly escaped death on the hazardous sea voyage to Canada. They had limited space and were given no vegetables or fruit to eat while on board the ship. Many of them developed scurvy after the long, rough passage. Survivors who made it to Victoria were quarantined on Albert Head for several days. There they were stripped of their clothes, and they and their belongings were fumigated with sulphur. After quarantine ended, they were sent by the railway contractor to a construction site. By the end of 1882, the total labour force on the railway had reached about 9,000 men, of whom 6,500 were Chinese and 2,500 white. It has been estimated that between 1881 and 1884, over 17,000 Chinese labourers worked on the railway and 10,000 of them had come directly to Canada from China.

During the construction of the railway, Chinese railway workers experienced harsh working and living conditions. Many Chinese died during blasting or were killed by collapsing tunnels. Chinese labourers who had come from the hot province of Guangdong in southern China found it difficult to endure the cold winters in British Columbia. They had only grass shoes and in winter wrapped their feet in potato gunny sacks to protect them from the cold. Wearing these sacks, they could not move about easily and, as a result, accidents happened at work sites. At these sites, neither medical equipment nor basic medical care was furnished by the government or contractors. Everything was left to fate.

The Chinese workers lived in crowded, ramshackle camps at Yale, Kamloops, and Savona's Ferry. Liang Qichao, a Chinese scholar and journalist during the final years of the Qing Dynasty, paid a short visit to Canada. He observed the poor living conditions experienced by the Chinese railway workers, writing in *Journey to the New Continent* that "the well-being of the Chinese in Canada was far more distressing than [that of] those in the United States." The Chinese were poorly fed, and, with very few or even a total lack of vegetables and fruit, many developed beriberi and scurvy and died of illness, freezing, or starvation in the first year after they arrived at a gold-mining site. When this happened at Yale, the townspeople feared that the Chinese had died of smallpox, but they had actually died of scurvy.

After they died, the bodies of Chinese workers were mostly wrapped up in scrap cloth, old clothes, or mats and buried in the bush, their bodies covered with rocks and earth. No coroner examined the corpses, no one paid attention to the causes of death, and there were no records kept of deaths. Many Chinese labourers died during the construction of the railway and their spirits rested on the track of the line.

Chen Jianzhong recalled that his maternal grandfather, Mr. Jian He, came by ship to Canada. After landing, he and other labourers were immediately put in jail cells in Victoria. In segregated rooms, they were fumed with sulphur to decontaminate them. Earlier Chinese labourers, who had been recruited by agents for railway construction, had jobs waiting for them when they arrived. Labourers who did not have jobs arranged by agents had to compete for a limited number of jobs and sometimes they fought among themselves over job opportunities. Chen Jianzhong's grandfather was lucky because his older brother, already in Canada, helped him get a job on the railway. The starting wage was twenty-five cents a day, much lower than what the white workers were paid. To save money for his family back in China, Jian He did not spend much money on food and often went to work hungry. After the railway was completed, he found a job at a sawmill in Port Moody. The wage was based on the number of shingles he finished, and therefore he worked extremely hard every day. One day he was so exhausted and tired that he cut off two of his fingers by accident. Fortunately, since he could speak some English, the mill did not lay him off—instead, he became a foreman.

The Canadian Pacific Railway Company started to lay off workers in spring 1883 as the line drew close to completion, initiating a period of unemployment and economic depression in BC. Some laid-off Chinese labourers returned to China, some moved to the west coast, and others went east to the Prairie provinces. In January 1884, the snow was twenty-five centimetres deep from the Okanagan to Yale and sixty centimetres deep at 37 Mile Post. Laid-off railway workers on their way to the coast had to struggle through the deep snow back to Vancouver or Victoria on foot, and many died of cold or hunger along the way.

On May 6, 1882, the United States passed an act that prohibited Chinese labourers from entering the country for the next ten years, and those Chinese already living in the United States were required to obtain a certificate of residence. Many Chinese labourers who had come north to BC from the United States were unaware of the new act and had not applied for the certificate of residence. As a result, they could not return to their homes in the US and were forced to stay in Canada if they did not have the fifteen or twenty dollars needed to pay for return passage to China.

On November 7, 1885, the last spike was driven at Craigellachie, BC, marking the completion of the transcontinental railway and the realization of the dream of a unified Canada. It reduced transportation time from east to west significantly, stabilized British Columbia's incorporation into Canada, and laid a foundation for national unification and prosperity. Chinese labourers had made tremendous sacrifices and a major contribution to the construction of the Canadian Pacific Railway, but they were subsequently abandoned by their fellow Chinese and their host country alike. Those who died during the construction of the railway were left in unmarked graves along the rail lines. The line "perished for the railway," written in English by an anonymous poet, reflected a sense of sorrow felt by these Chinese workers.

Yip Sang with his children and family members in front of Wing Sang Company building at 51 East Pender, prior to its expansion in 1901. Yip Sang is holding hands with his son Yip Kew Hong. Second from the right is Yip Sang's other son Yip Kew Gin. The other two family members are unidentified. City of Vancouver Archives, CVA 689-51. Photgrapher Bailey Bros.

EMERGING CHINESE COMMUNITIES

☸

Most Chinese immigrants who came to Canada during the gold rush and railway construction period lived in temporary Chinese camps at gold-mining sites or along the railway line. These camps were abandoned when the workers moved on to other work sites. But during this period, a few permanent Chinese communities also developed in Victoria, New Westminster, and a few of the larger gold-mining towns. Chinese businesses and residents were concentrated on a street that was called Tong Yan Gai (Tang People's Street) by the Chinese—and Chinatown by the mainstream society.[†]

THE CHINESE POPULATION

The great mobility of the early Chinese immigrants made it difficult to accurately estimate the population. It is thought, however, that there were about 2,500 Chinese people living in British Columbia by 1863, and that through the 1860s, the Chinese population ranged between 1,700 and 4,000 individuals.

After the gold rush had largely died down, most of the Chinese miners gradually moved to the main cities on the coast. By the late 1870s, only 33 per cent of the Chinese lived in Interior cities and towns or at gold creeks. Fifty-seven per cent had settled in Victoria and 11 per cent lived in Nanaimo, where they had found work in the coal mines.

The national census of 1881, which for the first time included British Columbia, recorded that there were 4,383 Chinese people in Canada. Almost all of them—4,350—lived in British Columbia, with a few in Manitoba (4), Quebec (7), and Ontario (22). By 1884, there were over 10,000 Chinese people in British Columbia. Most of them lived in Victoria; the coal-mining towns of Nanaimo, Wellington, and South Wellington; New Westminster; the gold-mining towns of Quesnelle Mouth and Yale; and at places along the route of the Canadian Pacific Railway, where thousands of Chinese labourers were by then employed building the railway.

---

† Tang refers to the Tang dynasty in China, a period regarded by many as the pinnacle of Chinese civilization. The southern Chinese were usually called Tang people.

Chinese communities were dominated by single male labourers. In 1884, for example, there were over ninety-two men for every woman. Married men among the first Chinese labourers could not afford to bring their wives to Canada and, furthermore, they often needed their wives to stay in their home villages to look after the old and young in their families. Only a few wealthy merchants could afford to bring their wives and children to Canada, usually to the Chinatowns of larger cities such as Victoria, New Westminster, and Nanaimo. Chinatowns in smaller cities such as Quesnelle Mouth, Quesnelle Forks, Lillooet, Yale, Lytton, and other small mining and farming towns did not have any Chinese women at all, except for a few prostitutes. There were fewer than 160 Chinese women living in British Columbia in 1885, and 70 of these women were prostitutes.

Most immigrants to Canada in the early 1880s were members of an extended family clan or had come from the same village or county in China.[†] Nearly 64 per cent had come from the four Siyi counties: Taishan, Kaiping, Xinhui, and Enping.[‡] About 30 per cent belonged to just three clans: Zhou, Li, and Huang. Ninety-five per cent of the immigrants with the surname Ma, 52 per cent of those named Lin, and 42 per cent of those named Li came from Taishan County, and 76 per cent of those with the surname Zhou came from Kaiping County. This reflects a process of chain immigration in which members of the same clan from the same county sponsored or otherwise helped their own people immigrate to Canada.

After arriving in Canada, most of the Chinese from the same clan or the same county tended to concentrate in one community. Although they were far away from China, they retained the Chinese tradition of building "villages" of people with kinship ties. These community patterns reflect the way in which residents of many villages in China belonged to just one or two clans; they continued to live in similar communities in Canada.

CHINESE OCCUPATIONS

The first Chinese immigrants were mainly gold miners or labourers on gold-mining infrastructure such as roads, with a few merchants and service

---

[†] Evidence for this and other demographic information comes from the archives of the Chinese Consolidated Benevolent Association (CCBA) in Victoria. When the CCBA was established in 1884 and 1885, it asked all the Chinese in British Columbia to donate two dollars as a membership fee. The association has in its archives 220 booklets of receipt stubs that reveal the names and county origins of 5,056 donors in 1884 and 1885, which likely represents most of the Chinese population at that time.

[‡] Siyi, which means "four counties," is a region in Guangdong. Sanyi, "three counties," includes Panyu, Nanhai, and Shunde counties. Siyi and Sanyi are both in the Pearl River Delta.

providers supplying the needs of these labourers. As time passed, Chinese men took up other jobs such as cooking, doing laundry, and working as servants for Euro-Canadian families. Others found work growing vegetables, chopping wood, cleaning fish in the canning industries, or working for coal-mining companies in Nanaimo, earning only $1.00 a day when white miners were paid at least $2.50.

By the beginning of the 1880s, the gold rush had abated but railway construction had not yet begun. In 1879, over 40 per cent of the Chinese still worked mining gold, 8 per cent worked in coal mines, and slightly over 10 per cent worked as servants or cooks for non-Chinese employers. A small merchant class had begun to emerge, and a few were variously employed as tailors, barbers, and butchers.

By the mid-1880s, the distribution among occupations had changed, largely due to railway construction. By 1885, there were 10,492 Chinese people in British Columbia, about 85 per cent of them labourers. Nearly 28 per cent were railway construction workers and 16 per cent continued to mine gold. A small number of labourers had managed to pay off their debts after a few years' hard work and had saved enough money to be able to start their own small businesses. These new entrepreneurs opened cafés and restaurants, laundries, and grocery stores. There were also by then forty-two doctors (herbalists) and eight teachers.

Chinese occupations varied from one city to another, depending on the local economy. In New Westminster, nearly 60 per cent of the Chinese worked on farms along the Fraser River, at fish canneries, and at sawmills. Not surprisingly, the majority of the Chinese living in coal-mining cities like Nanaimo and Wellington were coal miners.

After railway construction ended in 1885, many unemployed Chinese railway labourers found new work as cooks or domestic servants, in coal mines, or at fish canneries. Those who could not find work elsewhere re-turned to the two largest Chinatowns, in Victoria and New Westminster, where they begged for money, and some were reduced to stealing. The Lee Chuck Company, which had profited greatly from its labour contracts, made no effort to assist the unemployed Chinese workers. Huang Tsim Hsim, the Chinese consul general in San Francisco, wrote letters appealing to shipping companies to reduce their fares so that impoverished Chinese workers could return to China. In January 1886, he also wrote a letter to the newly founded Chinese Consolidated Benevolent Association (CCBA) in Victoria asking it to help destitute labourers.

One feature of the emerging Chinese communities was the monopoly of certain industries by people from certain counties or with shared clan origins, a tradition carried to Canada from China. In China, villagers favoured people who shared a common lineage and excluded outsiders or neighbours with other surnames. Most Chinese cooks, washermen, and servants in the early history of British Columbia came from Taishan County, while gardeners and farm labourers belonged to the Zhongshan clan. During the late 1880s, the four hundred Chinese residents in Winnipeg had come from Heshan County; most were surnamed Li. For many years, Li clan members would go to the Winnipeg railway station and prevent Chinese laundry workers coming from the west coast from leaving the train. They did not want any competition. The Chinese laundry workers who could not leave the train had to continue the journey eastwards. Eventually, the Li association in Vancouver persuaded their clansmen in Winnipeg to drop such hostile actions, and people from other clans were finally able to live and work in Winnipeg.

Speaking a common dialect was another factor affecting employment preferences. At this time, the Siyi dialect was the main tongue spoken by the Chinese in North America, followed by the Sanyi and Zhongshan dialects. A Sanyi or Zhongshan person who was unable to speak the Siyi dialect would not be employed by Siyi employers. Similarly, the Sanyi or Zhongshan employers would only employ people who spoke their dialects.

The Development of Chinatowns

During this period, the Chinese had no alternative but to live together in Chinatowns. Euro-Canadians discriminated against the Chinese, and white landlords usually did not wish to sell or rent their properties to them unless the lands were on the fringes of the settlement, far away from white neighbourhoods. In larger cities like Victoria and Vancouver, the Chinese established their living quarters on mudflats, the cheapest districts in these cities, where infrastructure was incomplete and living conditions very harsh. In Nanaimo and other coal-mining towns, mining companies housed Chinese miners in isolated areas, segregating them from white miners to avoid conflicts. Racial discrimination and efforts to segregate the Chinese from English-speaking communities resulted in a reluctance among the Chinese to integrate themselves into these communities. Even if it had been permitted, the Chinese would have feared living in isolation in communities dominated by a foreign, and racist, population. Chinatowns provided a safe haven for the Chinese.

Economic factors also played a critical role in the formation of Chinatowns. The Chinese labourers who came to seek gold were often penniless and shared what resources they did have. The Chinese merchants or contractors who recruited them cared neither about their living conditions nor their health. To keep their own costs to a minimum, these merchants built or leased wooden shacks in the cheapest district of a town and operated simple stores and restaurants to meet the labourers' needs. These clusters of buildings formed the nucleus around which the Chinatowns developed.

Cultural shock and a language barrier also contributed to the development of Chinatowns. Very few Chinese people could speak English and therefore most found it difficult to communicate with non-Chinese people. When they lived together, Chinese people could speak their own dialects, eat their own foods, and worship their own gods, enjoying a sense of comfort and security. Since they were unable to join mainstream society, a Chinatown became a self-contained enclave and functioned like a miniature China within a European country.

During the Fraser River gold rush, Chinese gold seekers lived in temporary "instant Chinatowns." These settlements consisted of groups of shacks or camps that were built quickly by gold seekers on their arrival at a mine site. Occasionally—for example, at Stanley and Keithley Creek—instant Chinatowns had a few small stores. Most of these instant Chinatowns disappeared after their residents left for other mining sites, and the abandoned shacks grew dilapidated and eventually disappeared.

After the gold rush ended and the Canadian Pacific Railway was completed, more permanent Chinatowns were established across Canada. Many of them experienced periods of growth followed by periods of diminishment. In the period from 1858 to 1885, most Chinatowns in British Columbia budded and then bloomed, although some also withered during this period as the gold rush faded.

In the budding stage, these new Chinatowns were dominated by single male Chinese residents—they were bachelor communities. Structurally, the budding Chinatowns were characterized by either a linear pattern or a cross-shaped pattern formed by two intersecting streets. The streetscape was dominated by rows of closely packed wooden shacks and cabins.

When Chinatowns entered the blooming period, the population had increased rapidly due to immigration, including some relatives and friends of earlier immigrants. As the populations of these Chinatowns expanded, the economies of Chinatowns became more diversified and prosperous. New grocery stores, rice shops, restaurants, and even theatres opened for business. Some labourers who had managed to save enough money opened small businesses, such as shoe repair shops or tailoring shops. An increasing number of Chinese people began to work outside Chinatowns as gardeners, laundrymen, and domestic servants or cooks for white families, extending the Chinese community beyond the boundaries of its Chinatown.

Temples, churches, schools, and other public buildings were built during the blooming period. County and clan associations were formed, born out of geographical, familial, or occupational bonds. Since most of the Chinese had emigrated from Siyi and Sanyi counties, close bonds existed among relatives and people who had shared a hometown in China. Although the number of married couples gradually increased as the Chinatowns bloomed, the population was still dominated by single male Chinese labourers for several decades. Gambling dens and brothels met the needs of this bachelor society.

As the Chinatowns bloomed, their cultural, economic, and spiritual status was strengthened among Chinese people, reinforcing the strong cohesive force needed for further development of the Chinatowns.

Chinese people first arrived in Victoria in June 1858. They lived in wooden shacks or tents on the northern mudflats of the Johnson Street ravine. This area became the first Chinatown in Canada. It was also the largest Chinatown in British Columbia for some decades and was called "Dabu" (the Big or First Port) by Chinese people.

Chinatown was accessible from the city centre across three narrow footbridges that spanned the ravine at Government and Douglas streets. Chinese labourers usually lived together in rented houses and shared expenses. Chinese-run laundries and snack bars were almost all located on Cormorant Street, later renamed Pandora Street. By 1862, Victoria's Chinese population was estimated at three hundred out of a total population of about five thousand. As the population grew, Chinatown expanded northward towards Fisgard Street.

By the early 1880s, Cormorant Street between Store and Douglas streets had become the commercial centre of Victoria's Chinatown. Nearly half of all Chinatown businesses were concentrated there. Behind the commercial façades of Cormorant Street were numerous wooden shacks or tenement buildings where most of the Chinese lived. In 1875, some Hakka residents—the Hakka are a Chinese ethnic group—raised enough money to purchase a small lot on Government Street, where they built the Tam Kung Temple.[†] In 1876, a mission school was opened by the Methodist church on Government Street near Chinatown.

To demonstrate that they recognized Canada as their new country, the Chinese community participated in the ceremony held to welcome Earl Dufferin, the third Governor General of Canada, when he arrived in Victoria on August 16, 1876. Three Chinese gates covered with evergreens and adorned with lanterns were built on Cormorant Street. On September 20, 1882, the Chinese community again built a huge gate on Store Street to welcome the Marquis of Lorne, the fourth Governor General of Canada, and his wife, Princess Louise, when they visited Victoria.

Howe Lee, curator of the Chinese Canadian Military Museum (and who served in the Canadian military for over thirty years, achieving the

---

† The Hakka are a group of northern Chinese who migrated to southern China. They had their own language and customs and were called Hakka, meaning "visitors," by the southern Chinese of Guangdong Province. Some Hakka were among the Chinese who came to Canada.

rank of colonel), recalled his grandfather's experience in Victoria's China-town:

> From Guangdong, my grandfather went to the United States to mine gold and then came to Victoria from the US. However, he did not actually go gold-mining but instead remained in Victoria, logging and helping out in a relative's store. He helped import rice, clothes, and other things necessary for Chinese labourers from China. Chinese labourers normally bought things in stores run by Chinese people for two reasons. One was that Chinese labourers spoke poor English and most of them could not communicate with the white people. They had to go shopping in Chinese stores. And the majority of them were Cantonese, who preferred rice over the bread made by the white people—despite a higher price, they bought rice. The other reason was that Chinese labourers did not trust the white people and also feared their bullying and discrimination. Lacking clear knowledge of the local currency, they were afraid that the change given by the white storekeepers could be incorrect, less than they were owed. My grandfather worked diligently and opened his own restaurant after saving enough money.

Like the first Chinese labourers, Chinese merchants from San Francisco played an important role in developing the economy of British Columbia. Soon after the gold rush started, three large Chinese import-export merchants from San Francisco established themselves in Victoria: Kwong Lee & Company, Tai Soong & Company, and Yang Wo Sang. In 1858, these merchants invested in real estate, purchasing seven lots on the northern fringe of Victoria, which became the site of the city's Chinatown. These companies had other functions besides importing goods. Some functioned as banks, keeping the savings of labourers and remitting money to China for them. They also acted as post offices, receiving and sending out mail for the labourers and writing letters for them. These merchants set up branches in Yale, Lillooet, Barkerville, and other gold-mining towns to supply the miners with goods.

These large merchants also operated opium factories. The opium trade was not outlawed in Canada until 1908. Before then, English merchants shipped raw opium from India to Hong Kong for partial processing, and then on to Victoria for final processing. Each opium factory in Victoria paid licensing fees to British Columbia and duty on the imported opium to the federal government. Opium processing and canning was a very lucrative business for Chinese merchants during this period.

In January 1860, the business of Kwong Lee & Company was valued at $3,000, Tai Soong & Company at $2,500, and Yang Wo Sang at $2,500.

By the 1880s, these companies were very prosperous. Imports from China to British Columbia in 1874–84 were valued at $1,369,888 and duties of $411,970 were paid to the federal government. In just two years, 1882 and 1883, Chinese merchants paid duties of $183,172 on goods imported from China. In 1884 alone, Chinese merchants in Victoria paid trade licence fees of $7,560, property assessment fees of $500, city taxes of $1,100, city water fees of $4,440, rents to non-Chinese landlords of $27,000, and cultivated land rents to non-Chinese landowners of $6,180, among other operating costs. In that same year, 708 Chinese merchants and labourers in Victoria paid personal income taxes. Although the Chinese at this time were often accused of not paying taxes, this accusation is clearly wrong. Chinese tax payments were high and contributed considerably to the economy of the province from its earliest days.

A few of these prominent merchants became the leaders of Chinatown and promoted the commercial interests of the Chinese community with mainstream politicians. For example, Lee Chong (known to the non-Chinese as Kwong Lee) was the manager of and a partner in the Kwong Lee Company. He could speak English and was described by one white writer as "quite a gentleman of most polite manners and very intelligent. Speaks English fluently in ordinary conversation." In April 1864, together with Chang Tsoo, he called on Governor Arthur Edward Kennedy to express concern about the unfair treatment of the Chinese in Canada and the government's plan to modify the colony's free trade policy. Governor Kennedy responded by saying that the government wished "to render equal justice to people of every nationality" and that "the Chinese population in this colony would be protected in their lives and property" just as well as any of Queen Victoria's subjects.

In 1860, a Chinatown began to emerge in Nanaimo. Nanaimo was a coal-mining town and Robert Dunsmuir's mining company (Dunsmuir, Diggle & Co.; later renamed R. Dunsmuir & Sons) recruited Chinese labourers to work in its coal mines. The company built shacks on Victoria Street to house the Chinese miners. This street, located far from the town centre, became the first of several Chinatown sites in Nanaimo.

During its budding stage, Nanaimo's Chinatown had only two or three small stores that provided for the daily needs of the small Chinese mining population; Yee Kee & Company was probably the largest shop. By 1874, Nanaimo's population had risen to 1,884 and its Chinatown had reached its blooming stage with two hundred Chinese residents, more than 10 per cent of the city's population. However, a decade later this Chinatown was approaching extinction: its residents and businesses were forcibly expelled in 1884 as rising land values made this area more valuable. By 1885, almost all the Chinese businesses and residents had moved to a new site situated in remote wilderness separate from the white community. In 1908, Nanaimo's Chinatown was again relocated to another less desirable site.

In 1870, the Dunsmuir company opened the Wellington Colliery about seven kilometres north of Nanaimo and established the mining village of Wellington. The company recruited Chinese labourers to work in its new mine, building scores of shacks for them some distance away from the main village. As an ever-increasing number of Chinese workers was recruited, more shanties were built. By the 1880s, half the workforce at the mine—about 275 out of 550 men—was Chinese. A small Chinatown thus emerged in Wellington. Two years later, the Dunsmuir company purchased the coal mine at South Wellington, where the Chinese were employed not only as coal miners but also as railway workers and in logging operations. A small Chinatown thus came into existence in South Wellington as well.

During the 1860s, New Westminster was an undeveloped frontier town on the north bank of the Fraser River. It consisted of a small group of wooden huts clinging to the hillside among fallen trees and blackened stumps. The Chinatown was established on the western end of Front Street, which ran east-west along the Fraser River. As its population increased, New Westminster's Chinatown began to expand uphill, covering a square block bounded by Front Street on the south, Columbia Street on the north, McInnes Street on the west, and McNeely Street on the east. New Westminster's Chinatown was thriving by the early 1880s, mainly because of the rapid development of the city's farming, lumbering, and salmon-canning industries. In 1882, there were thirteen stores in Chinatown: six grocery stores, four hand laundries, one restaurant, one butcher shop, and one tailor shop. It had become the second-largest Chinatown in British Columbia after Victoria's and was called "Erbu" (the Second Port) by the Chinese people.

Barkerville's Chinatown, established in 1862, had short budding, blooming, and withering periods tied closely to the waxing and waning of the gold rush. It was the main supply centre for Chinese miners in other settlements in the Cariboo region. For a short period, this flourishing Chinatown, located at the southern end of the town, had the largest Chinese population in British Columbia. During the first half of the 1860s, there was a population of several thousand Chinese people, and among its businesses were laundries, a restaurant, and several large stores, the largest being the Kwong Lee & Company store. However, its prosperity lasted for only a few years. In 1868, Barkerville was destroyed by fire and rebuilt. But by 1870, the Cariboo gold rush was virtually ended, and many white and Chinese miners left for other places. Barkerville's Chinatown declined in both population and economic activity.

During the gold rush, Yale, situated on the lower Fraser River, became not only an important gold-mining town, but also an important supply base for gold seekers. Its Chinatown, located at the eastern end of Front Street, had several stores that provided supplies to the Chinese labourers heading for the upper Fraser River and those returning to New Westminster and Victoria.

Chinese Culture in Chinatowns

Chinese immigrants brought Chinese customs to Canada, and Chinatowns had their own culture distinct from surrounding white neighbourhoods. Inside Chinatown, the residents spoke their hometown dialects, read Chinese newspapers and magazines, saw traditional Guangdong (Cantonese) opera, and celebrated traditional Chinese festivals such as the Chinese Lunar New Year, the Lantern Festival, and the Qingming tomb-sweeping festival.

The Chinese immigrants mainly spoke the Siyi, Sanyi, and Zhongshan dialects. People unable to speak these dialects found it difficult to survive in Chinatowns or to integrate themselves into these communities.

Life in Chinatown could be boring and lonely. Celebrating traditional Chinese festivals helped alleviate this. The most important social event of the year was celebration of the Chinese New Year, during which firecrackers were set off. All the shops closed and were tidied, cleaned, and decorated with pieces of red paper on which good luck verses were written. People dressed in their best clothing and exchanged visits. Visitors were entertained with Chinese wine, nuts, cakes, fruits, and other delicacies. Occasionally, wealthy merchants invited Cantonese opera troupes from San Francisco to travel to Victoria to perform.

There were strong folk spiritual and religious beliefs in China, incorporating principles from Buddhism and Taoism. The many gods the Chinese worshipped included Kwan Kung (God of Righteousness) and Choi Sun (God of Wealth), and temples were built in which to worship them. The Chinese desired blessings from these gods in the form of peace, wealth, and the elimination of misfortune. They built shrines or placed ceramic figurines of Buddha in kitchens, bedrooms, or other eye-catching places in their homes where they could pray for blessings and protection. Merchants would look for a lucky date on which to open their business and would create a shrine to the God of Wealth to ensure a booming business. Some craftspeople offered sacrifices to the founder of their craft on a regular basis. The early Chinese immigrants also attached great importance to feng shui, a system that considers the good and evil influences of natural surroundings, used when assessing buildings and building sites. They would examine feng shui when deciding to purchase real estate.

There were few educational opportunities for Chinese children at this time. In the early 1870s, wealthy Chinese merchants in Victoria hired teachers from China to tutor their children at home. For example, Dong Ji, owner of the Tai Soong Co., hired Chen Sunyi to teach his children. In March 1874, the first school in Victoria's Chinatown was founded. The Methodist Sabbath School offered classes to Chinese adults as well as children. The school aimed to teach English to the Chinese and to introduce them to the principles of Christianity.

The dominant young, male population without families combined with the fact that there were very few women in Chinatown led to the establishment of gambling clubs, brothels, and opium dens. These pastimes became an integral part of the Chinatowns' society and led to Chinatowns' reputation in mainstream society as "dens of evil." There were criminal cases launched over gambling in Chinatown and disputes over money. Having lost their savings to gambling, some Chinese committed thefts, thereby exacerbating social problems. To relieve loneliness and depression, some Chinese turned towards prostitutes. There were cases where women were kidnapped in China and shipped to Victoria for sale as prostitutes. However, not all the Chinese were in favour of such establishments. In May 1875, some concerned Chinese leaders sent a petition to the Victoria City Council requesting the suppression of the nine Chinese brothels in Chinatown, saying that they were "shocked and scandalized by the existence of these places." But because a bylaw to suppress Chinese brothels would also affect non-Chinese brothels, the petition came to nothing. Another practice the Chinese indulged in was smoking opium, through which many Chinese relieved pain and depression.

CHINESE ASSOCIATIONS AND SOCIETIES

The Chinese formed a number of types of organizations, including clan and county associations, dialect groups, religious groups, political organizations, and other associations. These organizations were often called "tongs." Although the word *tong* has sometimes been associated with criminal activity and gangs in the English media, it simply means society or association. The first tongs in Canada were formed in the 1880s; some were extensions of organizations that existed in China. Many helped members who were ill, provided friendship and entertainment to lonely workers, helped people communicate with their families back in China, and provided social services to the local Chinese people, at a time when such services were not offered by government.

In the late eighteenth century, an organization called the Society of Heaven and Earth, also widely known as the Hongmen society, was formed in China. It was a secret society established to overthrow the Qing dynasty and restore the Ming dynasty. For this reason, it was banned by the Manchu rulers of the Qing Dynasty. Branches of the Hongmen society were formed throughout China and were known by various names in different provinces. The lodge in Guangdong and Guangzi provinces was known as Hong Shun Tong. In Canada, the Hongmen society was also known as the Chinese Freemasons.

Most of the Chinese migrants to the United States and Canada in the nineteenth century came from Guangdong Province and many of them were already members of Hong Shun Tong. After they arrived in North America, they set up branches in various towns and cities. In the 1860s, there were three thousand Chinese people in Barkerville, BC, and 80 per cent of them were Hong Shun Tong members. They established the Hong Shun Tong there on March 21, 1863, and purchased a building to house its association offices. The Hong Shun Tong aimed to help its members when they were in financial and other difficulties and to protect them against persecution and bullying. If a member was involved in a legal case, the tong would bail him out; when a member was bullied, the tong would come to his aid; and when a member died in Canada, the tong would ship the deceased's bones back to China for burial in his home village. Chee Kung Tong, a branch of the Hong Shun Tong, was established in Quesnelle Mouth in 1876 and in Quesnelle Forks in 1882. In 1877, a Chee Kung Tong was established in Victoria's Chinatown. The Chee Kung Tong had many strict rules; a member who maintained connections with outsiders and damaged the reputation of the society would be punished.

The Hongmen organization included many sorts of people, not all of them law-abiding. As it developed into a more powerful organization in the nineteenth century, some members monopolized certain businesses—such as brothels and opium dens, or trafficking in workers and women. They managed and controlled these industries by violent means, including extortion of protection money. This segment of the Hongmen contributed to the society's negative reputation among the non-Chinese population.

A fangkou was a co-operative boarding floor or hut. Because they were single and shared family bonds and dialects, the early Chinese immigrants pooled their money to rent a floor of a building or a hut in Chinatown, where they ate and slept together and shared food and rent expenses. In Victoria's Chinatown, several men surnamed Wu lived together in one room that they called Ding On Fang, and several natives of Zengcheng County shared another room that they called Kun Ying Fang. The name of the fangkou was used as an address that was given to a store in Chinatown that dealt with their mail. When letters from China arrived at the store, they would be sorted by the name of the fangkou and picked up by their respective lodgers.

In time, some fangkou whose members were related to each other banded together to form a larger organization known as a clan association. Before 1885, there were five large clan associations in Victoria: Lee Long Sai Tong, Wong Kong Har Tong, Chan Wing Chun Tong, Chow Oylin Kung Shaw, and Lum Sai Ho Tong.

A shantang was a charitable organization for a particular county that raised money from people who had come to Canada from that county. At first, the shantang used these funds to collect the bones of deceased Chinese people to return them to China for burial. The Chinese believed that they should be buried in their home village in China; if not, their spirits would be unable to find peace. For example, natives from Taishan County contributed money to its shantang, which collected the bones of deceased Taishan natives and shipped them to Hong Kong. Family members from Taishan County would then come to Hong Kong to pick up the bones of their relatives and friends and take them home for burial.

As a shantang grew larger, it developed into a county association that dealt not only with the shipment of bones but also with helping its members in Canada. By 1887, eleven county clan associations existed in Victoria: Yee Hing Tong of Taishan County, Kwong Fook Tong of Kaiping County, Tong Fook Tong of Enping County, Fook Hing Tong of Xinhui County, Fook Sin Tong of Zhongshan County, Po On Tong of Dongguan County, Chong How Tong of Panyu County, Hang On Tong of Shunde County, Fook Yum Tong of Nanhai County, Yan On Tong of Zengcheng County, and Yen Wo Company, which was an association of the Hakka ethnic group.

In the early days, clashes between clan associations or between county associations occasionally occurred. A dispute between a person named Lee and a person named Wong might lead to clashes between the Lee association and the Wong association. In response to such conflicts and to assist the former railway workers who were now unemployed, a group of Chinese merchants in Victoria sent a letter in early March 1884 to Huang Tsim Hsim, the consul general in San Francisco, requesting the establishment of a consulate in Canada and a Chinese Consolidated Benevolent Association (CCBA) to help impoverished Chinese people, to mediate conflicts among the Chinese, and to unite the Chinese to fight against discriminatory acts made by the government.

Huang Tsim Hsim supported the merchants' proposal and instructed his secretary, Huang Sic Chen, and the interpreter, Dai Yong Xiang, to assist the Victoria merchants in establishing the CCBA. During his stay in Canada, Huang Sic Chen collected information about each overseas Chinese centre in British Columbia and assumed responsibility for drafting CCBA rules. A provisional board of directors comprising twenty Chinese merchants in Victoria was formed in April 1884. The board sent out a circular to all the Chinatowns or Chinese settlements in British Columbia to raise funds for the new association. The circular asked each Chinese person to donate two dollars for the dual purposes of fighting racial discrimination and forming the CCBA. The provisional board of directors meanwhile declared that the CCBA would not look out for the interests of any individual who had not paid the two-dollar fee by October 17, 1884. If any miner did not make a donation and later wished to return to China, he would not be permitted to depart until he paid one hundred dollars to the association.

In June 1884, the CCBA in Victoria was formally founded. Its two co-presidents were Lee Yau Kain and Wong Yin Ho. It also had six vice-presidents, twenty directors, and one secretary. The CCBA archives show that its income came from three sources: the foundation donations of two dollars, rental income from the ground floor of the association building, and annual donations by wealthy Chinese merchants to support a temple in the CCBA building. These merchants were also usually the major donors for any special events.

In March 1885, the CCBA purchased a lot at 554–560 Fisgard Street from Thomas D. Lindsay for $4,500 and raised almost $10,000 to build a three-storey brick structure on the site. In autumn the same year, the CCBA building was completed. A temple called the Palace of All Sages was housed on the top floor of the building. The custodian of the temple was supported by devotees' donations, rather than a salary from the association. The association's office was on the second floor. The ground floor was rented to stores. After the new building was completed, Huang Tsim Hsim came to Victoria in person from the consulate in San Francisco and hosted the opening ceremony.

The CCBA had many functions that served the Chinese community. It built a hospital and a school in Chinatown and a cemetery on the northern fringe of the city. It made significant contributions to the unification of the Chinese people in order to oppose racial discrimination. It also protected Chinese legal rights and interests and mediated and settled disputes within the Chinese community. Until China established diplomatic relations with Canada and a consulate in Ottawa in the early twentieth century, the CCBA was the most important Chinese institution governing relationships with mainstream Canada.

RELATIONSHIPS WITH WHITE AND FIRST NATIONS PEOPLE

During the years 1858–85, British Columbia's mainstream population was overwhelmingly of European, especially British, origin. Most interactions between the Chinese and the mainstream Canadian society were influenced by British values and judgments, and by Sino-British relations. Although the Chinese immigrants were tolerated to some extent during the gold rush period, relationships between the Chinese and Euro-Canadians became increasingly strained after it ended. As a result, many Chinese isolated themselves from mainstream society and, in some cases, lived on First Nations reserves.

THE RELATIONSHIP BETWEEN THE CHINESE AND THE BRITISH SETTLER SOCIETY

The discrimination the Chinese experienced in Canada had its roots in mid-nineteenth-century conflicts between the imperialist European nations and China. The mainly British people who dominated the new colonies in British Columbia during the gold rush and the railway-building era brought with them already-ingrained prejudice against the Chinese; this prejudice was played out in the relationship between the Chinese immigrants and Euro-Canadian colonists and demonstrated in the stereotypical view of the Chinese held by these colonists.

British settlers in BC felt that their culture was the pinnacle of civilization, and they considered the Chinese to occupy a much lower rung in a hierarchy of nations. In addition, they had immigrated to Canada with the intention of founding a new country in their own image. Chinese languages and ways of life, Chinese clothing and long braids, and non-Christian beliefs were not only thought to be innately inferior or irrational, they also countered the wish to construct a new homeland that imitated Europe.

British settlers also considered the Chinese to be temporary workers and thus an impediment to the colony-building project. The earliest Chinese immigrants indeed saw Canada mainly as a place for a temporary sojourn where they could earn more money than they could at home. Once they had saved enough money, they planned to return to China—although many never did—so the white settlers did not regard them as owners. Ironically, many European immigrants to North America were also destitute labouring people who had lost their lands in Europe, a point that was ignored when it came to the Chinese.

Prior to 1860, the Manchu government prohibited its citizens from emigrating to other countries, although it was unable to strictly enforce this policy, and Chinese people continued to leave China to find jobs in other countries. In 1860, after it defeated the Manchu government, the British pressured the Manchu to sign the *Sino-British Treaty*, which required the Manchu government to permit its citizens to live and work abroad. However, since China had been forced to sign this treaty after a military defeat, it continued to regard Chinese emigrants as betrayers of their country and was indifferent to their status abroad.

At this time, China was weak and unable to protect Chinese people living in foreign countries. The Manchu government had no consulate in Canada and could not have protected the basic rights and interests of the Chinese even if it had intended to do so. Consequently, the Chinese in Canada had little or no recourse when they experienced discriminatory behaviour and policies. Not only that, but most of the early Chinese immigrants were illiterate labourers, ignorant of how to protect their rights and interests in the Western world. They were unable to initiate interactions with white people due to the language barrier. And in a strange environment far away from their homeland, they were reluctant to protest and cause trouble.

During the gold rushes of the 1860s, there was anti-Chinese sentiment among the white miners, and occasionally violent incidents occurred. The mining towns were remote and often lawless places. Vigilante justice sometimes prevailed over the laws of the colony and at times, Chinese miners were bullied, assaulted, robbed, and even murdered. In 1861, two Chinese labourers were shot dead by white miners in Cayoosh in a dispute over a mining claim. White miners also used violent means to prevent Chinese miners from entering mountainous areas of the Cariboo and gaining access to the richest mine sites. Sometimes they robbed Chinese miners of gold sands they had extracted. In 1863, a Chinese man was hanged by a person whose reason was simply that he didn't like the look of him. Despite his admission, this murderer was released. A few years later, in 1865, another white man, Copeland, cut off a Chinese man's queue and fired his revolver into a group of Chinese men on board the steamship *Hope*. Although Copeland was arrested, he was released on bail; he then left the area and was never tried for his crime.

In spite of such violent incidents in the mining districts, the relationship between white people and the Chinese in the towns and cities of the colony was moderately good in the 1860s. Cheap labour was in great demand and Chinese workers were welcomed. There were few white women in British Columbia at the time and mainstream settlers employed the Chinese as servants to do washing, cooking, and other tasks considered to be women's work.

However, other Canadian residents began to express concern about the Chinese coming to British Columbia soon after their arrival. In March 1859, Leonard McClure, an editor of the *Victoria Gazette*, became the first person to publish a piece describing the threat he thought the Chinese posed in British Columbia. He protested the British government's attitude towards "this peculiar class of newcomers." R. Byron Johnson, a British traveller who toured British Columbia in the 1860s, described how the Chinese were treated:

> It is the fashion on the Pacific Coast to abuse and ill-treat the Chinaman in every possible way;... he is treated like a dog, bullied, scoffed at, kicked, and cuffed-about on all occasions, his very name made a slang term of reproach; and yet, withal, he betrays no sign of meditated revenge, but pursues his labours calmly, and is civil and polite to all.... He is insulted to a pitch that would not be endured by a person of any other nationality.

At a public meeting held in Victoria on March 5, 1860, a poll tax on all Chinese entering the colony of Vancouver Island was proposed. When Chinese merchants in Victoria learned of this proposal, they called upon Governor James Douglas, who assured them that he had no plan to impose a tax on the Chinese, a promise that was eventually broken. Despite the wish by many to impose a head tax, there were also some non-Chinese people who opposed such a tax because they viewed Chinese labourers as an asset that supported Victoria's economic interests.

Once the easily accessible gold sands were largely exhausted, gold mining in BC became dominated by large companies that had the financial resources to mine gold inside the mountains using expensive equipment. The mining population of the gold rush era gradually dispersed, creating a chain of economic effects in the colony. In some cases, merchants who had stockpiled merchandise and food for the miners were unable to sell these and went bankrupt. Some property owners lost their rent-paying tenants and were unable to pay their property taxes. The revenue of the United Colony of British Columbia declined and by the late 1860s, it had a debt of nearly £1.3 million, marking the onset of a period of economic depression.

Under such circumstances, many of the Chinese gold miners found it difficult to obtain work in the restaurants, laundries, and market gardens, sectors where the Chinese had been employed—there was now an oversupply of such workers. Instead, they began to search for jobs on ranches and farms or in coal mines. The Chinese led a simple lifestyle and were willing to work longer hours for lower wages. They could therefore find employment faster and more easily than white workers who demanded higher pay. As a result, white labourers began to feel that their own livelihoods were threatened, and antagonism between white and Chinese labourers intensified.

After British Columbia entered Confederation in 1871, the Chinese presence became a political issue for the province. The two Victoria newspapers, the *Daily Colonist* and the *Victoria Gazette,* published anti-Chinese editorials, feature articles, and letters to the editor protesting their presence. As public opinion shifted from the relative tolerance of the gold rush era, politicians also began to participate in anti-Chinese agitation. Both Arthur Bunster, Nanaimo's representative in the BC legislative assembly, and John Robson, editor-in-chief of the *Daily Colonist*, had a strong bias against the Chinese and favoured denying the Chinese the right to vote. During the first provincial election in 1871, in which votes were simply a show of hands, the Chinese were prevented from voting, even though they were Canadian citizens.

In 1872, the legislative assembly of British Columbia passed an amendment to the Qualification and Registration of Voters Act that disenfranchised both Chinese and First Nations people. This was the first of a series of discriminatory legislative acts passed in British Columbia at both the provincial and municipal levels. The Lieutenant-Governor of British Columbia thought this amendment might contravene the British North America Act, so he submitted the act to London for consideration before he approved it. It was unclear at that time, then, whether the Chinese could vote or not. In 1874, eight Chinese people voted in a Lillooet by-election because they came from Hong Kong, a British colony, and were considered to be British citizens. In 1875, a report in the *Daily Colonist* wrote that J. S. Drummond won Victoria's mayoral election by sixty-seven votes; it was estimated that out of ninety-two Chinese votes, seventy-seven went to "Lummond" (a mockery of the Chinese pronunciation of Drummond), who promised them "plentee workee" and pushed them into the ballot stalls.

The situation became clear after the BC voters act received royal assent on April 22, 1875. After this date, no Chinese or First Nations person could be included on the voter lists of any voting district or be eligible to vote in any legislative assembly election. Chinese Canadians in British Columbia would remain unable to vote for many years. By June 1, 1875, all voting officers had removed all naturalized Chinese Canadians from their provincial voter lists. The following year, an amendment to the Act Respecting Municipalities was passed that stipulated that no Chinese person would be entitled to vote in any municipal election for a mayor or town councillor.

During the federal election campaign of 1878, an anti-Chinese organization known as the Workingmen's Protective Association emerged. Its objectives were "the mutual protection of the working classes of British Columbia against the influx of Chinese, and the use of legitimate means for the suppression of their immigration." All persons, male or female, of any nationality, creed, or colour—except the Chinese—could join the association. On September 30, 1878, it organized a public meeting in Victoria so that the political candidates could express their views on the question of Chinese immigration. It was made clear at the meeting that the organization would only support anti-Chinese politicians. At another meeting, the names of white firms and families employing Chinese people were read out in order to disgrace these employers of Chinese workers; housewives were advised not to employ any Chinese people or to patronize their businesses. Such activities contributed to anti-Chinese sentiment in the white community. It was reported in the Victoria *Colonist* that many businessmen and politicians publicly denounced Chinese workers, although they secretly hired them, but the newspaper named no names. At the end of 1879, the association was reorganized and renamed the Anti-Chinese Association—its motto was "No Surrender."

The British Columbia legislature established a committee in 1879 to consider how to put a halt to Chinese immigration. The committee recommended that, since the provincial legislature had no power to impose a tax exclusively on Chinese people, a grievance should be sent to the federal government setting out the baneful effects of the Chinese presence and stressing the necessity of taking effective measures to prevent further immigration to the province. This grievance was subsequently drafted and sent to Ottawa. In May 1879, the House of Commons established a select committee to study the "Chinese question." It suggested that Chinese immigration be discouraged and that Chinese workers should not be employed on federal public works. However, this suggestion was ignored when railway construction began.

Anti-Chinese organizations tried unsuccessfully to prevent the federal government from employing Chinese workers on the railway. In 1878, Amor De Cosmos, then an MP for Victoria, sent a petition with a thousand signatures to the federal government, requesting that employment of people with hair longer than 5.5 inches be prohibited. The letter was obviously directed at Chinese labourers with their queues. This request was rejected, and once railway construction started with Chinese labourers, violent incidents at construction sites occurred. A Chinese railway construction gang at Camp 37 near Lytton objected when two of their members were fired. The Chinese workers assaulted the foreman and several other white people. In the evening, twenty white men launched a retaliatory raid on the Chinese campsite, burning down the Chinese cabins and brutally clubbing the Chinese men, killing one.

Chen Jianzhong, a Chinese Canadian descendent who came to Canada in 1996, recalled his grandfather's story of when he came to Canada to work on the railway:

My granddad lived a long life so I had a chance to learn from him about that period of struggle for Chinese people living in Canada. He came to British Columbia from Zhongshan during the construction of the Canadian Pacific Railway. Racial discrimination was severe back then. The white people called the Chinese "Chink" or "Chinaman" instead of their names. Chinese people were forbidden to enter theatres or department stores. Once, my grandfather's older brother entered a large store to take a look, but he was driven out of the store.

The anti-Chinese organizations spread anti-Chinese ideas beyond the borders of British Columbia. After 1882, anti-Chinese editorials appeared in several eastern newspapers, including the *Toronto Telegram*, the *Toronto World*, the *Toronto Globe*, and the *Ottawa Herald*. These newspapers made derogatory remarks, calling the Chinese "yellow pagans" or describing "unhygienic conditions in laundries." The anti-Chinese organizations tried to increase pressure on the federal government to enact anti-Chinese legislation by turning public opinion against them. More and more newspapers began publishing anti-Chinese propaganda, joining the chorus of protest.

In August 1883, the coal miners in Wellington, BC, went on strike, demanding an increase in their wages. Robert Dunsmuir, the mine's owner, rejected their demand and evicted many white miners from company housing. In their place, he hired several hundred Chinese labourers from Victoria to work in the Wellington coal mines, which increased already-existing anti-Chinese sentiment. White coal miners demonstrated in protest and sent petitions to local politicians, who in turn voiced the workers' grievances to the provincial government. Dunsmuir held his ground and eventually broke the strike.

The Wellington strike and other violent incidents allowed the BC legislature to adopt an ever-stronger line against Chinese immigration. It was argued that Chinese labour both undermined white workers' strikes and spread diseases, posing a threat to the community. Tougher legislation was needed to restrict and limit Chinese immigration, and three drastic acts were quickly passed in 1884 in the legislature. These were an Act to Prevent Chinese from Acquiring Crown Lands, an Act to Prevent the Immigration of Chinese, and the Chinese Regulation Act. These three anti-Chinese acts did not comply with federal laws, so they were never enforced. But the acts stimulated and intensified anti-Chinese movements across western Canada, with very adverse impacts for the Chinese.

As the construction of the Canadian Pacific Railway came to an end in 1884, the federal government started to adjust its formerly supportive views regarding Chinese workers, and in July 1884, a royal commission was set up to investigate the issue of Chinese immigration. Mr. Tuckfield, a deputy of the Knights of Labor in Nanaimo, testified to the royal commission in August:

> Having visited the Chinese quarters in Victoria... [we] have found the premises occupied by Chinese in a most unhealthy condition; that vice, including prostitution and gambling, is abundant in those quarters.... They are a non-assimilating race. Their vices are most disgusting. They turn their sick out to die in the streets, and their lepers to fill our prisons. They control the labor market in this city. As producers and consumers they are no benefit to the country.... Our children must seek employment in other countries to make room.... In fact, the results of our investigations, brings [sic] us to the conclusion that the Chinese are a disgrace to a civilized community, and we beg that steps may be taken to stop the influx of Chinese to our shores.

This testimony helped stimulate the federal government to adopt anti-Chinese policies and enact discriminatory legislation, beginning in 1885.

Despite their experiences with discrimination and exclusion, Chinese labourers hoped to establish a good relationship with mainstream Canadian society and thought that demonstrating loyalty to local governments would result in fair treatment. In 1869, when Musgrave, the governor of British Columbia, visited Barkerville, the local Chinese welcomed him with an arch over the street and a shower of firecrackers. Led by Kwong Lee & Company, local Chinese merchants addressed the governor:

> We, the Chinese merchants and inhabitants of Cariboo, beg to offer you a cordial welcome, and to assure you of our loyalty and devotion to the Government of Her Most Gracious Majesty the Queen. We further wish to express our satisfaction at the impartial and just manner in which the laws of government of Her Majesty are administered, affording equal privileges and protection to all.

Musgrave responded graciously that he appreciated the sentiments they expressed and assured them that he would "preserve to you and your fellow countrymen the uninterrupted enjoyment of all advantages which are afforded to you in this colony." Unfortunately, his assurances proved to be unfounded.

Despite their contributions to the provincial economy, on the whole Chinese labourers endured humiliation, exploitation, and discrimination. But when they encountered treatment that was too inequitable, the Chinese could also stand up for themselves. An Act to Provide for the Better Collection of

Provincial Taxes from Chinese was passed on September 2, 1878, by the BC legislature. This act stipulated that each individual Chinese person over twelve years old would have to pay ten dollars every three months for a "residence licence" to live in British Columbia. Any Chinese people who did not purchase this licence would have their personal belongings seized and auctioned publicly to recoup the fee.

In response, the Chinese merchants in Victoria filed a petition with the Governor General. The petition asked him to disallow the act on three grounds: first, that it applied to children over twelve, whereas other provincial taxes were paid only by residents over eighteen; second, that it was not graduated according to ability to pay, but was "a large and arbitrary amount payable by poor and rich alike"; and third, that it applied only to Chinese people, many of them British subjects. At the same time, the Chinese leaders in Victoria sent petitions to Guo Songtao, the ambassador from China to Great Britain. Ambassador Guo voiced grievances to the British government, which were in turn forwarded to Ottawa for consideration.

Meanwhile, Victoria had hired Noah Shakespeare to collect the residence tax. Accompanied by a policeman, Shakespeare went to Chinatown to hunt for Chinese people and seize their belongings for public auction if they did not have a residence licence. This kindled intense anger among the Chinese. On September 17, a city-wide strike was organized to protest the act. Factories, hotels, restaurants, and households that employed Chinese workers were all affected. The strike lasted five days and succeeded in forcing Shakespeare to resign and the government to return the impounded goods. Through the joint efforts of the Chinese people, Justice Gray of the Supreme Court of British Columbia declared the Act to Provide for the Better Collection of Provincial Taxes from Chinese unconstitutional and invalid on September 27, 1879. This outcome was a blow to the anti-Chinese force. However, such early efforts to fight discriminatory policies failed to change the overall anti-Chinese trend in Canada, and in western Canada in particular.

In 1882, the American government passed a Chinese Immigration Act that prohibited the entry of Chinese labourers into the United States for ten years. After the passage of this act, many anti-Chinese activists in Canada appealed to the federal government to pass a similar Chinese immigration act in Canada. Under pressure from the government of British Columbia, the federal government passed the Chinese Immigration Act on July 2, 1885, which imposed a fifty-dollar tax per head on Chinese immigrants to Canada, ushering in the era of restricted entry to Canada.

RELATIONSHIPS WITH FIRST NATIONS PEOPLE

Both Chinese and First Nations people occupied the lowest strata of the labour force. They earned roughly the same amount of money per day, whereas white workers earned much higher wages. Records show that a Chinese labourer made $1.00–$1.25 per day, a First Nations labourer earned $1.00–$1.50 per day, and a white labourer was paid $2.00–$3.75.

Although both Chinese and First Nations people were disadvantaged groups, their relationship was complex. There existed both common ground and conflicts between them. Gillian Marie wrote in her thesis, "Attitudes toward Chinese Immigrants to British Columbia 1858–1885":

> The antagonism and violent treatment of Chinese miners by whites was acknowledged by Indians who accepted the white man's racism. This situation was recognized by white contemporaries. The Bishop of Columbia wrote in 1860 that the Indians south of Lytton looked upon Chinese men with "an evident sense of their own superiority," holding the Chinese in great contempt. Commander R. C. Mayne spent four years in British Columbia from 1858 and in his experience the Indians refused to regard both blacks and Chinese with "any of the respect claimed by and shown to whites." He recounts an incident when a local Indian asked him about the Chinese and when told they were "carqua King George men [i.e., the same as Englishmen]," the Indian replied "Wake, wake! [No, no!]."

Historical records concerning the relationship between Chinese labourers and First Nations people are scarce. Traces of this relationship are largely based on oral family histories, the remaining official records, and observations made by European Canadians.

During the first decades of Chinese immigration, Chinese gold seekers competed with First Nations people not only in the search for gold but also in finding other employment. Evidence that some First Nations people looked down on the Chinese can be found in historical documents, although such documents do not contain enough evidence to prove that incidents of contempt or violence were necessarily the result of widespread ethnic or racial discrimination. There were instances where First Nations individuals murdered Chinese miners. One example concerns a Chinese miner named Pulingo. Pulingo hired a First Nations man to transport him by canoe to a spot eight miles above Hope on the Harrison River. This man, Tachnack, is believed to have murdered Pulingo and stolen his gold and other possessions. He served a year in jail with hard labour for the theft but he was never charged with the murder, because Pulingo's body was never recovered.

A letter from Port Douglas, titled "The Indian and Chinese Fight," was published in the Victoria *Daily Colonist* on September 12, 1860. The letter related:

Having just arrived from Cayoosh, I intend sending you a few items of interest concerning the Chinamen and Shuswap Indians. The former were attacked about the 20th of August, by a party of Indians, who carried away with them all the provisions they could find in the Chinese camp, and threatened to take the Chinamen's lives if they resisted. The Chinamen, not being armed, said nothing, but let the Indians plunder them. The next day the Indians came again on a similar errand, but did not want provisions; they wanted the Chinamen's blankets. The night before the Chinese had purchased some fire-arms from white men. The demand was refused, when the Indians fired on them, killing two Chinamen. The Chinamen returned the fire, killing two Indians and two clootchmen [Chinook word for First Nations women], and wounding several others. Both parties ran—one party up and the other down the river. The Chinamen came down in canoes to Big Bar. When I left Cayoosh, Judge Elwyn, with R. Flynn, constable, and two deputies, was up the river inquiring about the matter, and to arrest the guilty party, but had not succeeded at the last accounts. There are some Chinese at Big Bar yet, but a good many are coming down the river to work on the Lower Fraser.

The origin of the fight was the murder of Chinamen on Dancing Bill's Bar last April. They were supposed to have been murdered by white men for a long time. Their throats were cut from ear to ear, and the bodies rolled up in blankets, put in a canoe, and sent adrift down the river. All the Indians from Caycosh to Fort Alexander denied that any Siwash had murdered them, as Indians never cut the throats of their victims. But a large reward for the apprehension of the murderer at last brought it out. Three weeks ago the chief at La Fontaine lodged a complaint against an Indian as the murderer, and constables Flynn and Potts immediately went to La Fontaine to secure him.

When constable D. Potts approached him the Indian fired upon him, whereupon the constable fired two shots and killed him instantly. Since that time the Indians have been grumbling, and at last have broken out in open war against the Celestials.

In spite of such occurrences, there gradually emerged a shared sense that both Chinese and First Nations people were victims of the discriminatory practices of the mainstream British population. The First Nations people no longer considered the Chinese as aliens who threatened their livelihoods and, in some cases, Chinese men and First Nations women entered marital relationships. There were almost no Chinese women in BC and many First

Nations men had died of smallpox and other diseases brought by Europeans. Such unions were thus attractive to both parties, offering emotional support and a sense of community to Chinese men living far from their home villages.

The traditional cultures of First Nations people and the Chinese also shared traits that formed a solid basis for Sino–First Nations relations. On First Nations reserves, the Chinese discovered that First Nations people, like themselves, lived in extended family units that respected their elders and cared for the young, rather than in nuclear families. Also, like themselves, Chinese labourers found that First Nations peoples worshipped their deceased ancestors and other spirits. First Nations people believed that after death a person's soul left his or her body and became a ghost. Similarly, the Chinese believed that every person has a soul and that after death, that soul becomes a ghost. Both ethnic groups offered sacrifices to the spirits of heaven and earth at important festivals. They could share traditional medicines and herbs and knowledge of plants and their uses.

Neither the Chinese nor the First Nations people wanted close relatives to marry. They believed that children of marriages between relatives within five generations would have defects. Therefore, First Nations people preferred to marry those from a distant place, and Chinese men met this need. Today, there are still people in British Columbia with both a First Nations and a Chinese heritage. Quite a large number of people in the lō Nation bear Chinese surnames, showing their Chinese ancestry. In the Cheam First Nation and the Lillooet First Nation, there were also cases where Chinese men and First Nations women cohabited.

Larry Grant, the descendant of a marriage between a Chinese man and a First Nations woman, lives on the Musqueam Reserve in Vancouver. He told us in an interview:

> My father was named Hong Tim Hing and he was a Chinese labourer. My mother was Agnes Grant and she was a First Nations woman. So I have a mixed heritage. After arriving in Canada, my grandfather grew vegetables on the Musqueam Farm. Later he brought my father to Canada at the age of 14 or 15 years. Almost the same age, both my father and mother lived and worked on the Musqueam Farm in their youth. My mother was the only daughter in her family. She often ran into my father as she was fetching water. When she grew up and was around 22 or 23 years old, my father found that she was still single, so he proposed a marriage by asking for her father's approval. My mother's reply was that she did not want a husband. But my grandfather on my mother's side accepted my father and told her "this man is your husband." From

then on, my mother and father lived together and later gave birth to my brother and me. When I was young, others often called me "half breed." Because my father was a Chinese labourer, my parents could not live on the Musqueam Reserve, which was a First Nations reserve, so they sometimes lived in Chinatown. Many Chinese labourers who worked on the Musqueam Reserve used Chinatown as their mailing address because Chinatown was legitimate for them. My father died at the age of 51. After my mother died later, she was not buried with my father but in the First Nations graveyard.

In general, most First Nations women who lived with Chinese men were unwilling to legally marry them. Under the system that existed then, First Nations people with legal Indian status were entitled to welfare and benefits, whereas the Chinese men were not. Marriage to a Chinese man would result in a loss of legal status for a First Nations woman and she would have to leave the reserve and lose her entitlement to benefits. As a result, most women chose to live with Chinese men rather than marry them. However, there were some cases where First Nations women chose marriage over status. Senator Lillian Eva Dyck, whose father, Yok Leen Quan, was from Kaiping, in Guangdong Province in China, and whose mother was a First Nations woman, reported that after her parents married, her mother lost her status under the Indian Act. In addition to losing their status, it was stipulated that where on-reserve cohabitation between Chinese labourers and First Nations women was not permitted, they would have to live apart or cohabit elsewhere. Many Chinese labourers who worked and lived on First Nations reserves therefore recorded Chinatown as their mailing address in order to disguise the fact that they were living on a reserve. For Chinese labourers, even cohabitation with First Nations women was not easy.

The federal government inadvertently played a role in the developing relationship between Chinese labourers and First Nations people. In 1877, it permitted some Chinese men to rent lands on the Musqueam Reserve to farm. The government's purpose was to have the Chinese, who had been farmers in their home province of Guangdong, show Chinese methods of farming to the Musqueam people, so they could earn a living from farming rather than following their traditional way of life. The rents paid by the Chinese were distributed to band members through the Indian Affairs department, providing a source of income to the Musqueam Nation. In this way, Chinese labourers made a unique contribution to a First Nations economy.

Since the sale of fish they caught was prohibited by the government, First Nations fishers traded salmon with Chinese farmers in exchange for rice and vegetables. These first Chinese farmers raised pigs, chickens, and ducks and grew vegetables they sold to the surrounding Euro-Canadian community. Payments for rent, food, and animal feed depleted their income and many lived in poverty, but the First Nations people were even poorer. Later, with newly invented transportation vehicles, Chinese farmers became able to sell vegetables in Chinatown, and their economic status began to improve.

Racial discrimination against both Chinese and First Nations people in this early period was not only expressed in daily life but also evident in burial practices. Neither deceased Chinese people nor First Nations people were allowed to be buried in Christian Euro-Canadian cemeteries. First Nations people established their own burial grounds on their reserves and allowed those Chinese people with whom they had developed relationships to be buried there too. Evidence of these early Chinese burial sites on reserves may still be found today in the territory of the lō First Nation. Sonny McHalsie, the executive director of the lō Aboriginal History and Culture Research Centre, said that protection of ancestral relics and burial grounds is a tradition of the lō people and that without the tradition, stories of the Chinese who came to live and work in lō territory could not have been handed down through the generations.

Between 1858 and 1885, when the gold rushes, railway construction, and early development of fisheries and agriculture in BC occurred, a different relationship was forged between the Chinese labourers and First Nations people compared to the relationships between both peoples and the dominant Euro-Canadians. In spite of some misunderstandings and conflicts, on the whole, Chinese labourers and First Nations people sympathized with each other, helped each other by participating in two-way exchanges, and learned from each other. The mutual exchange of goods and effective co-operation between First Nations people and Chinese labourers can be considered a prelude to the relative harmony among ethnic groups that characterizes multicultural Canada today.

PART II

THE HEAD TAX ERA, 1885–1922

Chinese winter quarters near North Bend, BC, 1886. Major Mathews Collection. City of Vancouver Archives, Out P41.

THE HEAD TAX AND
ITS IMPACT ON IMMIGRATION

❦

After the CPR was completed in 1885, several factors converged that made a head tax seem likely to provide a solution to the perceived problem of Chinese immigration. The economy moved into recession and there were many unemployed workers, including former Chinese railway workers, which increased resentment among non-Chinese labourers. The railway itself facilitated better communication between the centres of power in the east and the west coast, and, as the western provinces were created and gained parliamentary seats in Ottawa, the political influence of the west in national affairs (like immigration) increased. The anti-Chinese prejudice prevalent in the west began to spread eastward, helped by the media and influencing political actions taken by provincial and federal governments.

THE ROYAL COMMISSION ON CHINESE IMMIGRATION, 1884

Responding to anti-Chinese pressure from BC, the federal government decided to appoint a royal commission both to ease the situation in BC and to obtain evidence that would justify imposing restrictions on further Chinese immigration to Canada. The Royal Commission on Chinese Immigration was formed in July 1884. The commissioners appointed were Dr. Joseph Adolphe Chapleau, federal secretary of state, and Dr. John Hamilton Gray, a British Columbia supreme court judge. The secretary of the commission was Nicholas Flood Davin, the editor of the Regina newspaper, the *Leader*.

The commission conducted its enquiries mainly in San Francisco and British Columbia. Since some of the first Chinese to enter Canada had previously participated in the California gold rush and settled in San Francisco, the commission first made enquiries there, taking testimony from a leading American merchant, the president of the Immigration Association of California, the chief of police, a detective, a police magistrate, a customs officer, and a white scholar of Asian studies. The only Chinese people consulted were the consul general and the consul. In British Columbia, the commission visited Victoria, Nanaimo, New Westminster, and Yale.

Opposite: Canadian Pacific Railway Chinese labourers' camp at Kamloops. Courtesy of the Royal BC Museum and Archives, image D-04712.

The commissioners asked twenty-seven questions and received responses from fifty-one witnesses in British Columbia, including lawyers, the provincial tax collector, farmers, bank managers, lumbermen, railway construction contractors, mining company owners, and a single female witness, a non-Chinese prostitute addicted to opium. These witnesses were directed questions such as the following:

- What classes of people come here as emigrants from China? Are they chiefly laborers, mechanics or traders?...
- Have you any system of public poor relief, and do they often become a burden on that fund, or upon the private charity of white citizens?
- Are they industrious, sober, economical and law-abiding or are they lazy, drunken, extravagant or turbulent?
- Do they respect their engagements with white men, and carry out their contracts?
- Do they show any disposition to interfere with the prospects of the white population in any way beyond the competition which they offer in the labor market?...
- Is there anything in their habits or mode of living injurious to the public peace, or to the public health?...
- Is their presence here any longer necessary or desirable?
- What would be the effect upon the comfort and prosperity of the people of this Province, if they were to go hence voluntarily or otherwise?

Although most of the testimony exhibited prejudice against the Chinese, there were exceptions. Railway contractor Andrew Onderdonk, who employed many Chinese labourers, testified that they were efficient workers. He stated that Chinese labourers "are industrious, sober, economical, and law-abiding; they are not drunken, extravagant, or turbulent. The development of the country would be retarded and many industries abandoned [without them]." His opinion was echoed by Thomas E. Ladner, who stated that "if the canneries in British Columbia had to depend on white labor, every one, without any exception, would be closed up and the industry be entirely killed..."

Mr. Samuel Robins, superintendent of the Vancouver Coal Mining and Land Company, however, testified:

When the Chinese first came to this province they no doubt supplied a want then felt, and their coming was encouraged and welcomed, especially I may add by the Vancouver Coal Mining and

Land Company (Limited), which I represent; but the laboring population were always strongly averse to their introduction. At the time of their coming here my company had been suffering from a strike of the white laborers, and we accepted the Chinese as a weapon with which to settle the dispute.... The encouragement given to the Chinese by employers of labor has not been withdrawn up to the present time, whilst the anti-Chinese feeling seems to have grown stronger every year....

The presence of the Chinese has no doubt contributed to the development of the province....

In fact, wages are high enough to attract the best class of white labor. Of nearly 400 white laborers employed by my company, not one earns less than $2 a day.... [The Chinese laborers] earn from $1 to $1.25 per diem.

Evidently, Robins felt that paying lower wages was an acceptable practice when Chinese labourers were employed, and other business owners concurred.

Among the prejudiced statements made to the commission, three common opinions stood out. The first was that the Chinese were morally corrupt and disease-ridden. In John A. Bradley's testimony, he contended that the Chinese smuggled, violated sanitary regulations, defied and despised laws, smoked opium, had introduced leprosy on the west coast, and contributed to the corruption and depravity of the youth of the coast.

The second common opinion was regarding unfair competition between Chinese and white labourers. Gilbert Malcolm Sproat explained that "the ordinary Chinese labourer [lived] a low animal existence with a few coarse enjoyments," so did not require wages as high as the non-Chinese labourers. It was widely held that the presence of Chinese labourers reduced wages and limited positions available to non-Chinese workers. The British Columbia chapter of the Knights of Labor testified:[†]

They are thus fitted to become all too dangerous competitors in the labor market, while their docile servility, the natural outcome of centuries of grinding poverty and humble submission to a most oppressive system of government, renders them doubly dangerous as the willing tools whereby grasping and tyrannical employers grind down all labor to the lowest living point.

[†] The Knights of Labor was an early labour organization, initially formed in the US in 1869. The first local in BC was formed in 1883 and other locals followed. Most members were miners or railway workers. The Knights of Labor maintained an anti-Asian stance and lobbied for the exclusion of Chinese workers from BC.

The third common assertion made by the witnesses was that the Chinese were unable to be assimilated into the mainstream society. Alexander E. B. Davie, the attorney general of British Columbia, expressed this view in his testimony: "They are a foreign element, and certainly there was no desire for it [assimilation] from the whites, and probably none on the part of the Chinese, and apparently always will be so."

In his conclusion, Commissioner Gray felt that opinion was divided among three camps:

First: Of a well meaning, but strongly prejudiced minority, whom nothing but absolute exclusion will satisfy.

Second: An intelligent minority, who conceive that no legislation whatever is necessary—that, as in all business transactions, the rule of supply and demand will apply and the matter regulate itself in the ordinary course of events.

Third: Of a large majority, who think there should be a moderate restriction, based upon police, financial and sanitary principles, sustained and enforced by stringent local regulations for cleanliness and the preservation of health.

Dr. Chapleau did not agree that white people were deprived of employment because the Chinese accepted lower wages. He also believed that the contrast between the Euro-Canadian and Chinese peoples was not a contrast between civilized and barbarian peoples, but a contrast between two very different kinds of civilization, and that the attack in BC on Chinese labourers was derived from prejudice and ignorance.

Despite this dissenting opinion, both Commissioners Gray and Chapleau aligned themselves with the third group, siding with the anti-Chinese forces. In order to impose some restriction on Chinese immigration, the commission proposed that a moderate head tax of ten dollars be levied on incoming Chinese immigrants. Their proposal was submitted on April 10, 1885.

Many British Columbia residents attacked the report of the royal commission, finding its moderate recommendations unacceptable, and several public meetings were held in various communities in British Columbia to protest it. On May 2, 1885, only a few weeks after the report was released, a public meeting was held in Victoria, presided over by the mayor of Victoria, Robert Rithet. One of the participants, Geo. Powell, complained:

The working classes of British Columbia, at public meetings and through their representative in the local parliament, have repeatedly petitioned and protested against the introduction of Chinese in preference to white labor; and the Dominion Government, aided by Chinese supporters and admirers in this province, have paid no attention to the just and lawful demands of the people, but have added insult to injury by preparing a farcical measure to restrict Chinese immigration, which does not become operative until the services of Chinese are no longer required on public works. Therefore the working classes of British Columbia and all others who are suffering from the effects of Chinese competition call upon the trades unions of Canada for such active and political support as may be deemed necessary to cleanse the government of tricksters and the country of Chinese vampires.

At the meeting, many participants claimed that the Chinese were ruled by secret societies and called upon the trades unions to ratify a boycott against employing them. Judge Gray became a target for unbridled satire. One person suggested that he ought to go and live with the Chinese since he maintained that the majority of people in British Columbia had no issue with them.

After this meeting, the anti-Chinese committee met again on May 4 and developed a plan to deliver its resolution to Ottawa. The committee also advertised in the *Daily Colonist* of May 20, informing the public of its decision to hold a mass meeting and demonstration on May 21 to protest the royal commission report and the new immigration act, and to call for all employers to boycott Chinese labour.

The Head Tax of 1885

In spite of the protests from BC that the commission had proposed too weak a solution, on July 20, 1885, the federal government passed an Act to Restrict and Regulate Chinese Immigration into Canada, based on anti-Chinese public opinion in BC, sympathetic views held in eastern Canada, and the findings of the royal commission. It came into effect on August 20, 1885, one month later. This was the first legislation enacted in Canada based on discrimination against a specific nationality, and it marked the end of an era in which Chinese immigrants could enter Canada freely.[†]

Rather than the relatively moderate ten dollars proposed by the royal commission, the government instead levied a much heavier tax of fifty dollars. The act also exempted certain immigrant groups from the tax. Section four of the act required that:

> every person of Chinese origin shall pay... on entering Canada, at the port or other place of entry, the sum of fifty dollars, except

---

† Records were kept of each Chinese immigrant who paid or was exempted from the head tax. The General Registers of Chinese Immigration were kept from 1885 to 1949 and are available today online in a searchable database, Immigrants from China, maintained by Library and Archives Canada.

the following persons who shall be exempt from such payment, that is to say, first: the members of the Diplomatic Corps, or other Government representatives and their suite and their servants, consuls and consular agents; and second: tourists, merchants, men of science and students, who are bearers of certificates of identity, specifying their occupation and their object in coming into Canada, or other similar documents issued by the Chinese Government or other Government whose subjects they are; and every such certificate or other documents shall be in English or French language, and shall be examined and indorsed (*visé*) by a British consul or Chargé d'Affaires or other accredited representative of Her Majesty, at the place where the same is granted, or at the port or place of departure....

In the act, the word *merchant* was not defined and it was left to the immigration officers to interpret it. Chinese children and youths who came to Canada also had to pay the head tax, but if they could prove that they had attended school for at least one year after their arrival, the head tax would be refunded. In addition to the fifty-dollar head tax, no vessel carrying Chinese immigrants to any port in Canada could carry more than one immigrant for each fifty tons of its weight, and the owners of such vessels would be liable for a fine of fifty dollars for each person it carried in excess of this number. In comparison, a ship transporting European immigrants to Canada was allowed two immigrants for every two tons of vessel weight, and there was no head tax payable.

The ship's master of any vessel bringing Chinese immigrants to any port in Canada had to collect the head tax from the immigrants and submit the money, along with a complete list of crew and passengers, to port authorities. No one could disembark till these formalities were complete. In addition, the quarantine officer had to examine the passengers before they left the ship and issue a bill of health certifying that no one on board had leprosy or an infectious disease (clause 9).

Amendments to the act were made in 1887, 1892, 1900, and 1903. The amendment of 1887 expanded the list of exemptions to include Chinese people who were just passing through Canada on their way to somewhere else, usually the United States. And Chinese women who were married to non-Chinese men were exempted because they were considered to have become citizens of their husband's country on marriage. The amendment of 1892 required Chinese residents of Canada who wished to leave the country temporarily to register with an immigration officer before departing.

The amendments of 1900 and 1903 raised the head tax to try to stem the continuing flow of Chinese immigrants. The Chinese Immigration Act of

1900 doubled the tax, to one hundred dollars per person. In 1903, it was again raised, to the very punitive level of five hundred dollars. The head tax on Chinese immigrants increased the income of both the federal and provincial governments. Between 1886 and 1924, Chinese immigrants paid nearly twenty-four million dollars in head tax. This revenue was shared between the federal government and the provinces—mainly British Columbia, where almost all the Chinese immigrants entered Canada. The head tax fund helped the federal government pay for the construction of the Canadian Pacific Railway and the British Columbia government to build the provincial Parliament building in Victoria.

THE ROYAL COMMISSION ON CHINESE AND JAPANESE IMMIGRATION, 1900

In 1900, responding to continuing anti-Chinese agitation, another royal commission was appointed to investigate the continuing immigration of Chinese people to Canada. This commission also investigated Japanese immigration, because, by this time, Japanese newcomers had also become an issue in British Columbia.

On September 21, 1900, the federal government appointed three commissioners. They were R. C. Clute, a distinguished lawyer from Toronto, who served as chairman of the commission; Daniel James Munn, a bookkeeper at a cannery in New Westminster; and Ralph Smith, a union leader and politician from Nanaimo. Ralph Smith resigned after he was elected to a federal seat and was replaced by Christopher Foley, a union organizer and political activist.

In the introduction to its report, the commissioners refer to a large number of petitions that had been submitted during the 1890s to the federal government protesting Chinese immigration and demanding more restrictive legislation. In 1897 alone, petitions were submitted signed by 1,934 people from Vancouver, 600 people from Nanaimo, and 2,700 BC residents from a variety of places; other petitions from Port Haney, Burnaby, Kaslo, Vernon, and other communities were also submitted. The common message among these petitions was that the head tax of fifty dollars had proved inadequate to stem the flow of Chinese immigration, and that the large influx of Chinese into Canada was considered a serious menace to the prosperity and general welfare of this country and British Columbia in particular, for the following amongst other reasons:

> ... that these Chinese are non-assimilative and have no intention
> of settled citizenship, are in moral, social and sanitary status below
> the most inferior standard of Western life, and being usually single
> (the most of them being imported as coolies by labour-contracting

organizations) accept less than the lowest living wage of white labour, yet expend but little of their scanty earnings in the land of their temporary adoption.

The anti-Chinese sentiments related to Chinese labour practices in Canada were augmented by political events in China. The Boxer Rebellion of 1900, in which China attempted to expel all foreigners from its territory, had failed, and China was forced to sign submissive treaties with the Western nations, including Britain. These events exacerbated anti-Chinese feeling in Canada around the time of the royal commission.

The commission took testimony from the Chinese Board of Trade in Victoria about occupations and family composition there. They also interviewed the Chinese Consolidated Benevolent Association in Victoria, Japanese social groups, and Chinese and Japanese employers and merchants. A few hundred people, most of them not Chinese, were interviewed in Victoria, Nanaimo, Union, Vancouver, New Westminster, Kamloops, Vernon, Revelstoke, Rossland, Nelson, Sandon, and Kaslo, as well as in Portland, Oregon, and San Francisco.

The conclusions of this royal commission were similar to the ones reached by the earlier commission. Although it was admitted that Chinese labour was essential in some industries, such as the canning industry or to supply domestic servants where they "are found valuable, useful and convenient," the report in general did not favour the Chinese and far more witnesses opposed the Chinese presence in Canada than supported it. The commissioners reported regarding the possibility of assimilation that "there is absolute unanimity with respect to the Chinese, that they would not assimilate and it was not desirable that they should." The report stated that, except for the merchant class, the Chinese did not pay their fair share of taxes. On the issue of further restrictions or exclusion, both skilled and unskilled labourers favoured complete exclusion. Among professional, industrial, agricultural, and other employers, fewer than ten favoured unrestricted immigration; and "of the rest, a few took the view that the tax now imposed was, for the present, at all events, sufficient, but the general consensus of opinion was in favour of higher restriction, or total exclusion."

The commission also considered whether more restricted or exclusionary policies would have a negative impact on trade between Canada and China. After examining the effects of the American exclusion act, the commission concluded that, since US trade with China had increased during the time it was enforced, "we are of the opinion that further restriction or exclusion will not appreciably affect the trade of Canada with China."

The final conclusion reached by the commission was that increasing the head tax from fifty dollars to one hundred dollars was inadequate and that their recommendation was to increase it to five hundred dollars, a goal they achieved.

Joe Dang is a Chinese Canadian who lives in Coquitlam, BC. His parents immigrated to Canada during the head tax era. Joe described some of his parents' experiences in the early 1900s:

> My father was Dang (Deng) Yee Gee. He was born in Nanhai county in Guangdong province on August 22, 1882. In 1908 he had to borrow money from fellow villagers in order to emigrate to Canada. Besides the fare for the ship, there was also the Head Tax of $500 that the Canadian government assessed for Chinese to enter. He began physical work in a limestone quarry [now occupied by the Butchart Gardens in Victoria, BC]. All the Chinese working in this quarry were assigned to all the dangerous chores including blasting the rocks to make cement. There were many fatalities from this work. Working in the quarry, Yee Gee, along with the others, had to live in tents, also known in Chinese as "fangkou." Father said that he worked 12 hour days for only 12 cents per hour. This of course, made the Head Tax a tidy sum to be paid off. My mother Soo Hoo had a very difficult life as a child because her father died when Soo Hoo was very young. When Soo Hoo's mother remarried, they were socially rejected because a woman remarrying in those days was not acceptable. They were having great difficulties in surviving and this resulted in Soo Hoo being sold to a Zhou family in Vancouver. So in 1913, at the age of 8, Soo Hoo along with her 6-year-old brother travelled to North America. During the long six-week voyage, her younger brother fell sick and died. Soo Hoo finally made it to Victoria where she became a servant for the Zhou family.

EVADING THE HEAD TAX

Because the head tax was so high, many Chinese people wishing to come to Canada found ways to avoid paying it. In 1910–11, Justice Dennis Murphy headed a royal commission that investigated the illegal entry of Chinese immigrants, and his report describes a number of fraudulent methods used to enter Canada in the years 1904–10.

One method was to stow away on a ship coming to Canada. Chinese stowaways used the three major passenger ship lines or tramp cargo steamers to get to Canada. Most of these ships had Chinese crews who hid the stowaways in coal cabins or other concealed locations, supplied them with food on the voyage, and helped them leave the ship once it had arrived in Canada. Stowing away took advantage of the loose security at Canadian ports. In Vancouver, there was only one government watchman to watch the ship after it docked. Chinese stowaways could secretly leave the boat to go ashore when the watchman was not on guard. Some swam to shore; others were picked up by pre-arranged boats and taken ashore. The port on Vancouver Island at Union Bay where ships stopped to refuel with coal was even less guarded; no watchman was employed at all. This was also the case at Nanaimo.

In his report, Justice Murphy described a case in August 1910 in which American and Canadian authorities apprehended fifty-three Chinese stowaways on board the *Kumeric*, a Bank Line ship commuting between Asia and the coastal ports of the Pacific Northwest. Among those captured was Yuen Jen Hing, who told the authorities that in March 1910, twenty stowaways had landed successfully at Vancouver. Justice Murphy concluded that "the number of stowaways who have entered Canada in the past is only limited to the number that have attempted that route"—that is, in all probability, quite a large number.

Another method by which Chinese crew members illicitly entered Canada was by trading places with Chinese on shore who wished to return to China. There were about 80 to 120 crew members on each of the large ships and, by trading places, people who wished to return to China permanently could do so at no cost, and the crew who wished to stay could simply take their places. Justice Murphy concluded that such exchanges could have been accomplished very easily but that the number of people who traded places would not have been great.

The sale of re-entry certificates was a third method used to gain entry. Before 1913, Canada's Chinese entry documents lacked photographs. Identifying the re-entrants was done by comparing a set of physical characteristics that had been recorded at the time of the person's first entry into Canada with the characteristics of the person holding the re-entry certificate. Chinese labourers who had saved enough and wanted to return permanently to China could claim they were merely going for a visit and apply for a re-entry permit. Since they had no intention of coming back to Canada, they then sold the permit to a person in China who wanted to come to Canada. A black market in re-entry documents thus flourished.

The man employed as the government's interpreter in Vancouver, Yip On, was involved in this scheme. When a ship whose ultimate destination was Vancouver arrived at Victoria, Yip On went to Victoria with a white officer and boarded the ship. On the way to Vancouver, Yip On was able to talk to the "re-entering" people in a language his white companion did not understand and to make arrangements with them so that they could land in Canada without any difficulties. Since he had the job of reading out the physical characteristics of the re-entrants, he could easily omit any that did not apply. Estimates suggest that Yip On helped Chinese immigrants avoid paying as much as a million dollars in head taxes and helped two thousand entrants using false papers between 1906 and 1910.

A last method was to take advantage of the head tax exemptions for certain categories of immigrants. Between 1886 and 1923, 89,652 Chinese immigrants arrived in Canada, of whom 7,908 were exempted from the head tax. In 1921 alone, of the 2,435 Chinese who arrived, 1,550 were exempted from the head tax. The exemption categories most successfully used were the exemption for merchants and the exemption for students (described on pages 76–77).

The immigration law allowed a merchant to bring in his wife, sons, and daughters free of the head tax. The Chinese did not bring in many wives or daughters, but they did bring in many so-called "sons"—the number grew from 16 in 1904 to 462 in 1910. Many Chinese labourers registered themselves in Canada as merchants for the express purpose of bringing in such sons. Canada's procedures made head tax evasion in this way simple. Chinese immigrants could easily memorize a coaching book that contained the right answers to the standard questions asked by immigration officials. Most false papers came with these coaching books, along with contracts that required immigrants to consistently maintain the appearance of belonging to their paper family.

Chinese merchants themselves were also exempted from paying the head tax. So-called merchants could enter Canada without having to bring a minimum amount of money to invest in Canada or engaging in a business in Canada. Local Chinese and brokers developed a network dedicated to assisting Chinese people to avoid paying the head tax by posing as merchants. Yip On's brother opened an immigration agency active in the Pearl River Delta area of Guangdong, and the brothers operated an immigration network. In 1910, Mak Wai of Taishan County wanted to emigrate to Canada. In China, he gave his name and photograph to unnamed "gentlemen" in his village. These gentlemen arranged for a Chinese passport that stated that Mak was a rice merchant, and the British consul approved his application as a head-tax-exempt merchant. However, when Canadian officials in Vancouver questioned him without Yip On's expected aid, Mak cracked and admitted that his father was a Chinese laundryman in Philadelphia, which was his most likely destination.

NEGOTIATIONS WITH CHINA

Levying a heavy head tax on Chinese immigrants did not accord with prevailing international practice, and several attempts were made to remove it. The Chinese Consolidated Benevolent Association in Victoria feared that the federal government would prohibit Chinese entry to Canada completely.

In March 1903, the association sent a letter to Yang Shuwen, the Chinese consul general in Canada, and Lin Shiyuan, the consul in Vancouver, asking them to advise the Chinese government to ban Chinese emigration to Canada, only lifting the ban when jobs became available in Canada. Their advice was not heeded.

In March 1909, W. L. Mackenzie King, then the federal deputy minister of labour, attended the International Opium Conference in Shanghai. While in China, he went to Beijing to meet Liang Tun-yen, the Chinese minister for foreign affairs, and proposed to him that if China, like Japan and India, restricted emigration by issuing only a limited number of passports, Canada would remove the head tax on Chinese immigrants. But Liang Tun-yen replied only that Mackenzie King should discuss the proposal with the newly established Chinese consulate in Canada, and this idea was dropped.

The CCBA again sent information in 1913 to both China and the Chinese consul general in Ottawa advising against further Chinese immigration, but its efforts were ineffective. In 1914, after the Manchu government had been overthrown and the Republic of China established, China tried to open negotiations aimed at removing the head tax. The Chinese government proposed to Canada that only a thousand visas to Canada would be issued per year, on the condition that the Canadian government abolish the head tax and ensure that Chinese immigrants would be entitled to the same rights and privileges as other ethnic groups. The Chinese also indicated that, should more than a thousand Chinese labourers be needed for public works projects, it would issue enough visas to satisfy the need. The federal government refused these conditions because overruling the discriminatory legislation of the provincial governments, especially in BC, would create strife between the two levels of government domestically. Collection of the head tax continued.

THE EFFECTS OF THE HEAD TAX ON IMMIGRATION

Initially, the head tax did restrict the number of Chinese immigrants to some degree. In 1885, fifty dollars was a large sum of money for most of the Chinese who wished to come to Canada. According to the 1885 royal commission report, a Chinese immigrant earned an average monthly wage of twenty-five dollars, or three hundred dollars a year. After paying $130 for food and clothing, $24 for rent, $28 for taxes, medication, religious donations, and other expenses, and deducting three months' wages of $75 for "winter costs" (meaning that a labourer would be laid off for three months during the winter, earning no wages), a Chinese immigrant could save only $43 a year.

Many non-Chinese people were disappointed to find that the fifty-dollar tax did not halt Chinese immigration, and the anti-Chinese movement successfully started agitating for the federal government to raise the tax, first to a hundred dollars, and then, in July 1903, to five hundred dollars. The increased head tax proved to be a very heavy financial burden. In the case of newcomers who had borrowed money to emigrate, they had to pay the debt incurred to make the voyage to Canada, as well as the money for the head tax. The head tax thus increased their indebtedness, further impoverishing already-poor Chinese labourers. The tax also meant that these immigrants could not afford to bring their families—who would also have to pay the tax—to Canada, nor could they afford to return to China to visit them.

Once the head tax was raised to five hundred dollars, the number of Chinese immigrants briefly dwindled from 245 in 1903 to 8 in 1905 and 22 in 1906, although by 1913–14, the number had risen again, to about 13,000 new arrivals. Despite the steep (temporary) decline in the numbers of immigrants, the Victoria Trades and Labour Council still maintained that the head tax was too low to be effective and suggested in a letter to Prime Minister Wilfrid Laurier that the Chinese should be totally excluded from Canada or that the head tax should be increased to a thousand dollars. It was not raised beyond five hundred dollars, but it was later replaced by an act excluding the Chinese altogether.

Although the head tax was a large sum for a Chinese labourer in the late nineteenth and early twentieth centuries, it was still more lucrative for a Chinese person to work in Canada than in China, where economic and political conditions were very unsettled in the early twentieth century as the empire was overthrown and replaced by a republic. A Chinese labourer could earn ten to twenty times more a month in Canada than he could in China. Therefore, in spite of the heavy head tax, Chinese people continued to come to Canada to find work. Although many Chinese returned to China permanently during the head tax era, the Chinese population continued to grow. Between 1901 and 1921, the Chinese population in Canada grew from 17,312 to 39,587; two-thirds of the Chinese lived in BC.

ANTI-CHINESE DISCRIMINATION IN THE HEAD TAX ERA

❦

During the head tax era, the Chinese continued to experience the racism and discrimination that began in the gold rush period. Anti-Chinese sentiment was widespread in British Columbia. Racism was relatively weak in the mid-1880s in the other provinces, where there were far fewer Chinese residents. After the CPR was completed, a growing number of Chinese moved to the Prairies and the eastern provinces. Racist attitudes also spread eastward and were expressed in discriminatory policies and in some cases erupted into violent conflicts.

DISCRIMINATION IN DAILY LIFE

Throughout the head tax era, newspapers in British Columbia contributed to the development of racist attitudes by spreading negative information about the Chinese people. Newspaper reports frequently stated that Chinese labourers depressed wages paid to white workers and reiterated the stereotypical view that the Chinese were opium-smokers, gamblers, and thieves who practised poor hygiene and spread diseases—in short, that they were uncivilized.

On June 7, 1900, the *Ledge,* the newspaper of the mining town New Denver, published a cartoon depicting (presumably Asian) rats eating a piece of cheese representing the wealth of BC and chewing up a paper labelled "Act to Exclude Mongolian Labor." The same issue included the political platforms of federal candidates in the upcoming election. John Keen, a Conservative candidate, stated in his platform: "I believe the influx of Chinese and Japanese subjects into this country to be a distinct detriment to our future welfare..."; he advocated that the newly elected government should aim for "the consolidation of the British Empire for the benefit of British subjects." Geo. T. Kane, a Liberal candidate, advised taking "a firm stand... with a view of discouraging the spread of Oriental cheap labor in this Province." The Vancouver *Daily Province* published a cartoon on March 6, 1908, that demonstrated the fear that uncontrolled immigration by Asians would result in a decreased standard of living and fewer job opportunities for non-Asian Canadians.

Newspapers in other provinces also published negative reports on the Chinese. Toronto's scandal sheet *Jack Canuck* published an article on September 16, 1911, suggesting that the Chinese posed a threat and described the "Yellow Peril" on streets where Chinese laundries and restaurants were concentrated:

> One need only stroll through the above mentioned block [King, Queen, Yonge, and York streets] and notice the throngs of Chinamen lounging in the streets and doorways to realize the "Yellow Peril" is more than a mere word in this city. The average citizen would stand aghast did he but realize the awful menace lurking behind the partitions or screens of some of these innocent appearing laundries and restaurants.

In addition to being defamed in the news media, the Chinese were discriminated against in many aspects of daily life, mainly in British Columbia. Chinese people were not permitted to sit on the lower floor of the Victoria Opera House but instead had to sit in the upper gallery. They were not permitted to swim in the city's Crystal Swimming Pool. A store manager in that city prohibited Chinese customers from entering the store every Saturday night from 7:00 p.m. to 10:00 p.m., claiming that many white women liked to shop at this time and did not want to be watched by Chinese men in the store.

Chinese men were also prohibited from marrying white women. A permit from the local sheriff was required in BC for marriages between white women and Chinese men, and such marriages could end mysteriously. Despite the prohibition, Lee Land, a Chinese store owner in Victoria, married Amanda Clapton, a white woman, in September 1908. After spending their honeymoon in Vancouver, they boarded the ferry to return to Victoria—but the couple disappeared before the ferry reached Victoria. In the same year, when Amy Morris, a white woman from San Francisco, wished to marry Lee Bai Kai, a Chinese merchant in Victoria, she was deported by the police, who claimed she was "undesirable."

The ability of Chinese people to enter certain professions was also affected by discriminatory policies. Some professional organizations in British Columbia—including doctors, lawyers, pharmacists, and accountants—did not allow membership to those who did not have the right to vote. Since the Chinese had been disenfranchised, they could not enter these professions, even if they held university degrees in them.

ANTI-CHINESE RIOTS IN VANCOUVER, 1887

After Vancouver was incorporated in 1886, the BC government needed labourers to clear local land for settlement. To encourage Chinese labourers, a parcel of forested land on the north shore of False Creek was leased to the

Chinese rent-free for ten years, and a small Chinatown began to emerge. When a group of Chinese labourers were brought from Victoria in January 1887 by a contractor to clear the forested Brighouse Estate on the western edge of Vancouver, a large group of white men came to pull down the Chinese labourers' tents and ordered them to return to Victoria. Soon after this violence against the Chinese, R. D. Pitt, a key member of the Vancouver Knights of Labor, organized a public meeting at which some three hundred people signed up to do all in their power to discourage the Chinese from living in Vancouver. A notice was sent to the residents of the small Chinatown asking them to leave Vancouver on or before January 15, 1887.

On February 2, 1887, an Anti-Chinese League was formed in Vancouver by white labourers that advised citizens not to do business with Chinese people or to employ them. (A similar organization was formed in Nanaimo two days later.) On the morning of February 24, two hundred members of the league went to the CPR wharf to await the arrival of a steamer from Victoria, which, according to rumour, carried a hundred Chinese labourers who had come to clear the Brighouse Estate. In the afternoon, a large crowd of league members marched to storm the Chinese camp on the estate. The Chinese labourers were beaten and their bedding and clothing thrown into a fire. During the attack, some Chinese men managed to escape into the bush, but others were forced to run into the icy waters of the ocean, only to emerge half-frozen after the mob left. The crowd was dispersed by the police with some difficulty.

The following day, the Chinese labourers left their camp and took refuge in Chinatown. As Chinatown residents themselves had received a notice to leave, many of them barred the doors and windows of their houses and departed for New Westminster. The Chinese labourers from the Brighouse Estate joined the exodus. Eventually, the provincial government sent special constables from Victoria to restore order. Under the protection of the "Victoria specials," the Chinese residents gradually returned from New Westminster to their Chinatown in Vancouver.

LAUNDRY INCIDENTS

After the CPR was completed, many Chinese people opened hand-laundry businesses in various communities. Recalling his father's experience in the laundry business in Vancouver, Gim Wong, a now-deceased ninety-one-year-old Chinese senior citizen, said:

> My father came to Canada from China in 1906 when he was fifteen. He borrowed $500 to pay the head tax. After he arrived at Canada, he first worked as a farmhand. Later he rented a house between Keefer and Main streets in Chinatown and opened a

small laundry. He was responsible for door-to-door collection of dirty clothes. He was often called "Chink" or other nasty words. Someone yanked his braided queue. On several occasions, a group of white children turned his wooden laundry cart upside down, spilling out all the clean clothes. He had to pay somebody himself to re-do this laundry. That's not all. Sometimes white people broke our windows. Many Chinese families in the Chinatown suffered similar treatment. Just to survive, my father had to endure these things. In 1921, my mother came to Canada to be reunited with my father. She also paid the $500 head tax. The two of them paid a total of $1,000 head tax—this was almost enough to buy two houses in those days.

Some of the Chinese railway workers who moved to Calgary were also verbally and physically abused. They also became the victims of the widespread fear that the Chinese spread diseases.[†] In June 1892, a Chinese resident working in a laundry in Calgary's Chinatown contracted smallpox, and the building and its contents were burned by civic authorities; as well, its occupants were quarantined in a shack outside town. Nine Chinese people fell ill, and three later died. When four of the Chinese people were released from quarantine on August 2, a mob of over three hundred men smashed the doors and windows of the Chinese laundries, trying to drive the Chinese out of town. For three weeks, the North West Mounted Police had to protect Chinatown and its residents against further attacks by the local white population.

Chinese laundry workers did not only experience verbal and violent physical abuse; municipalities across Canada also enacted local bylaws that targeted Chinese laundries and attempted to control their activities. For example, there was a small budding Chinatown in Hamilton, Ontario, in the 1910s. In part, this Chinatown was created by two discriminatory municipal bylaws aimed at Chinese laundries. One bylaw prohibited the Chinese from building or using buildings as laundries, stores, or factories in areas close to the city hall and the central business district. Another bylaw required Chinese laundrymen to renew their licences every year and stated that renewal would be denied if any nearby residents objected. Under such restrictive

---

† The fear that Chinese people spread more diseases than any other people was unfounded. The report of the royal commission of 1902 pointed out that out of 183 cases of infectious diseases that occurred in Vancouver in 1900, only 6 occurred in Chinatown. In fact, the reverse was often true as many Chinese were infected by European diseases after arriving in Canada—for example, with tuberculosis—but such cases were not reported in the English-language media. Europeans carried many contagious diseases to North America, evident in the massive depopulation due to smallpox and other diseases among First Nations people.

bylaws, Chinese laundrymen could set up their businesses only in or near their tiny Chinatown and not in other parts of the city. In 1913, fifteen Chinese laundrymen applied to relocate their laundries to other areas in Hamilton, in order to serve their non-Chinese clientele more easily, but the city refused them after local residents objected. Similar restrictive bylaws were passed in other Canadian communities, including Vancouver, Kamloops, and Toronto.

ANTI-CHINESE RIOT IN VANCOUVER, 1907

With a growing Chinese population in British Columbia, anti-Chinese feeling continued to gain momentum. In 1907, the Asiatic Exclusion League was formed in Vancouver. Its objective was to exclude all Asians from Canada, but it was primarily aimed at the Chinese.

On September 7, 1907, the league organized an anti-Asian parade that included hundreds of American agitators from Bellingham and Seattle who had come to take part. The parade marched to city hall, carrying placards with slogans such as "White Canada" and "Yellow Peril." On arriving at city hall, Robert Dunsmuir, the coal-mining magnate whose son James had since become Lieutenant-Governor of BC, was burned in effigy since his family business was known for hiring a large number of Chinese at low wages. A. E. Fowler, secretary of the Seattle Asian Exclusion League, spoke to the crowd. He told how, in Bellingham on September 5, five hundred white men had attacked the Sikhs and Hindus, dragging them from their beds and driving them out of the city. Fowler suggested that Vancouver could achieve with the Chinese what Bellingham had accomplished with the Indians.

Incited by his speech, a mob marched the short distance to Chinatown. It threw stones at Chinese storefront windows, breaking every one, and dozens of Chinese people were beaten. Having had no warning of the impending attack, most of the Chinese simply barricaded their doors, although some hid in the Japanese neighbourhood nearby. The mob then surged to Japan Town, where the Japanese put up a fight because they had been warned about the attack and were better prepared. The white mob did not disperse until midnight. On Sunday morning, it tried to raid Japan Town again. The Japanese, armed with sticks and guns, beat off the rioters, who then returned to their assault on Chinatown. By that time, however, police reinforcements were able to drive the rioters off. Stones, broken glass, and bricks littered Chinatown. On the Monday following the riot, a salesperson at McLennan, McFeely & Company reported that when their store opened that day, "there was a steady stream of Chinese in search of revolvers. And no cheap guns, either, for the Chinese buy better guns than the average white man. This morning the cheapest gun we sold at $15, and one Chinaman ordered fifteen at $20.50 each. I daresay we must have sold over a hundred before the police asked us to shut down on the sale." To protest the assault, the Chinese closed all their businesses, holding a general strike for three days that interfered with work in many Vancouver homes and businesses.

After the riot, regret was expressed by public figures and the media. News reports in the *Daily Province*, the *Vancouver Daily World,* and the *Daily News Advertiser* all condemned the riot. Since there was no official Chinese representation in Canada at this time, little regret was expressed regarding the damage inflicted on the Chinese. Japan, on the other hand, was already a military power, and the Japanese consul in Vancouver immediately lodged a protest. Prime Minister Wilfrid Laurier quickly replied: "His Excellency the Governor General has learned with the deepest regret of the indignities and cruelties to which certain subjects of the Emperor of Japan, a friend and ally of His Majesty the King, have been victims and he hopes that peace will be promptly restored and all the offenders punished." A month later, Laurier also cabled his regrets to the Emperor of Japan, assuring him that such violence would be prevented from recurring in future. Nothing similar was expressed regarding the Chinese.

The federal government set up a committee in 1907 to investigate the losses sustained by the victims and to recommend compensation amounts. The commissioner, W. L. Mackenzie King, recommended compensation for the Japanese right away but did not suggest compensation for the Chinese until mid-1908. The committee then agreed to compensate the Chinese $26,236 for their business losses and $3,185 for damage to their properties, amounts later paid by the federal government.

DISCRIMINATION IN THE PUBLIC EDUCATION SYSTEM

Victoria had more children in its Chinatown than other communities did. The very few Chinese students who studied with white children in those communities did not draw the negative attention of their parents. In Victoria, it was a different case, and Chinese children there were discriminated against in the public school system by non-Chinese parents and school officials alike.

In 1900, there were 108 Chinese children of elementary school age in Victoria, and 15 of them studied alongside white children at Rock Bay Elementary School, the public school closest to Chinatown. In February 1901, a few white parents of the white children asked the school board to move the Chinese children to a separate school because they were unclean, untidy, and rude, and they had a demoralizing influence on their own children. The school board surveyed the teachers, who thought the Chinese students behaved well and were clean and hard-working. The school board did not have sufficient funds to set up a separate school for Chinese children and, in addition, thought the provincial school act prohibited the establishment of schools based on creed, colour, or nationality.

As a result, the school board did not pursue the matter of segregation. When the school term began in September 1902, Chinese children continued to study alongside the white children at Rock Bay Elementary School.

The unhappy parents then sought help from Victoria's Trades and Labor Council in support of their request. Under pressure from the organization, Victoria's city council passed a resolution that permitted the school board to create a new school district in Chinatown. Some school trustees did not support this resolution because a separate school in Chinatown would benefit the few Chinese children more, since schools in other districts were overcrowded. When the school term began in January 1903, the fifteen Chinese elementary students were placed in a separate, ungraded classroom in Rock Bay Elementary and the few older Chinese students attended public schools with non-Chinese students in other districts.

The racism of their parents influenced the white students and there were cases when Chinese school children became the victims of assaults by white children. The *Daily Colonist* of April 6, 1904, describes how a Chinese boy, in trying to escape from an assault by a group of white boys, was run over by a street car and had to have one of his legs amputated. This case went to court, but the court eventually decided that the defendants were not guilty.

The Chinese Immigration Act of 1903 stated that even when Chinese teenagers declared themselves to be students, they still had to pay the five-hundred-dollar head tax to enter Canada. After spending a year in a public school and obtaining a certificate of attendance, they could receive a refund of their head tax. Victoria's school board charged that the Chinese children from China were not genuine students and only attended school to receive the head tax refund. In August 1907, the school board ruled that no Chinese children would be admitted to public schools until they could understand enough English to comprehend the school rules. This meant that Chinese youths newly arrived from China could not attend a public school and collect their tax refund. When some Chinese children took private English lessons and applied for admission to the public schools in August 1908, the school board passed another ruling that only Canadian-born Chinese children would be permitted to attend public schools. When Lee Mong Kow, a prominent Chinese community leader and a naturalized British subject, applied to have his three children attend the North Ward School, the school board allowed them to register only if they could pass an English examination. In other words, even native-born Chinese children or the children of naturalized Chinese citizens had to pass an English test before they could register in a public school.

The Chinese Consolidated Benevolent Association engaged a lawyer to grapple with the school board. After many negotiations, in November 1908, the school board eventually rented rooms at the Chinese Methodist Mission in Chinatown for all the Chinese students from grade 1 to grade 4, provided that they understood enough English to follow school rules and procedures. (The Chinese Methodist Mission in Chinatown was then known as the Fisgard Street Chinese School.) After they completed grade 4, students would be allowed to enter other graded schools and study with white children. In response, the CCBA built the Chinese Imperial School in Chinatown to teach Chinese children both Chinese and English.

In 1911, under pressure from the British Columbia government, the Immigration Department in Ottawa redefined the term "student" in the Chinese Immigration Act of 1903 as "a person of Chinese origin who goes to attend a university." According to this new definition, no Chinese children who had paid the head tax could get a refund because none of them attended university.

In the 1920s, the education of Chinese students again became an issue in Victoria. The Victoria Chamber of Commerce feared that "Oriental children sitting side by side with White children tended to develop the idea of social equality," and recommended that the school board segregate the Chinese children from the non-Chinese children.

On January 11, 1922, George Deane, the school inspector, reported to the school board that 216 Chinese children in Victoria were studying in four schools. On the morning of September 5, the Chinese students in the Boys' Central School and the George Jan School were lined up and taken to the King's Road School, a school in which they would be segregated. Instructed by their parents, the Chinese students walked out and went home. This walkout marked the beginning of a year-long boycott of the public schools by the Chinese children.

The CCBA organized an Anti-Segregation Association (ASA) to fight the school board's actions. It sent letters to commercial, literary, and academic circles in Beijing, Shanghai, Guangzhou, and Hong Kong, and to other Chinese communities across Canada, informing them of the segregation and asking for financial and moral support. In response, the Chinese Benevolent Associations in Vancouver and New Westminster and many other Chinese organizations donated generously to support the campaign. The ASA organized a Chinese Free School on November 1 for the striking students. At the same time, it sent Yang Qizhuang, a prominent community leader, to Shanghai to publicize the news about segregation in Victoria and to urge the Chinese government to protest to the British and Canadian governments. Eventually, under pressure from Ottawa, the churches, and the public, the school board informed the CCBA that out of the 232 Chinese students in Victoria, 100 of them would be permitted to return to their original, non-segregated schools but the 132 remaining Chinese students who were already assigned to the Rock Bay and Railway Street schools near Chinatown before the strike would remain in these two segregated schools until they completed grade 4. The ASA accepted this arrangement and instructed the Chinese children to return to school when the term began in September 1923. After Rock Bay Elementary School was demolished in the later 1920s, all its Chinese students were transferred to the dilapidated Railway Street School, which they called *Jizaiwu* (Chicken's Coop). The partial segregation of the Chinese children ended only after World War II.

Employment of White Women

Many Chinese business owners hired English-speaking white women to work in their laundries and restaurants, to better serve English-speaking customers. This practice came under attack in 1912, when a Chinese restaurant owner in Moose Jaw, Saskatchewan, was arrested after a non-Chinese waitress lodged a complaint against him of assault after he smacked her ankle with a broom. He was convicted of indecent assault. This case was widely reported in local newspapers and resulted in the passage of the Female Employment Act in 1912 by the Saskatchewan legislature. It stipulated that all Chinese, Japanese, or other Asian people were prohibited from employing any white woman or girl in their restaurants, laundries, and stores. (The words "Japanese or other Oriental persons" in the act were deleted after the Japanese protested.)

This legislation was a blow to Chinese businesses, especially restaurant owners, who often had difficulties communicating with English-speaking customers. It also posed a problem for the many young English-speaking women who wanted such work; such acts deprived them of jobs and infringed on their right to work. As a result, both Chinese business owners and white working women opposed the act. In 1913, Wong Guangrong, the manager of a Chinese restaurant in Saskatchewan, was fined one hundred dollars for employing a white woman. Wong appealed the fine all the way to the Supreme Court of Canada, but his appeal was rejected. The Chinese continued protesting and later the Chinese consul general in Ottawa negotiated with Saskatchewan. As a result, the act was amended in 1919 to abolish the restriction on Chinese restaurant managers from employing these women but instead, it required them to apply for an annual licence if they wanted to hire white women. This act was not repealed until 1969.

In 1913, Manitoba passed a similar act, but it was never officially proclaimed and was only sporadically enforced. In 1914, Ontario also passed a law forbidding "Oriental" business owners from employing white women, and in 1919, the legislature of British Columbia followed suit.

THE CHINESE IN WORLD WAR I

As part of the British empire, Canada went to war in Europe in 1914, and the Chinese in Canada participated. In Vancouver, Chinese Canadians bought one hundred thousand dollars worth of government bonds to support the war effort.

The Canadian government exempted the Chinese from conscription, in order to preserve their status as non-citizens. Nevertheless, the Chinese Benevolent Association called on young Chinese men to volunteer to serve Canada in the Canadian Expeditionary Force. One example was Private Frederick Lee, who joined the 172nd Battalion—known as the Rocky Mountain Rangers—in Kamloops in March 1916. Two brothers from the Shuswap area also volunteered. Wee Tan Louie tried to enlist in Kamloops but was rejected because of his race. Rather than accept this, he rode on a horse across the mountains in winter and successfully enlisted in Calgary in February 1918. His brother, Wee Hong Louie, was allowed to enlist in Kamloops in April 1917 and served as a gunner, wireless operator, and driver. These were just a couple of individuals among the almost three hundred native-born Chinese Canadians and new immigrants who volunteered.

Despite the wartime contributions of Chinese Canadians, the federal and provincial governments continued to discriminate against them after the war. Returning Chinese volunteers, having served the country, petitioned for the right to vote in 1920 but the Dominion Elections Act of 1920 ruled that people unable to vote provincially—for example, in British Columbia and Saskatchewan—were also unable to vote in federal elections.

Even though Canada had a labour shortage towards the end of the war, and many Chinese workers were employed, especially on farms, the postwar period was a period of economic depression. Many returning soldiers faced unemployment as too many people competed for scarce jobs. Many thought that the jobs that had been filled by Chinese and other Asian people in 1917–18 should instead be given to returning white veterans.

In 1919, anti-Chinese incidents began to arise across Canada. The first occurred in Halifax, which had a large military presence. On February 19, 1919, a drunken soldier quarrelled with a Chinese restaurant owner, smashed the restaurant's windows, and damaged the furnishings. The police arrested the offender, provoking outrage among other veterans. About three hundred soldiers and other rioters attacked the restaurant, causing damages of fifteen thousand dollars. The next day, several hundred soldiers and civilians vandalized the six Chinese restaurants in the city for two hours; local police failed to stop the mob. In another part of the city, a man started arguing with the Chinese woman who owned the Busy Bee Café. He wrecked furniture, broke dishes, and hurled the cash register through the window. A crowd of bystanders pushed into the café, shouting "Beat her up." Damage in this case amounted to only three hundred dollars because the police managed to stop this riot.

Such events led to the appointment of a grand jury to investigate the situation. Its report called for co-operation between civil and military police to stop any future "uprising." Nevertheless, between December 1919 and August 1920, there were at least four more attacks on Chinese staff and café property. Although some Haligonians believed that foreigners controlled the city's restaurants, the city found that Chinese people ran only nineteen of the city's fifty-five restaurants and employed just 145 Chinese workers.

Chinese laundry owners were also harassed in Halifax. In 1919, the *Halifax Herald* featured an article that asked "Why Should Chinamen Do Canadian Laundry?" and urged white Canadians to regain control of the laundry business.

BUSINESS RESTRICTIONS

There were many instances in which Chinese businesses were perceived to be a threat to similar white-owned businesses. Examples from Vancouver and Toronto were typical of the time.

In the early history of Vancouver, there were many itinerant Chinese peddlers who sold produce door-to-door. They were supplied with fresh produce by their compatriots who had established market gardens, and their customers included restaurants and the many homes that employed Chinese servants and cooks. White grocers perceived them as a threat, and the city passed a series of bylaws, beginning in 1894, when they were prohibited from selling their produce outside normal business hours. An amendment to the Market Bylaw in 1908 further restricted the peddlers' businesses.

After 1910, Vancouver's city council was pressured to take stronger action against Chinese produce peddlers because it was believed by some that they controlled too large a share of the vegetable retail market, with adverse price effects for consumers and reduced profits for non-Chinese retailers. In 1915, the council passed a bylaw requiring the Chinese to pay a fifty-dollar licence fee, compared to the twenty-five-dollar fee paid by non-Chinese. By 1918, the Chinese itinerant produce peddler with his shoulder pole, walking through the neighbourhoods of Vancouver, was beginning to be replaced by the Chinese-owned truck, operating from a few central produce distribution stations. That year, the peddlers organized the Vegetable Sellers' Association and attracted between three and four hundred members. Also in that year, the city council doubled the licence fee to a hundred dollars. The outraged association hired a lawyer to file an appeal to the Supreme Court. Although the appeal failed, the association did manage to have the fee reduced back to fifty dollars by June 1919.

Even then, many refused to pay because stores paid only ten dollars for a business licence. To protest the fee, the peddlers went on strike for three months starting in November 1919. Their lawyer, F. M. MacLeod, submitted to city council a petition from over five thousand customers calling for a fee reduction so that the peddlers could resume work. But city hall remained adamant, and the Chinese had no choice but to pay the fifty-dollar licence fee. After paying, the peddlers demanded additional police protection from thieves who frequently pilfered goods from their wagons. As a result of the licence fee, the number of door-to-door peddlers in Vancouver gradually diminished and, instead, more and more storefront produce stores were opened by the Chinese. White storekeepers also protested the "invasion" of white districts by Chinese grocers and complained that they kept their shops open for longer hours. In 1922, the Retail Merchants Association, the local board of trade, and local newspapers all called for a boycott of Chinese-run stores. These groups pushed for laws to limit the number of businesses that non-British Canadians could own.

Similar legislation was introduced in Toronto, but with a more positive outcome. In March 1919, Toronto's city council passed a regulation that stipulated that a business licence would not be issued to any foreign resident. Chinese business owners asked Consul General Yang Shu-wen to negotiate with the city council. After he intervened, the regulation was amended so that a business licence would not be issued to anyone from an enemy country, only to merchants from countries allied with Canada. Since China was one of the allied forces during World War I, all Chinese laundries and restaurants were issued business licences.

Although not all non-Chinese Canadians supported the discrimination that the Chinese faced in the head tax era, broadly speaking, it was a time when the Chinese faced many racist policies and even organized violence against their persons and property. From children in the public education system to returning World War I veterans to business owners in the cities, the Chinese were restricted in what they could study, whether they could vote, and in what sectors of the economy they could work.

Chinese girl and boy in traditional dress taken in North Kamloops, c.1907. Photo by Spencers Studio. Courtesy J.A. Chute.

A Changing Chinese Population

❦

During the head tax era, the Chinese population in Canada changed greatly in its number, composition, and geographical distribution. By the end of the head tax era, the Chinese population had dispersed across Canada. The Chinese were no longer primarily employed in gold mining or railway construction, and they began to diversify their economic base by entering new businesses and working at a greater variety of jobs, especially in British Columbia, where they participated more broadly in the economy of the province.

Demographic Changes

Despite the head tax, the Chinese population continued to grow, in part because of a second, Canadian-born generation of Chinese children, in part because of continued legal and illegal immigration. The Chinese population was 9,129 in 1891, grew to 27,831 by 1911, and reached 39,587 by 1921.

The Chinese population between 1885 and 1923 had several noticeable characteristics. New arrivals were mainly middle-aged or young people, so the Chinese population had a greater proportion of young people than the population as a whole. Some wives and their children were able to join their husbands in Canada, increasing the proportion of both within the total population. However, the population was still mainly male. In 1885, it was reported to the Royal Commission on Chinese Immigration that women comprised only 1.2 per cent of BC's Chinese population. By 1921, there were a total of 37,163 Chinese males and 2,424 females in all of Canada, with a ratio of male to female of 15:1. Since many of the Chinese immigrants had been peasant farmers or labourers in China, there was also a larger proportion of working-class people among the Chinese than there was in the total Canadian population.

The Chinese in Canada were concentrated in British Columbia until the late nineteenth century—over 97 per cent of Canada's Chinese population lived in BC before 1891. After the CPR was completed, many of the Chinese left BC and moved east to the Prairies and the eastern provinces. By 1921, only 59.4 per cent of the Chinese lived in British Columbia, and the Prairie provinces (19 per cent), Ontario (14.2 per cent), and Quebec (5.9 per cent) accounted for most of the rest (a tiny percentage lived in the other provinces).

The home county origins and clan affiliations in the head tax era were similar to those of the gold rush and CPR-building years. CCBA records made between 1892 and 1915 show that most of the Chinese population came from six counties in China: Siyi counties—Taishan, Xinhui, Kaiping, and Panyu—and Zhongshan and Enping. Most belonged to just five clans: Li, Huang, Ma, Zhou, and Chen. Most of the Mas and Huangs came from Taishan County, and most of the Lis and Chens came from Taishan and Xinhui counties. The CCBA records of Chinese people buried in Victoria's Chinese cemetery between 1902 and 1920 confirm these records. Out of a total of 849 burials, 66 per cent were people from Siyi counties; of these, a third were surnamed Li, Zhou, or Huang. The home counties and surnames in these records were similar to those in CCBA donor records made in 1884 and 1885. These CCBA records show that 80 per cent of the Chinese in Canada were from Siyi (Four Counties), Sanyi (Three Counties), and Zhongshan counties, with four dominant surnames: Li, Ma, Huang, and Zhou.

OCCUPATIONS AND JOBS

After the large-scale gold rushes and railway construction ended, the occupations of Chinese people began to diversify in British Columbia. Due to the language barrier and the legislative and other restrictions the Chinese faced, there was a limited number of occupations they could work at. Many worked at unskilled or semi-skilled jobs in the natural resource industries like mining, logging, and sawmills, and in the fish canneries. Some became market gardeners or worked as farmhands or ranch hands. Others worked as merchants and storekeepers in Chinatowns, selling groceries and other goods to their fellow Chinese, or as peddlers selling produce in the non-Chinese community. There were also Chinese-owned restaurants and cafés in many communities. It was very difficult for the Chinese to find white-collar jobs or jobs in mainstream manufacturing in this era, and not many were skilled artisans, although there were a few who opened tailoring shops and similar trades and crafts businesses. The Chinese also worked as domestic servants and offered personal services, such as laundry, in the mainstream community. There were very few Chinese women in the labour force, even in industries like laundries or domestic service that were traditionally dominated by females. By the 1920s, the census data show that 23 per cent of the Chinese worked in personal services and another 20 per cent worked as store or laundry owners and restaurateurs. These two sectors remained important sources of employment for the next several decades. In particular, outside of British Columbia, most Chinese worked either at laundries or at restaurants and cafés in the head tax era.

There were several reasons that laundry businesses were started by the Chinese. Before washing machines became widely available to homeowners in the 1920s, doing laundry by hand was very hard work and those who could afford to hired laundry services. Doing laundry by hand was very tiring, tedious, and low paying. As was the case in several unappealing industries, non-Chinese people were happy to let the Chinese dominate this sector. Setting up a laundry business was accessible for the Chinese as well: not much capital was required, the inability to speak much English was not a big problem, and little skill was required of workers. Although laundry work paid poorly, it was still the most profitable industry for the Chinese. At the turn of the twentieth century, laundry owners earned between forty and one hundred dollars a month. By comparison, the Chinese who worked in mines and forestry, on farms, or in shoe factories or hardware stores earned only twenty to forty dollars per month.

After the turn of the twentieth century, the Chinese opened restaurants or cafés in many communities across Canada, usually serving Western foods until after World War II, when they began to serve Chinese foods. In many small towns, the Chinese restaurant owner would be the only Chinese person in the community. Chinese restaurants were passed down through Chinese family networks that allowed young people to learn the business and then buy out their elders. Like the laundry business, running a café or restaurant was very hard work, with long hours and often primitive working conditions, especially in small towns and villages. In an interview, Dr. Liang Lifang (Leung Laifong), a professor emerita in the Department of East Asian Studies, University of Alberta, described her family's restaurant:

> My grandfather Liang Fengmin (Leung Fungmin) was born in Taishan, Guangdong, in 1900. He came to Canada via Hong Kong in 1918. After a short stay in the residence of the Chee Kung Tong [the Chinese Freemasons], he moved to the Prairies. He used to work as a chef in Prince Albert, Saskatchewan. Trained as a professional chef, he could make large wedding cakes. His older brother came to Canada much earlier. My grandpa quit his job to take care of him. They and my uncle started a restaurant selling Chinese and western cuisine in a small town, Lacombe, in central Alberta. They lived on the second floor and the restaurant was on the ground floor. They worked very hard but felt quite lonely. Grandpa told me that Chinese restaurant owners were sometimes bullied by the white people who refused to pay for a meal unless they could beat them in a fight. After the establishment of the People's Republic of China, our family moved to Hong Kong. At that time, my great-grandmother was too old to come to Canada. My grandpa was a dutiful son. He thought that if we all moved to Canada leaving her alone, he would be too worried about her.

So, he did not file an application for us to emigrate to Canada. My grandmother did not come to Canada until 1968.

Another service that the Chinese provided to Chinese and non-Chinese alike was tailoring, since mass-produced clothing was not yet ubiquitous. By the end of the 1920s, Vancouver's Chinatown was home to numerous tailor shops, including the Modernize Tailors. Bill Wong (whose older brother was Milton K. Wong, a prestigious Vancouver philanthropist) spent all his life in Vancouver's Chinatown working in the family business. At the age of ninety-one, he described his father's tailoring business, which celebrated its hundredth anniversary in 2013:

> The white people were not fond of Chinatown but I am emotionally attached to Chinatown. My father, Wong Gongli, came to Canada from Guangdong province in China on August 11, 1911, and found work as a servant in a white person's home. In 1913, he opened "The Modernize Tailors" shop in Vancouver's Chinatown. His shop was renowned for fine handwork and delicate material. There were about forty tailor shops in total run by Chinese and Japanese people back then. The Chinese worked long hours every day for a very low wage. The lower price was an advantage in attracting more customers. After my father made a sum of money by doing tailoring, he got married and managed to feed the whole big family. When I was young there were not many mixed sorts of people in Chinatown and we all knew each other and helped each other. After businesses closed at the end of a day in the early Chinatown, nobody locked their doors and no one worried about theft. It was very safe.

By 1900, salmon was BC's second-most valuable export, and fish canneries could be found all along the Pacific coast. Many Chinese people found work in these canneries butchering and canning fish. White workers avoided cannery work because it was seasonal; canning was done mainly in July and August. Chinese workers were so prominent in the canneries that when the Smith Butchering Machine was introduced in 1906 to automate the canning process, it was known popularly as the "Iron Chink," using a derogatory term for the Chinese.

Many of the Chinese found work in agriculture, either as farmhands or as market gardeners. Most of the Chinese immigrants had come from rural areas in China and had farming experience. They bought or rented abandoned fields and transformed them into fertile farmlands for the cultivation of crops, flowers, vegetables, and fruits. Mah Bing was one example of a successful Chinese market gardener. In 1918 he bought 160 acres of land in what is now Richmond, on the fertile delta lands of the Fraser River. He employed over thirty Chinese workers on his farm. Like other market gardeners in the region, he sold most of his produce in Vancouver.

The Chinese adopted greenhouse cultivation techniques so they could grow vegetables during winter. On the Musqueam First Nation land in Vancouver's Southlands area, eleven parcels of land varying in size from one to five acres were rented to Chinese farmers who grew vegetables in greenhouses. Until 1923, eleven Chinese farmers owned 120 greenhouses with an area of 546.052 square acres in total, accounting for 28.7 per cent of greenhouse capacity across the province. The minister of agriculture said, "90% of vegetables and more than 55% of potatoes in the markets of Vancouver are produced by the Chinese. The Chinese own 2,500 acres of lands in Ashcroft and Lillooet and also rent 1,905 acres of land. In Victoria, all of the greenhouses except two are owned by the Chinese." By 1925, the Chinese had 158 greenhouses in Victoria alone.

ANTI-CHINESE WORKPLACE LEGISLATION AND CHINESE BUSINESS ASSOCIATIONS

One reason for the limited fields the Chinese could work in was restrictive legislation passed by the BC legislature in response to widespread anti-Chinese sentiment. From the late 1880s to the mid-1890s, an anti-Chinese bill was proposed or passed at almost every session of the British Columbia legislature. A number of the bills were related to hiring practices. In 1886, an act was passed prohibiting the employment of Chinese workers on a railway line to be constructed between Victoria and North Saanich. Also in 1886, an act prohibiting the employment of Chinese by the Vancouver Electric Light Company was enacted. Between 1888 and 1890, the BC legislature proposed several bills in a row related to the employment of Chinese in mining. In 1890, the provincial government amended the Coal Mines Regulation Act to prohibit the employment of Chinese in underground mines—they were only able to work on the surface. Additionally, it later rejected some Chinese immigrants to Canada by imposing occupational restrictions on incoming labourers. In 1916 and 1917, BC prohibited the entry of skilled and unskilled artisans and labourers (which caused a reduction in Chinese immigration during those years).

Nevertheless, there remained some non-Chinese who favoured the Chinese workforce and were opposed to the head tax because it reduced the number of potential employees. In 1907, Vancouver's white housewives signed a petition asking the government to exempt the Chinese from the head tax so that they could afford domestic servants at a monthly salary of thirty-five to fifty dollars, the amount charged by Chinese labourers. The housewives' request was rejected.

The exterior of Lim Gong fresh fruits and vegetables store at 157 2nd Street, 1910. City of Vancouver Archives, Bu P670.

Various restrictions were passed by municipalities to restrict the activities of Chinese businesses that were perceived to be competing with non-Chinese businesses, including laundries and the sale of fresh produce. To combat such restrictions, the Chinese began to form business associations to protect their interests. In 1893, a group of Chinese merchants in Victoria's Chinatown formed the Zhaoyi Gongsuo, which functioned like a chamber of commerce. Three years later, another group of Chinese merchants in Victoria formed a second business association, the Gongyi Gongsuo. In 1908, the two societies merged to become the Victoria Chinese Merchants Association. In response to efforts by the non-Chinese to limit the activities of Chinese peddlers, they formed the Shangman Xiaofan Lianhehui (which means United Door-to-Door Peddlers Association, and which was known in English as the Chinese Vegetable Peddlers Association) in 1922. In Vancouver's Chinatown, the Vancouver Chinese Chamber of Commerce was organized in 1909. The Vegetable Retailers was formed to fight against discrimination similar to that which occurred in Victoria. In Montreal, merchants formed the Chinese Chamber of Commerce in 1909. In the same year, the Chinese Merchants General Chamber was established in Toronto's Chinatown. Among these Chinese business associations, Vancouver's was the most active; those in Toronto and Montreal did not last long and dissolved soon after they were formed.

The Chinese in the Labour Movement

By 1900, the labour movement in most parts of Canada was well developed. Outside BC, there were not many Chinese labourers, and these few did not participate in the labour movement. In BC, however, Chinese workers, learning from the example set by white labourers, began to organize labour unions to resist exploitation and discrimination. In August 1901, Chinese cannery workers in Vancouver struck to secure their employment contracts. In summer 1906, Chinese laundry employees in New Westminster demanded a wage raise and a six-day work week. Despite the fact that they were unorganized workers, they struck one day in November and managed to achieve a wage increase from fifteen to twenty-five dollars per month.

In 1916, Chinese workers in the lumber industry organized the Chinese Labour Association to bargain for treatment comparable to that of non-Chinese workers. White Canadian labour, which had led the anti-Chinese movement, began to recognize the power of these Chinese unions. Some unions discussed Chinese membership and began to see advantages to forming an alliance with the Chinese workers, but such alliances did not occur until after 1930.

In April 1918, Chinese, Japanese, and Indian lumber workers launched an even more successful collective strike. They wanted an eight-hour workday paid at their ten-hour wage. Employers refused the request at first, but two days later they had no other option but to accept, since there was a labour shortage and the striking workers were needed to keep the mills running.

In 1919, in response to the Vancouver Shingle Mill's attempt to reduce their wages by 10 per cent, Chinese labourers took on their greatest challenge. The Chinese, who represented the majority of workers in this industry, refused to submit and formed the industry-wide Chinese Shingle Workers' Union. After a forty-day strike, they successfully secured their old wages.

500 block Carrall Street, 1906. Vancouver Public Library, 5240. Photographer Philip Timms.

THE DEVELOPMENT OF CHINATOWNS

As the Chinese population in Canada grew, the Chinatowns developed. In general, a growing population led to prosperity and a decreasing population resulted in their decline. During the head tax era, the Chinatowns in the cities prospered while those that had emerged in temporarily prosperous mining towns tended to decline. Most of the Chinese in Canada lived in blooming Chinatowns located in major cities and towns. Population distribution, county origins, and the male-to-female ratio within the Chinese population had an impact on the living conditions, business structures, and cultural patterns in specific Chinatowns. Chinatowns were also shaped by the basic everyday needs of the local community and by market opportunities offered by the surrounding non-Chinese population.

LIVING CONDITIONS IN CHINATOWN

During the head tax era, most Chinese labourers earned far lower wages than did white Canadians—only two-thirds or even half what white workers were paid. Because of this disparity in wages, many Chinese labourers eked out a scanty living in the bottom economic strata. They not only had to buy the necessities of life, in many cases they also needed to send money home to support their families in China. Some owed money for their voyage to Canada and the head tax, which they paid in instalments from their meagre wages.

To save money, the Chinese labourers scrimped on food and housing. Their diet was restricted to rice and vegetables. Sometimes several persons shared a little meat if it could be bought at a low price. As many as ten Chinese labourers crowded into just one room—often with poor ventilation and unhygienic conditions. After a visit to Chinese labourers' dwellings, the report of the 1902 Royal Commission on Chinese and Japanese Immigration gave a detailed and unsympathetic description of the living conditions of Chinese labourers at the time. The report says of boarding houses of the "best class":

> Ascending a narrow stairway we enter what had apparently once been a large room… but which had an additional floor, occupying a position nearly midway between the floor and the ceiling, thus making two stories out of one. The lower floor was divided off into

small rooms reached by a number of narrow hallways, each room containing three low bunks covered with a Chinese mat. In many cases a double tier of these bunks was observed. The covering, in a moderately clean condition, consists of a mat and one or two quilts. The second or upper floor was reached by a short stairway. Here no attempt seems to have been made at a division of space, at least by partitioning, but at intervals a small mat is spread out on the floor with some regularity, by which each individual is enabled to locate his own particular claim. In many cases even a third floor exists, reached usually by a narrow [rickety] stairway, into which the occupant crawls upon his hands and knees. Here we found an almost entire absence of light and ventilation, the occupants using a small smoky, open lamp, to discover their respective locations, the fumes from which add to the discomfort of the surroundings.

The conditions as to style of dwellings described here [convey] some idea of the close economy of these people in small things which enables them to live at but a fraction of the expense necessary for the maintenance of our people of the same class.

On the dwellings of the "common labourer":

We enter a small 10 x 10 foot room without a ceiling. A small table occupies the centre of the room, upon which stands a small, open, badly smoking oil lamp; at its side an opium bowl containing a thick, dark substance resembling coal tar, which is being stirred at intervals by one of the occupants of the room, with a small iron spoon.

Three low bunks surround the room (often a double tier of them), covered with the usual Chinese mat, no other covering being observable; which, with a stove used in common, a few dishes, a stool or two and some shelving constitute the furniture of the room. The walls are blackened with smoke that is constantly drifting around the room. The walls and floor, which are composed of rough lumber, are absolutely bare, and the starry heavens are observable at intervals through the roof. The bunks are all occupied, some of the occupants apparently sound asleep, others gazing vacantly, others again turn an idiotic gaze upon you, but each hugging his pipe with a smile of security and content. Here again we found an entire absence of any attempt at ventilation so characteristic of those people. The atmosphere of the room is fairly stifling, the smoke from the oil lamp intermingling with that of the opium, constitutes an atmospheric condition well calculated to prevent a prolonged visit.

In contrast to Chinese labourers, a small percentage of Chinese merchants, shopkeepers, and small business owners were much better off. They could afford to bring their families to Canada, and their homes were no worse than those in mainstream society. After visiting a Chinese merchant at home, a commissioner of the 1902 royal commission recalled, "We were admitted into that gentleman's private apartments, consisting of four rooms well furnished after the Oriental style. Here we were introduced to his family, consisting of wife and three small children. The surroundings here were sufficiently neat and orderly to satisfy even the most fastidious taste."

Law Hong Tim, the great-grandfather of fourth-generation Chinese Canadian Gail Yip (Law), was a Chinese merchant. He established Ying Tai & Co. in New Westminster's Chinatown. Gail Yip has done extensive research into her family's history and told us:

> My great-grandfather came to Canada from Shunde, Guangdong province of China in 1889, bringing with him my great-grandmother and grandfather, Law Chong. They started Ying Tai & Co. in New Westminster as a wholesale importer of Chinese products that were resold to other Chinese stores in Chinatown. The company was also a Chinese labour contractor. For a period of time, Ying Tai & Co. had ninety employees who were paid $15 a month including room and board, as labourers for two sawmills and a shingle mill in New Westminster. The company prospered, so my grandfather could afford three voyages back to China, where he married. My grandmother did not come to Canada until 1913 with my grandfather and their two sons. She was exempted from the head tax because of her status as a merchant's wife. After my great-grandfather returned to China, the company was managed by my grandfather and his cousin Law Soong. The Ying Tai building had a bunkhouse, dining hall, and kitchen located on the western end of the first floor for the labourers and the mercantile was in the opposite end. The dining hall was large enough for fifteen tables. The Law Soong family lived on the second floor, and the top floor had a kitchen, living room, and bedrooms where the Law Chong family lived. The families prospered as shown in family photos. At Chinese festivals, such as New Year, they celebrated with fireworks. My great-grandfather's business was very successful and he became a wealthy merchant. He was respected in the Chinese community and was a member of the Chinese Empire Reform Association.

The Chinese were united in coping with discrimination from mainstream Canadian society, but within Chinese society there existed wide gaps

Group studio portrait of the Chinese Empire Reform Association. Left to right: Won Alexander Cumyow, unknown, Yip Yin, nephew of Yip Sang (standing), unknown, Yip Sang. City of Vancouver Archives, CVA 689-53.

between the rich and poor classes and between the lifestyles of the wealthy merchants and the poor labourers.

Between 1885 and 1922, the largest Chinatowns in Canada were in Victoria and Vancouver. In the three Prairie provinces, there were six significant Chinatowns in Calgary, Edmonton, Lethbridge, Saskatoon, Moose Jaw, and Winnipeg. In Ontario, half the Chinese population lived in Toronto's Chinatown; the other half was divided between Ottawa and Hamilton. In Quebec, 90 per cent of the Chinese lived in Montreal's Chinatown, which overshadowed the small Chinatown in Quebec City. In the Atlantic provinces, the Chinese communities were very small and no Chinatowns had formed. Most of the temporary or "instant Chinatowns" that had budded and flourished during the gold rush and railway construction periods had declined or disappeared by the beginning of the twentieth century.

STREETSCAPES AND ARCHITECTURE IN CHINATOWN

A distinctive aspect of the Chinatown landscape was the pattern of streets and the arrangement of buildings along them. Larger Chinatowns usually had one or two main streets, such as Victoria's Fisgard and Cormorant (Pandora) streets and Vancouver's Pender and Keefer streets. Perpendicular to these main streets were numerous side streets and alleys, and narrow laneways between them allowed access to interior courtyards. A unique pattern formed, where there were streets within streets. The buildings were densely spaced, built right to the street and taking up the whole street frontage of the lot. Interior courtyards allowed light to enter the buildings from the back. Many of the buildings had storefronts at the street level and residences and association offices accessed by long, steep staircases on the upper floors.

Some of the alleys became very well-known for the commercial activities situated there. in Victoria's Chinatown is named for the gambling game played there. In Vancouver's Chinatown, Shanghai Alley was the site of Chinese residences after the 1890s, and in 1898 a theatre was built there. Canton Alley, also in Vancouver, could be closed off by an iron gate, to protect residences from incidents like the anti-Chinese riot of 1907.

Most of the buildings in Canada's larger Chinatowns were built between the late 1880s and the 1920s. The most important buildings were Chinese association buildings and buildings that housed public institutions like schools. Many of the earlier wooden structures were replaced by two- or three-storey brick buildings. Although the buildings in Chinatown were designed in Western architectural styles by Western architects, they contained some unique features and decorative elements that did not exist in buildings outside Chinatown, forming a unique hybrid architectural style.

One feature was the recessed balcony. These were balconies with a full roof set back into the building. These covered balconies were places where residents could observe activities in the street below; they were also used as a place of worship. The so-called cheater floor was another feature of buildings in Chinatowns. Tax assessments in these years were based on the number of storeys a building had. To reduce taxes, Chinese property owners built a low-ceilinged mezzanine between the ground floor and the second floor. Since the mezzanines had no windows, city tax collectors did not notice them from outside. A building with two storeys and an invisible mezzanine would be taxed as a two-storey and not a three-storey building. After city tax collectors learned about these mezzanines, they referred to these intermediate, untaxed storeys as cheater floors. In addition to these unique features of Chinatown architecture, Chinese buildings incorporated traditional Chinese architectural elements such as upturned eaves and roof corners, extended eaves covering main balconies, and structural components such as tiled roofs and moon-shaped doors.

Chinatown streetscapes were notable for their colourful decorative motifs of dragons, phoenixes, and lions carved or painted on columns, walls, and shop signs. A wide variety of colours, especially golden yellow, mandarin red, emerald green, and imperial gold were used to highlight decorative details, and numerous ornamental components such as pagodas, lanterns, chopsticks, and artistic Chinese characters enhanced and emphasized the Chinese nature of these structures. Distinctive Chinese signs hanging on storefronts and buildings contributed to a feeling of vitality.

Chinese arches were a significant temporary architectural feature in Chinatown. The Chinese erected arches with wood plates, branches, flowers, and leaves to welcome visiting dignitaries, both Chinese and Canadian. After their visits, these temporary arches were dismantled. In 1896, the Chinese community in Vancouver spent over two thousand dollars on an impressive arch built to welcome Li Hongzhang, governor of Zhili Province and the representative of the Manchu emperor. In September 1906, when Earl Grey, the ninth Governor General of Canada, visited Victoria, a large Chinese arch was erected to greet him. In 1912, an impressive arch featuring electric lights and the English message "Welcome" was built to greet Duke Connaught, the tenth Governor General of Canada.

BC's CHINATOWNS

By 1885, Victoria's Chinatown had sixty-eight businesses. Some larger firms imported dry goods, opium, and other merchandise from China and redistributed it to smaller Chinatowns in British Columbia. Between 1885 and 1911, the number of businesses increased from 68 to 155; among these, opium manufacture was a major business. In the 1890s, Victoria's Chinatown boomed and the Chinese population in Victoria grew from the 2,080 people recorded in the 1891 census to 2,978 in 1901.

Between 1880 and 1900, Victoria's Chinatown began to bloom. New businesses and a new class of small businessmen emerged. Many two- or three-storey brick buildings were erected. After the 1890s, the business centre of Chinatown expanded from Cormorant Street to include Fisgard Street. The CCBA, the Imperial Chinese School, the Chinese Methodist Church, the Chinese Hospital, the Chee Kung Tong, and some other clan associations were all located on Fisgard Street.

Victoria's Chinatown had once been a garbage-choked place with over-crowded lodgings and unhygienic conditions. The major transformation of the townscape did not take place until 1907, when bubonic plague raged in Seattle. Fearing a similar outbreak in Victoria, the city council carried out drastic improvements in Chinatown. Unsanitary wooden sheds on platforms and dilapidated back verandahs were demolished. Many frame structures were replaced by brick buildings.

Victoria's Chinatown reached its height in the early 1910s; according to the 1911 census, the Chinese population had grown to 3,458. About a third of the Chinatown businesses were on Fisgard Street, another third on Cormorant Street, and the remaining third in other parts of Chinatown. The older, more established import and export companies and stores remained on

Cormorant Street, but new smaller grocery stores, fish markets, and restaurants opened up on Fisgard Street. There were ten opium factories, twenty voluntary associations, two opera houses, one hospital, three Chinese schools, two churches, and more than five temples or shrines. Behind the commercial façades of the buildings was a crowded maze of courtyards, picturesque arcades, and narrow alleys. These interconnecting passageways, closed off from public view by wooden gates, led to tenements, opium dens, gambling clubs, and brothels, and housed a variety of other activities.

After the turn of the twentieth century, Quesnelle Forks, Keithley, and other small mining towns were abandoned after their gold was exhausted, and their Chinatowns approached extinction. Nevertheless, these instant Chinatowns were still flourishing in the 1880s. An instant town of about seven hundred people, including two hundred Chinese, sprang up in Granite Creek after gold was discovered there in 1885; the whole town had two restaurants, two saloons, one butcher shop, and seven stores. But as soon as the earnings from gold diminished in the spring of 1886, the non-Chinese miners abandoned this mine. A few years later, many of the Chinese miners also left and the instant Chinatown was abandoned.

Quesnelle Forks had a booming Chinatown during the 1860s gold rush but it had declined by the late 1910s and was abandoned by 1922, since no more gold sands were to be found in the nearby rivers. Similarly, miners deserted Keithley's Chinatown in the 1890s since they could no longer eke out a living. Barkerville's Chinatown, once the largest in Canada during the gold rush, entered the withering stage in the 1910s, when it had only six Chinese stores. By the 1920s, only one store remained and the Chinese population had dwindled to thirty-five people.

During the late 1880s and early 1890s, Nanaimo's Chinatown was blooming because it was a commercial hub. Small satellite Chinatowns existed in the surrounding coal-mining communities of South Wellington, Wellington, Extension, Ladysmith, Bevan, and Cumberland.

In 1901, Nanaimo had a Chinese population of about six hundred, most of whom lived in Chinatown. The Western Fuel Company of San Francisco owned the land occupied by this Chinatown. In 1905, Mah Bing Kee and Ching Chung Yung, two wealthy merchants in Nanaimo, bought forty acres of the company's land, on which a second Chinatown was built. But soon after, they increased the rents in Chinatown and merchants and residents pooled their resources and bought a piece of land on Pine Street where they established a third Chinatown in 1908. This Chinatown consisted of an array of wooden houses on both sides of an unpaved street. The plain frame houses had false fronts, overhanging balconies, and wooden sidewalks. During the 1910s, this Chinatown was blooming; it expanded northward along Hecate Street and westward along Machleary Street, becoming

U-shaped, with a deep gully separating the two arms of the U. The coal-mining industry in Nanaimo began to decline in the early 1920s as coal deposits were depleted and as competition from oil as a fuel increased in the United States and elsewhere in Canada. Nanaimo's Chinatown began to wither.

South Wellington was about nine kilometres south of Nanaimo. In the 1890s, about a hundred Chinese people lived there. By the turn of the century, however, coal reserves in the region had begun to wane, and the mine closed in 1902. As a result, most of the Chinese moved away and the small Chinatown at South Wellington disappeared.

Wellington's Chinatown boasted several hundred Chinese residents during the 1880s. In the late 1890s, the Wellington pits, owned by Wellington Collieries, were worked out, but the company discovered a rich deposit on the southern slope of Mount Benson, about eight kilometres south of Nanaimo. The company opened a new mine there and a new mining village emerged, called Extension. A port for its coal was constructed at Oyster Harbour, eighteen kilometres away from Extension. As a result of a fire in the Wellington mines in 1899, the remaining buildings were moved to Oyster Harbour, which was renamed Ladysmith in 1900. Wellington's Chinatown was abandoned after the Chinese miners were transferred to Extension and Ladysmith. In 1901, the Chinese living quarters at Extension and Ladysmith had a combined population of about seven hundred. After the 1920s, the Chinatowns in Extension and Ladysmith continued to decline as coal production decreased. The Extension mines were finally closed in April 1931, and its Chinatown was deserted.

In 1888, Dunsmuir's Union Colliery operated a small mine on the northern slope of a steep-walled, east-west valley at Union, ninety-seven kilometres north of Nanaimo. The main road, Dunsmuir Avenue, ran through the mining village above a railway line on the valley bottom. A small lane branched down Dunsmuir Avenue to the southern slope of the valley, where the Chinese lived. When the townsite of Union was planned in 1893, its population had reached about three thousand, but since the town was hemmed in by steep slopes, it was poorly suited for expansion. Therefore James Dunsmuir, eldest son of Robert Dunsmuir, chose a new townsite east of Union called Cumberland. In 1897, the town of Cumberland was incorporated. However, Chinatown and other ethnic settlements remained in the mining village of Union. During the early 1920s, two explosions shattered the Union mines. As a result, the mine was closed and many Chinese labourers left. The Chinatown then began to decline.

In 1910, the Wellington Collieries Company, which owned the mines in Cumberland and Extension, was sold to Canadian Collieries (Dunsmuir) Ltd. The new company continued to operate with as many as 540 Chinese miners in 1920. The Chinatown in Union was abandoned after its miners went to work for Canadian Collieries, moving into Cumberland's China-town, which had become a self-sufficient community of several hundred people. Cumberland's Chinatown contained scores of one- or two-room wooden shacks, each with a tiny vegetable garden. There were also many boarding houses. At its peak, Cumberland's Chinatown had eighty business establishments, including twenty-four grocery stores, four restaurants, five drugstores, two four-hundred-seat theatres, a temple, and eighteen gambling houses. The Lum Yung Club, housed in the largest wooden structure in the Chinatown, was a popular gambling establishment. The Dart Coon Club, a social organization of the Chinese Freemasons, and the Chinese Nationalist League also had established branches in Cumberland's Chinatown.

New Westminster's Chinatown held a special position among the western Chinatowns. After Victoria, it was the second-largest Chinatown in British Columbia till it was overtaken by Vancouver's Chinatown during the 1890s. Although it was levelled by fire in 1898, reconstruction began immediately and a new Chinatown quickly emerged. In addition to new structures for businesses and residents, two new institutions were established at that time—the Chinese Methodist Church and the Chinese Empire Reform Association.

Chinatown entered the blooming stage in the 1910s and many of its wooden structures were replaced by brick buildings during that decade. The commercial centre had gradually shifted northward, and several blocks away was a Chinese cemetery. By the 1920s, most of the Chinese in New Westminster were concentrated along two streets, Columbia and McInnes. In 1921, seventeen of thirty-eight Chinese business concerns in Chinatown were located on Columbia Street between Eighth and McInnes streets. That year, the Chinese population in the city was 750.

After the railway was completed, many Chinese labourers remained in Kamloops, working on farms and ranches, in mines or canneries, or as cooks or domestic servants in the white community. In 1892, Chinatown had a population of about a hundred people, including six merchants. The following year, a large part of Chinatown was destroyed by fire, but it was rebuilt immediately. It was divided into northern and southern sections by the CPR track. New structures such as the Chinese Methodist Mission Hall, the Chinese Freemasons building, and the Chinese Nationalist League building were built after the fire. When the CPR track was moved north in 1914, the northern half of Chinatown was levelled.

Vancouver was incorporated on the former site of Granville Village in April 1886. In short order, Vancouver became the economic, cultural, and transportation centre of British Columbia. Its Chinese population and businesses grew so rapidly that very soon it surpassed New Westminster's Chinatown in size, becoming the second-largest Chinatown in the province. Although Vancouver's Chinatown developed much later than many other

Chinatowns on the BC mainland, its rapid growth soon overshadowed all other Chinatowns in the province.

Vancouver was virtually burnt to the ground by a great fire on June 13, 1886, but the city was rebuilt immediately. The government needed labourers to clear land for settlement, so it leased 160 acres of forested land on the north shore of False Creek to the Chinese rent-free for ten years, on the condition that they clear and cultivate the land. By the end of 1886, a tiny Chinatown had emerged there with a population of about ninety, most of whom were railway labourers and some laundrymen. In the summer of 1887, several hundred Chinese workers were laying track to extend the CPR from Port Moody to Vancouver. On May 22, 1887, Vancouver welcomed the first train to cross Canada from the Atlantic to the Pacific Ocean, becoming the western terminus of the transcontinental railway.

Vancouver's Chinatown was still in the budding stage in the 1880s, but it was growing rapidly and entered the blooming stage in the 1890s. By 1889, there were twenty-nine Chinese businesses in the city. Except for three laundries, they were all located in Chinatown. There were ten merchandise and grocery stores, seven laundries, two opium importers, two labour contractors, two tailors, one butcher, and one boot- and shoemaker. Chinatown was situated adjacent to the city's red light district, where Hart's Opera House, brothels, saloons, gambling dens, and other entertainments were available. Most of the Chinese lived in a very small area and Chinatown was crowded almost to the point of suffocation.

Several organizations that had been established in other Chinatowns soon expanded to Vancouver, providing its Chinese residents with educational and social activities. The Methodist Mission was probably the first important institution in Vancouver's Chinatown. In 1889, the mission opened the Chinese Methodist Church, followed by the Chee Kung Tong in 1892.

Because Vancouver's Chinatown was situated on a mudflat by False Creek, it was impossible to lay deep foundations for strong building construction. During the early days, many houses were much like the crude wooden shacks that had housed the Chinese on the campsites during the gold rushes. Some of the shacks eventually collapsed, creating a trail of debris. In addition, there were no sewers to drain off waste. As a result, the Chinatown was dark and filthy.

The Vancouver city government passed a bylaw in 1896 that required all commercial laundries to meet certain sanitary standards. Sewers were built and the wooden shacks on the muddy flats were pulled down. The mud flats were filled with earth and street levels were elevated. Three years later, in 1899, the Vancouver municipal government passed a regulation regarding lodging houses, aimed at forcing the Chinese to improve the sanitary and living conditions in Chinatown. The city council sent health inspectors to inspect Chinese living quarters. On one occasion, the *Chinese Daily News* warned, "Our reporters have received information that the city council will raid Chinatown, and that four council members and two sanitary inspectors together with city lawyers will check sanitary conditions in every lodging house in Chinatown. We ask you to ensure improved sanitary conditions so that the inspectors will have no excuse to close the lodging houses."

During the early 1900s, an increasing number of Chinese businesses were established. As the demand for commercial and residential premises increased, Chinatown expanded. Some white businessmen on Hastings Street were afraid that Chinatown might expand into their territory. Because of their complaints, the government restricted Chinatown's expansion to the north and Chinatown instead grew westward along the north bank of False Creek. By the end of the decade, Chinatown covered about four city blocks bounded by Canton Alley on the west, Hastings Street on the north, Keefer Street on the south, and Westminster Avenue (renamed Main Street after 1910) on the east.

After the turn of the twentieth century, Vancouver's Chinatown outstripped Victoria's in both population and importance. Since it had a deeper harbour and was the western terminus of the Canadian Pacific Railway, Vancouver took over the shipping that had formerly passed through Victoria, gradually replacing Victoria as the premier port on Canada's Pacific coast. Meanwhile, Vancouver's Chinese population grew larger than Victoria's in 1911, becoming Canada's largest Chinese community. Its Chinese population continued to grow, reaching 6,484 in 1921.

During the early 1920s, Chinatown was virtually self-contained, with two Chinese theatres, six schools, a hospital, a library, and a large number of clan, county, and other associations. The headquarters of some of the associations—such as the Lung Kong Kung Shaw, the Shon Yee Association, and the Yue Shan Society—moved from Victoria to Vancouver because there were more members in the latter city. The townscape of Vancouver's Chinatown was dominated by mixed Chinese institutional buildings and Western structures such as city hall, the Vancouver Public Library, bank buildings, and hotels operated by non-Chinese people.

CHINATOWNS ON THE PRAIRIES

After the CPR was completed, Chinatowns were established along the railway line in Calgary, Edmonton, and Medicine Hat. The Chinese in the prairie Chinatowns worked mostly in service industries such as laundries and restaurants, or on farms.

Calgary began to grow after the CPR line reached it in August 1883. Its small town centre developed along Centre Street north of the railway station. A few Chinese laundrymen came to Calgary and started businesses near the station; by 1888, several Chinese laundries were operating. A few Chinese residents were concentrated on the eastern fringe of the town centre, which became the site of a small Chinatown.

After the hostile and destructive riot in Chinatown in 1892, the Chinese were discouraged from coming to Calgary. By 1901, there were only sixty-three Chinese people in Calgary, just 1.5 per cent of the city's population. But by 1909, Calgary had two small Chinatowns separated by the railway tracks and, in 1911, there were 485 Chinese people. The first Chinatown had eight restaurants, a grocery store, a tailor shop, and several laundries. The second Chinatown, established around the Chinese Mission, included three restaurants, six laundries, three grocery stores, a tailor shop, and a row of Chinese dwellings. In 1910, the Canadian Northern Railway announced the route into Calgary it was planning and the location of a hotel near the CPR station. After their announcement, property values in the two Chinatowns soared, and the landlords expelled the Chinese tenants and sold their properties. The Chinatowns disappeared.

In September 1910, Chinese people bought a piece of land near the Centre Street Bridge over the Bow River and established a third Chinatown in Calgary. It entered the blooming stage in the late 1910s. There were several associations there, including the Chee Kung Tong, the Chinese Nationalist League, the Chinese Public School, the Shuo Yuan Association, the Mah Association, and the Calgary Chinese Mission. Its Chinese population was 485 in 1911. Calgary's Chinatown continued to grow into the 1920s but began to decline after the 1923 Exclusion Act.

In 1891, there were three Chinese laundries in Lethbridge. Local white landlords were reluctant to lease their properties to Chinese people if the land was attractive to the white community, so the Chinese could only rent wooden shacks on the edge of town. A few Chinese businesses were established on Ford Street (now Second Avenue South) on the northern edge of a coulee, and a Chinatown began to emerge. In 1904, a few hundred Chinese workers went to work on the Knight Sugar Company's sugar beet farm in Raymond, a small town southeast of Lethbridge. Some of these workers later moved to Lethbridge and opened laundries or established market gardens. By 1909, the Lethbridge city directory included 102 Chinese people, 81 living in Chinatown. It also listed five Chinese laundries, two Chinese restaurants, and two Chinese stores. In 1915, a branch of the Kuomintang (Chinese Nationalist Party) was established, the first Chinese political institution in Lethbridge. Seven years later, the Chee Kung Tong also established a lodge there. The Chinese population in Lethbridge remained very small, numbering only 170 in 1921.

Edmonton was incorporated as a city in 1904, a year before Alberta became a province. It was chosen as the provincial capital. By the early 1910s, a small Chinatown had emerged on the eastern fringe of downtown Edmonton. Its Chinese population grew from 130 in 1911 to a high of over 500 in 1921. It contained a few clan associations, such as the Mah, Gee, Wong, and Lee associations, as well as a Chinese mission. In the early 1920s, the Chinese Freemasons (known as Hongmen in Chinese) and the Kuomintang were also established in Chinatown.

Saskatchewan became a province in 1905, and its development was closely related to the path of the CPR. Moose Jaw became a booming railway town virtually overnight when in 1882 it was chosen as the divisional point of the CPR. Soon a few Chinese hand laundries had appeared in the town. By the 1910s, a small Chinatown had emerged on River Street with a population of about 150 and a few restaurants and stores. A Chinese elder recalled that around 1913, Moose Jaw had about 450 Chinese men and two women, thirty-five to thirty-eight Chinese laundries, and three Chinese restaurants. The Moose Jaw Chinese Mission was organized in 1911, but other political organizations and the Chee Kung Tong were not formed there at that time.

It was only after the CPR was completed that Chinese people came to Winnipeg in larger numbers from the west. Most of them were surnamed Lee and had come from Heshan County in Guangdong. By 1886, they had opened eight Chinese laundries and were trying to prevent Chinese people who were not from Heshan County from settling in the city. It was not until 1909 that a few stores concentrated at the intersection of King Street and Alexander Avenue formed the centre of a Chinatown.

In 1901, there were only 109 Chinese residents in Winnipeg, but by 1911 the Chinese population had reached over 500. Winnipeg's Chinatown entered the blooming stage in the 1910s, when branches of the Chee Kung Tong, the Chinese Christian Association, and the Kuomintang were founded. The Chinese Christian Association organized English classes for Chinese residents and played an important role in assimilating them into the mainstream. Winnipeg's Chinatown reached its peak in the 1920s when the Chinese Benevolent Association and various clan organizations such as Gee How Oak Tin Association were formed. In 1921, Chinatown covered six city blocks. About a third of the eight hundred Chinese people in Winnipeg worked in the city's three hundred laundries. The remaining two-thirds worked as cooks, domestic servants, or labourers.

CHINATOWNS IN ONTARIO, QUEBEC, AND ATLANTIC CANADA

Even before the construction of the Canadian Pacific Railway began, a few Chinese people had arrived in Ontario, probably coming from the United States. In 1881, there were only twenty-two Chinese people in Ontario, and they were so scattered that no Chinatowns formed. After the CPR was completed, a steady stream of Chinese immigrants started to move from British

Columbia to Ontario. In 1894, Toronto had a Chinese population of only about fifty, but by 1900, the population had grown to two hundred people. The Chinese people and their businesses were widely scattered, although a few laundries and stores were concentrated on Church and Yonge streets and along Queen Street East and West. Chinese associations were not yet in existence, although Chinese Sunday schools had been organized by various churches—for many years, these schools were the focal points of Chinese activities in Toronto.

In the early 1910s, two embryonic Chinatowns emerged. Several businesses and residences were located on York Street, as was the Chee Kung Tong lodge. Another group of Chinese businesses were located on Queen Street East, and the Chinese Empire Reform Association established a local office there. After the fall of the Manchu dynasty, the Chinese Empire Reform Association declined and Chinese businesses located near its office moved out of this area. Meanwhile, the budding Chinatown on York Street was growing and expanded northward on Chestnut and Elizabeth streets to Dundas Street West. After the 1920s, Toronto's Chinatown was the third-largest Chinatown in Canada after Vancouver and Victoria. In addition to a great variety of small businesses, Toronto's Chinatown had many clan and county associations, Chinese churches, schools, theatres, and opera houses.

During the 1890s, Montreal's Chinatown began to emerge on De la Gauchetière Street West between St. Urbain and Clark streets. During the 1910s, Montreal's Chinatown consisted of about twenty Chinese businesses, and by 1911, it had nearly 1,200 residents (compared with only 68 in Quebec City).

The Montreal Chinese Benevolent Association was established in 1912 and attempted to issue its own departure fees for Chinese residents in the city. However, in 1914, the CCBA in Victoria responded that it would not issue exit permits to any person holding a departure permit issued by the Montreal CBA.

Montreal was the starting point for Chinese people heading for the Atlantic provinces and also served as a supply base for the Chinese in eastern Canada—the Chinese in the Atlantic provinces depended on Montreal for both supplies and information about China. Montreal's Chinatown was thriving through the late 1910s, and by 1921, it had a Chinese population of 1,735, becoming the fourth-largest Chinatown in Canada. A large number of Chinese businesses and institutions such as the Chee Kung Tong, the Chinese Hospital, and the Chinese Methodist Church were concentrated on De la Gauchetière Street West, which was the commercial spine of Montreal's Chinatown.

Chinese communities in New Brunswick, Nova Scotia, and Prince Edward Island were very small, due to the small total population, the climate, and their industrial traditions. In 1921, the total Chinese population in the three provinces was less than six hundred. Except for Saint John and Halifax, which each had a Chinese population of about 140, Chinese communities in other towns had only ten to twenty people. No Chinatowns formed because most of the Chinese worked as laundrymen and were scattered among the towns. Newfoundland had about eighty Chinese residents in 1922, mostly in St. John's.

CHINESE VOLUNTARY ASSOCIATIONS

Chinese voluntary associations expanded between 1885 and 1923 because of the growing Chinese population, and many new organizations appeared. Chinese community leaders encouraged membership in the associations because they felt that greater unity among the Chinese would strengthen them in their dealings with others. Another external factor was the intensifying political contests taking place in China that stimulated greater political participation among overseas Chinese. The voluntary associations included clan associations, county associations, dialect associations, youth and recreation clubs, business associations, and political parties. All these voluntary associations were united under the umbrella of the Chinese Benevolent Associations.

Bonds among clan members played an important role during the head tax era. Clan associations provided temporary lodgings for members, helped them to find jobs, offered relief and social services to members in need, and helped members conduct funerals. Some clan associations maintained funds for their members' education.

Clan associations in British Columbia were characterized by large memberships and they owned many of the buildings in Chinatown. In Victoria, the Lee clan formed the Lee Long Sai Tong (later renamed the Lee's Benevolent Association). In 1909, it purchased a lot on Fisgard Street where it built two brick buildings. The Lee association celebrated the birthday of the clan's founder, Lao-Tsu, on February 15 of the lunar calendar—this was their most important celebration.[†]

There were at least twelve clan associations in Victoria in 1909 but after Victoria's Chinatown declined in the 1920s, many clan associations closed due to lack of members. The Lum Association declined after many of their members moved from Victoria to Vancouver in the early 1920s. As Victoria's Chinatown declined, Vancouver's grew rapidly. New clan associations were set up there and many clan associations moved their headquarters from Victoria to Vancouver. The Mah, Wong, and Lum clans all established asso-

---

† Lao-Tsu (also known as Laozi) was a philosopher and poet in ancient China, and is reputed to be the author of the *Tao Te Ching*, the fundamental text of Taoist thought, and one which influenced Confucianism and Buddhism.

ciations in Vancouver in the 1910s and 1920s. The Chinatowns in Calgary, to, and Montreal were established later than the Chinatowns in British Columbia, but their clan associations followed the same development pattern as those in western Canada.

These clan associations depended on the efforts of their members to purchase buildings. The Wu clan rented a building on Pender Street in Vancouver, but they were evicted by the owner in 1919. They then moved to a few huts near False Creek but were once again evicted. To prevent yet another eviction, the association realized it needed its own building. It raised enough money from clan members to buy a property in 1920, which they could occupy without fear of eviction. The clan association buildings and their temples are a significant element of the cultural heritage of Chinatowns to this day.

Liu Winston, chairman of the Lew Mao Way Tong in Vancouver, described some of the history and activities of his association:

> Lew Mao Way Tong was established in 1920. At that time, villagers bearing the surname Lew from Xinhui and Shadui counties in Guangdong province in China, came to Canada together. They were all bachelors and felt lonely! More seriously, the Chinese were bullied by the whites. Under such circumstances, the Lew clan organized Lew Mao Way Tong to establish a foothold in Canada and to help fellow villagers keep in contact with one another. The association did not have its own premises at first. Lew Baizihui (literally, one-hundred members organization) overcame financial difficulties and raised sufficient funds to purchase 349 East Pender Street in 1920. Lew Mao Way Tong was thus officially established and it is still present today.
>
> The reason why it was called Lew Mao Way Tong is that Mao Way is a Chinese place located in the middle part of Gansu province. More than two thousand years ago, our ancestor Lew Yinning was the eleventh-generation grandchild of Lew Ge Cheung, a Zuoweizhen General under Emperor Wu of the Jin Dynasty in 276 AD. He was given the title Mao Way Taishou by the emperor. The position is equivalent to provincial governor in the modern sense. The ancestor of Lew Yin Ning is the very famous Lew Fa from the Three Kingdom Period. Back then, Mao Way was a crucial place in China. We used the fame of the place to name the association Mao Way. Nowadays, many local Lew clan associations use the name Mao Way.
>
> In the early days of the Lew Mao Way Tong, it did not hold many activities because the early Chinese earned little money and

could not afford the fees. But on the Tomb-Sweeping Day every year, Lew Mao Way Tong members would go to Mountain View Cemetery near Fraser Street in the early morning to worship their deceased ancestors. Afterwards they held an association celebration. All the clansmen with the surname Lew would gather at the Lew Mao Way Tong to worship the clan's ancestors. They placed a whole pig as well as chicken, pork, and fish with scales on the altar. In 1985, a fire burnt the original building to ashes. Several clansmen raised funds from fellow clansmen and also took out a bank loan. Finally in 1990, a new building was erected on the current site. This symbolized the immortal Mao Way spirit. Today, Lew Mao Way Tong has a history of ninety-two years. Its long standing was hard earned.

County associations formed by groups of Chinese who had come from the same county in China were another pillar of the Chinese communities. They began as loose rudimentary associations with rented offices and, over time, developed into more formal, mature organizations. Like the clan associations, as their membership grew the county associations also raised funds to build association office buildings in Chinatowns, replacing rented premises. These associations promoted communication among members, offered assistance to members in need, resolved conflicts, and organized charity events. Victoria's county associations were established earliest. Vancouver's emerged later, beginning in the 1890s, followed by other associations as the Chinese population dispersed across Canada.

Speakers of the same dialect also formed associations. The Hakka ethnic group, which had migrated from northern China to Fujian and Guangdong provinces before coming to Canada, shared a dialect and formed an association, the Yen Wo Tong, in Victoria in 1905. Speakers of the Sanyi dialect also formed an association. Its Sailor Charity Division, located in Vancouver, was established in 1919 to help sick sailors and other travellers.

The period from the 1890s to the 1930s witnessed not only the development of clan and county associations, but also the establishment of new types of associations, including business associations. Chinese youths also formed associations to organize activities of special interest to young people. They were very concerned about their future and anxious to be equal with white youths. A group of local Chinese students formed the Chinese Young Men's Progressive Party around May 1911 to lobby for equality. The members appealed to police to prevent gambling in Chinatown and sent a letter to the British monarch recommending that "the law as regards all immigrants from Hong Kong to this country be ameliorated so that their reception on landing may be easier for them." In 1914, a few Chinese youths organized a social club called the Victoria Chinese Canadian Club (Tongyu-anhui, meaning Common Origin Association). Its members included both Canadian-born Chinese youths and China-born youths. The club organized social and political activities, and staged benefit performances to raise funds to donate to victims of natural disasters in China. Victoria's Chinese Public School also had a Student Autonomous Society (*xuesheng zizhi hui*). Its visitors included Lee, an interpreter and educator who served as the chief interpreter of the Chinese immigration services from 1889–1920 and who had helped found the Lequn Yishu in 1899. Seto Ying Shek, who was active in lobbying to repeal the head tax and give Chinese residents in Canada the same rights as other foreign residents, also gave a speech to the society.

The Chinese Benevolent Associations (CBA) were formed by a coalition of overseas Chinese associations and their directors were elected from various other voluntary associations in Chinatowns. The purpose of these umbrella associations was to unite the Chinese community, to protect the rights and safety of Chinese immigrants and Chinese Canadians, and to mediate any conflicts among the member associations. Before China appointed a consul in Canada in 1908, the CBAs actively performed a liaison role as a spokesperson between the Chinese communities and the various levels of government.

The first CBA in Canada was formed in 1884–85 in Victoria, where it was known as the Chinese Consolidated Benevolent Association (CCBA), and the second was formed around 1892 in New Westminster. In 1895, a rudimentary CBA was established in Vancouver but it was another decade before Vancouver's CBA was officially founded. Six Vancouver merchants— Yip Sang (Ye Chuntian), Shum Moon, Wong Yuk Shan, Li Sai Fan, Zhou Tang, and Liang Qi (Liang Qirui)—registered the CBA as a charitable organization in BC on November 21, 1906. In its early history, Vancouver's CBA did not have its own rules and managed all its affairs according to the rules established by Victoria's CCBA. It also had no permanent location till 1910 and, as a result, did not organize many activities. As the association grew, it was able to raise funds and built premises on Pender Street (where the CBA remains today). On October 21, 1910, the CBA held an unveiling ceremony at its new building. The association's office was installed on the second floor; the Chinese Hospital occupied the ground and first floors. The Chinese characters on a plaque installed on the balcony were a copy of the original calligraphy created by the noted Chinese scholar-official and calligrapher Zhu Ruzhen, held by the CCBA in Victoria. Later, Chinese Benevolent Associations were founded in many other cities across Canada.

EDUCATION AND CULTURE IN CHINATOWNS

The Chinese maintained their cultural traditions in Chinatown. They spoke Chinese, ate Chinese food, and wore Chinese clothing. In addition, they followed their traditional religious and spiritual practices and enjoyed artistic traditions they had brought from China. The education of Chinese children was of special concern, and this period also saw the emergence of new Chinese schools.

THE EDUCATION OF CHINESE CHILDREN

In the early 1880s, there were few Chinese children in Chinatown. Children in wealthy merchants' families were taught at home by private tutors. Labourers' children attended classes run by missionaries. John Endicott Gardiner rented the third floor of the Chinese Consolidated Benevolent Association (CCBA) building in Victoria and opened a Chinese Mission School in February 1885 for twenty-five Chinese students.[†] He received financial support from Loo Chock Fan and other Chinese merchants. In March 1891, the Chinese Mission School moved to the upper floor of the Chinese Methodist Church.

By the late 1890s, there were about a hundred Chinese children in Victoria's Chinatown and the CCBA saw a need to provide them with a Chinese education. With support from the Chinese community, the association opened the Lequn Yishu (the Sociability Free School) in July 1899 on the third floor of its building; thirty-nine students enrolled. This was the first free Chinese-language school in Canada.

At this time, the idea of public education was just emerging in China, and students were not taught mathematics, sciences, or the other subjects taught in Western public schools. Two Chinese teachers, Li Yanguang and Huang Jieshi, were brought from China to teach the students Confucian ideals, Chinese poetry, and classic Chinese texts. The students were divided into upper and lower classes.

---

† Gardiner was born in Guangzhou, China, the son of missionary parents, and spoke Cantonese fluently. He came to Victoria in 1885 to serve as a translator at the trial of a Chinese person and was then hired as an interpreter by the Custom House. He remained in this job till 1887, when he was ordained as a Methodist minister.

Younger students in the lower class were taught the *Three Character Classic*, the *Hundred Family Surnames*, and the *Thousand Character Classic*, the universal introductory literacy texts for young students in traditional Chinese education. After a young student had memorized all three texts, he or she would be able to recognize and pronounce approximately two thousand Chinese characters. Knowledge of these characters was needed before students could read texts or write on their own. The first four lines of the *Three Character Classic* are:

People at birth (*rén zhī chū*),

Are naturally good and kind-hearted (*xìng běn shàn*),

Their natures are similar (*xìng xiāng jìn*),

But their habits make them different from each other (*xí xiāng yuǎn*).

The three-character verses state the core creed of Confucianism as developed by the influential philosopher Mencius—that is, that human nature is inherently good.

The senior students in the upper class were taught the *Si Shu* (the Four Books: *Great Learning, Confucian Analects, Doctrine of the Mean*, and *Mencius*), and *Wujing* (the Five Classics: the *Book of Changes*, the *Book of Documents*, the *Book of Rites*, the *Book of Odes*, and the *Spring and Autumn Annals*). The Four Books and Five Classics collectively lay out the foundation of Confucianism. They were the basis of the civil examination in imperial China and can be considered the Confucian canon.

In addition to the Lequn Yishu, several other schools were operated by various associations and churches. The Yue Shan Society ran a primary school for children speaking mainly Three County dialects. The Hongmen Chee Kung Tong operated its own school, Qinge Xuexiao (Educating Youth School). Both the Chinese Methodist Church and the Chinese Presbyterian Church organized English classes. The Chinese Empire Reform Association opened the Aiguo Xuetang (Patriotic School) in Victoria in 1907 and in Vancouver in 1908 to teach Chinese culture and advocate for political reforms in China.

After the Victoria School Board ruled in 1907 and 1908 that Chinese children who could not speak English and who were not born in Canada could not attend public schools, the small Lequn Yishu rapidly became overcrowded. In February 1908, the CCBA decided to build a new and larger school to teach both Chinese and English to Chinese children. Within half a year, it raised more than seven thousand dollars and purchased a lot on which to build the school. The new school, Zhonghua Xuetang (the Imperial Chinese School) was opened on August 7, 1909, by Xu Bingzhen, the Chinese consul general in San Francisco.[†] In 1915, the school graduated its first full high school class, a group of twelve students.

After the CBA was established in Vancouver, it opened the Huaqiao Xuexiao (Overseas Chinese School) in 1917. The school was managed by Zeng Shiquan and Chen Shuren, who were leading members of the Kuomintang party. After Zeng Shiquan and Chen Shuren returned to China one after the other in 1922, governance of the school's affairs was poor, and student numbers plummeted from a high of two hundred. Because of insufficient funds, as well as fewer students, the school closed its doors in 1932.

Other Chinese schools were opened in the larger Chinatowns. Toronto's Huaqiao Xuexiao opened in 1914, initially governed by the Chinese Presbyterian Church. Lei She'an, He Lin, Ma Chuben, and other community leaders established Calgary's Huaqiao Xuexiao in 1916.

On July 16, 1921, Qinge Xuexiao (Educating Youth School), created by the Hongmen Chee Kung Tong in Victoria, was officially unveiled. Representatives from all walks of life gathered in the school. Teachers at the Chinese Public School and the secretary of the Hoy Sun School Association gave speeches and encouraged the students to study hard.

The University of British Columbia was barely established when its first Chinese student enrolled. Susan Yipsang, a daughter of the pioneer merchant Yip Sang (also known as Ye Chuntian), enrolled in 1914–15. She was the first woman student with a Canadian-born Chinese background to attend UBC, and went on to become the principal of a girl's school and a professor of English at Sun Yat-sen University in Guangdong, China. Other Chinese Canadian students quickly followed and, in addition to the new generation of Chinese Canadians, students began to come from China to attend Canadian universities. The first of these attended McGill University as early as 1906. Others, including the Kuomintang activist Chan Sue-yan, who was a part-time student, found their way to the University of British Columbia.

A unique but short-lived Chinese Aviation School was organized in 1922 by Chan Dun and Lee Quong Yee, members of the Chinese Nationalist League in Victoria. The main objective of this school was to train Chinese pilots for the National Chinese Air Force or for commercial Chinese airlines. A World War I pilot, Harry Brown, became an instructor in the school, and it purchased a plane for the eight students. In 1923, one of the students crashed the plane in Victoria's harbour and that was the end of the flying school.

[†]   Initially the new school was called the Imperial Chinese School at the request of the Manchu government. After the Manchu government fell in 1912 and was replaced by the Republic of China, the school was renamed the Chinese Public School.

ARTS AND MEDIA

In their leisure hours, many of the first Chinese immigrants enjoyed Cantonese opera—a strong cultural tradition in their homeland.[†] Cantonese opera, unlike its European counterpart, is an exciting spectacle combining music, theatre, acrobatics, and martial arts. These operas are drawn from traditional stories and legends, and from Chinese history. Characters include emperors and empresses, generals, and scholars, as well as ghosts and other spirits. The singing style, costumes, and gestures are highly stylized and convey detailed information about the characters to the audience. In the early twentieth century, even though there were elaborate costumes, the stage sets were minimal and all the roles—both male and female—were played by men. The audience interpreted the actions and stage props a character used to understand what was occurring. A character could crack a whip to show he was riding, step very high to show he was entering a building, or run around the stage to show he was travelling a long distance.

Cantonese opera appeared early in Canada. Once a Chinatown had emerged in Victoria, theatrical troupes began to visit from San Francisco to perform operas on special occasions such as weddings, birthdays, and anniversaries. By the 1880s, there were three theatres for opera performances in Victoria, one with a seating capacity of eight hundred. In November 1882, the mail steamship G. W. *Elder* landed no fewer than eighteen trunks filled with costumes for the new Chinese theatre on Cormorant Street. Besides the costumes, the shipment contained stage properties for the theatre. One costume is said to have cost $1,600 in China before it was imported by a San Francisco troupe, which in turn sold it to the Victoria theatre.

From the 1880s onwards, opera troupes regularly toured in Canada, not only from San Francisco, but also from China and Hong Kong. In 1898, Vancouver's first Chinese theatre opened. The five-hundred-seat Sing Kew Theatre on Shanghai Alley was built by the Sing Kew Dramatic Society. Through its performances, it helped preserve Chinese culture in Vancouver and provided familiar entertainment to the local Chinese community. In addition, members of both the China Empire Reform Association and Sun Yat-sen's revolutionary party used the theatre as an assembly hall. When Sun visited Vancouver in 1911, he delivered a speech to the Chinese community at the theatre. Cantonese opera was performed at several theatres in Vancouver throughout the head tax era.

Cantonese opera troupes in the 1910s included the Zhu Shengping Theatrical Troupe, the Guo Feng Nian Theatrical Troupe, the Zhu Min'an

---

[†] In 2009, Cantonese opera was added to the Representative List of the Intangible Cultural Heritage of Humanity by UNESCO.

Theatrical Troupe, and the Le Qianqiu Theatrical Troupe. All these troupes travelled to perform in other Canadian Chinatowns. Theatrical troupes were also established in other cities; the Shijie Jing Opera Company was founded in 1917 in Toronto.

Opera performances were also important fundraising events in China-town, in spite of the fact that performers earned very little at this time. Benefit performances helped support various social and political causes, in both Canada and China. In January 1915, members of the Guotaiping Theatrical Troupe gave two performances in Vancouver to help unemployed Chinese people. In April 1915, the Xing Zhongqun Theatrical Troupe gave a benefit performance in Cumberland of *Wuchang Uprising,* which told of the uprising in the city of Wuchang that successfully overthrew the Manchu government. The income was donated to the Cumberland Saving China Society. In 1917, at the invitation of the CBA, the Xianxiang Jushe Theatrical Troupe gave a charity performance in the Royal Theatre in Vancouver to raise funds for the Chinese Public School.

Sound recording for gramophones had been invented in about 1890 and commercial recordings of Cantonese operas were made as early as 1904 by the major commercial labels. The Berliner Gram-o-phone Company in Montreal produced many recordings of Cantonese opera for the Chinese communities in Canada.[†] The ability to listen to sound recordings helped maintain the popularity of Cantonese opera.

In the early Chinese communities, newspapers also played an important cultural role. Since most of the Chinese did not understand English, they could read only Chinese-language newspapers. The newspapers provided local information as well as political news from China. Most papers were strongly partisan and actively encouraged the Chinese in Canada to join whichever political movement in China the particular newspaper favoured. They played a key role in promoting particular political agendas, keeping information flowing from China that enabled the Chinese in Canada to continue to play a political role in their home country. They also provided basic information and distributed local news that the Chinese community needed to thrive in Canada.

---

† The recordings made by this company are now extremely rare, but the Canadian Museum of History has a collection of Cantonese operas recorded between 1915 and 1920 that were collected by a Montreal shopkeeper who sold his recordings to Kiang Kang-hu, then chairman of McGill University's department of Chinese studies, when he needed funds. From there, they were eventually donated to the Canadian Museum of History.

The Chinese in Canada did not have their own Chinese-language newspaper in the nineteenth century, so readers subscribed to *Hua Yam Yat Po,* published in San Francisco. In August 1903, the Chinese Empire Reform Association began to publish *Jih Hsin Pao* (known in English as the *Chinese Reform Gazette*), which advocated for the establishment of a constitutional monarchy in China. This was the first Chinese-published newspaper in Canada and continued until 1911, when the empire was replaced by the republic.

In 1906, two Christians, Zhou Tianlin and Zhou Yaochu, established the *Hua Ying Jih Pao (Chinese English Daily)* in Vancouver, which promoted Sun Yat-sen's revolutionary agenda. The paper hired Cui Tongyue, who had been the editor in San Francisco of the Chee Kung Tong paper *Morning Sun,* as editor-in-chief. This newspaper ceased publication in 1908 due to financial problems. Several local Chee Kung Tong members purchased the printing presses and began publishing *Da Luk Bo,* which also advocated revolution. But in less than a year, this newspaper ceased publication because of a shortage of funds.

The best-known Chinese newspaper in Canada was *Tai Hon Yat Bo* (the *Chinese Daily News*), established in 1907 in Vancouver. Funding to establish the paper was raised by Chen Wenxi of the Chee Kung Tong. Its pages included daily news, reviews, health care information, advertisements, and even a poetry page where classical poetry often appeared. Feng Ziyou, a former secretary of Sun Yat-sen and a veteran of Sun's Zhongguo Tongmenghui society (known in English as the China Alliance Society), was hired in 1910 to come from Hong Kong to serve as editor-in-chief and promote Sun's revolutionary agenda. In 1915, *Tai Hon Yat Bo* was renamed *Tai Hon Kong Bo* (the *Chinese Times.*) The *Chinese Times* continued to publish a variety of articles about Chinese and local events until 1992. Mr. Wu Zelian, a senior member of the Chinese Freemasons and former chairman of the *Chinese Times,* spoke about the newspaper in the early twentieth century:

> The *Chinese Times* started publication in 1907. It was originally named the *Chinese Daily News* and later renamed the *Chinese Times.* At the beginning, the *Chinese Daily News* started in the basement of a house owned by a Chinese Freemason. Due to financial and labour shortages, it had only one sheet and for each issue, just two to three hundred copies were printed. In the early days, its major theme was the overthrow of the Qing Dynasty and restoration of the Ming Dynasty. It also contained other information but not many advertisements. The newspaper was funded mostly by donations from members of the Chinese Freemasons.

As the *Chinese Daily News* established itself and its circulation increased, it contained more advertisements and expanded to two larger sheets and a printing of over 5,000 copies. It was delivered to those regions in Canada that had Chinese Freemasons organizations. Although its head office was in Vancouver, a lot of the information it published was about China and the various Canadian provinces. Information about China was reported from correspondents hired in China. Information about Canada was telegraphed from Chinese Freemasons branches across the country.

The *Chinese Times* survived difficult times but the lack of funding was always a big problem. During my term as chairman, one of the most important jobs was to look for money. When the newspaper lacked funds, we tried to borrow from the Royal Bank but were rejected. Then I borrowed money using my own credit. For some time, we had no money to pay staff salaries. I called the bank and asked them to lend money to the newspaper. We paid salaries once with borrowed money. When circulation increased, a flat press could not meet the demand so we purchased a drum machine. In 1979, the paper expanded to three large sheets and then to six. With the immigration wave of Hong Kong people to Canada, the *Chinese Times* lost in the competition to *Sing Tao Daily*, which had adequate funds and published much more information. The *Chinese Times* survived until 1992 when it ceased publication due to economic problems.

Xinminguo Bao (the *New Republic*) was founded by Victoria's Tongmenghui president, Huang Bodu, along with other Tongmenghui members such as Gao Yunshan, beginning in 1912. *Xinminguo Bao* criticized the former Manchu government for its corruption and incompetence and disseminated the principles of Sun Yat-sen and the Tongmenghui. It influenced the overseas Chinese community considerably. The main columns in *Xinminguo Bao* were China News, World News, Guangdong News, Overseas Chinese News, and advertisements. The *New Republic* ceased publication in 1984, when, in addition to financial problems, it faced increased competition from Hong Kong and Taiwan newspapers.

The *Shing Wah News*, the newspaper of the Zhongguo Kuomintang (Chinese Nationalist Party), was established in Toronto in 1917. This was the longest-running Chinese newspaper in eastern Canada. In 1922, it was converted to a daily newspaper. The *Shing Wah Daily News* became the voice of the Kuomintang abroad. Its flag featured a reproduction of the handwriting of Chiang Kai-shek, at that time the president of the Kuomintang.

RELIGION AND SPIRITUTAL BELIEFS

Chinese immigrants continued to worship their traditional patron gods after they arrived in Canada to express gratitude and seek protection. In Victoria, the Chinese Consolidated Benevolent Association installed the Palace of All Sages (*Lie Sheng Gong*), which housed shrines for the worship of Tian Hou Niangniang, the Goddess of the Sea, who protected fishers, sailors, and sea-going people; Zhao Yuantan, the God of Wealth, who helped the worshipper become rich; other deities such as Hua Tuo, the God of Medicine; and Confucius—the greatest of all Chinese scholars—who was consider the "God" of knowledge. The Hakka (northern Chinese who had migrated to southern China, where they maintained their own dialect and customs) established the Tam Kung Temple, where they worshipped their patron god, Tam Kung, who protected seagoing people. The Hongmen Society (also known as Chinese Freemasons) built shrines where they could worship the founders of their society and Guan Yu, the God of Righteousness.

Many clan associations in Canada had shrines in their association buildings where they worshipped their ancestors. Wong's Benevolent Association in Vancouver has a shrine to worship Mon Keang Kung, their ancestor. Huang Jingyang, president of Wong's Benevolent Association in Vancouver, relates:

> The first Wong clan association in Vancouver was Wong Wun Sun Zong Gongsuo, established in the winter of 1913. Afterwards, the clansmen organized the Wong's Benevolent Association. It recruited members in 1920 and began to raise funds. Later it purchased a four-storey building at 121 East Pender Street in Chinatown. On October 10, 1922, the Wong's Benevolent Association was officially established. Mon Keang Kung, who had been the Chief of the Secretariat in the Donghan Dynasty, is revered as the ancestor of the clan, so there is a portrait of him in the building for worship. We have two worship ceremonies each year, one in March and the other in October. In doing so, we aim to demonstrate filial piety, to commemorate our ancestors, and to promote unity among clan members.

Although many Chinese claimed to be Buddhists, most of them actually just worshipped the statues of Buddha and other Buddhist deities, rather than adhering to the philosophic principles of Buddhism. Among the early Chinese immigrants, none were followers of Taoism, the native religion of China. Instead, the Chinese beliefs at that time among the common people were a combination of elements drawn from Buddhism, Taoism, and Confucianism. Nevertheless, in the census records between 1901 and 1921, almost 70 per cent of the Chinese were recorded as Confucians and Buddhists.

The temples or shrines in Chinatown were called "joss houses" by Western people. Joss refers to the sticks of incense that were burned in ceremonies of worship. Christian Westerners considered the Chinese temples to be idolatrous, leading their churches to try and convert the Chinese to Christianity.

❀

The earliest missions in western Canada were established by the Wesleyan Methodist Church in 1859. Although missionaries in the Protestant churches tried to convert the Chinese to Christianity as soon as they arrived in Canada, their efforts met with sporadic success until the 1880s. Through education, entertainment, and community services, churches in Canada eventually attracted large Chinese congregations.

After the CPR was completed, many Chinese people moved to New Westminster to work in the salmon canneries. Chinese membership at the New Westminster Wesleyan Methodist Church rose from nine in 1890 to forty-eight in 1893.

In Victoria's Chinatown, there were two Christian churches: the Chinese Methodist Church and the Chinese Presbyterian Church. Although some members of the white community in Victoria strongly objected to the acceptance of Chinese as Christians, the Methodist Mission Board hoped to introduce Christianity to the Chinese community, and some philanthropists in the church supported this idea. John Endicott Gardiner, who had opened a Chinese Mission School in Victoria in 1885, continued to extend his missionary work in the Chinese community. With a grant of $10,000 from the Methodist Mission Board, he purchased a lot on Fisgard Street for $3,500 and built the Chinese Methodist Church. It was officially opened on March 13, 1891. Every day, young women from the Chinese Girls' Rescue Home attended a service (see p. 127-128 for more information on this home). A weekly Bible class, Sunday school, and morning and evening services were also conducted in the church. Under Gardiner's leadership, the Chinese mission in Victoria continued to grow, from twenty-four members in 1888 to fifty in 1889. The religious service at the evening school sometimes attracted more than a hundred Chinese people. After Gardiner's tenure, the Reverend Chan Sing Kai served the church throughout the 1890s and 1900s and was succeeded by the Reverend Chan Yu Tan in 1912 after Chan retired to Hong Kong.

One notable convert among the Chinese in Victoria was Tong Chue Thom. Beginning as Gardiner's assistant, in 1894, he was asked to start a mission in Nanaimo and he subsequently devoted his whole life to the Chinese mission.

Not only did Christians try to convert the Chinese in Canada; there were also Christian Chinese missionaries in China. Victoria Cheung, who was a second-generation Chinese Canadian, became a devout Christian and started to prepare for missionary work in China when she was still a teenager. After she graduated from high school, she received a scholarship from the Women's Missionary Society of the Presbyterian Church to attend the University of Toronto's medical school. After she graduated, she became the first female Chinese intern at Toronto General Hospital. In 1923, Dr. Cheung went to China as a medical missionary, working as a doctor at the Marion Barclay Hospital, run by a mission in Jiangmen, Guangdong.

Another Christian organization in Victoria's Chinatown, the Chinese Presbyterian Mission, was started by the Reverend A. R. Winchester in April 1892. In January 1899, the mission became the First Chinese Presbyterian Church. Winchester was assisted by C. A. Coleman, who could speak both the Cantonese and Shanghai dialects fluently. They started an evening school, Sabbath service, and later, a boys' day school. The First Chinese Presbyterian Church was led by the Reverend Leung Moi Fong throughout the 1910s. The Chinese congregation in Victoria had increased to fifty-seven by 1914.

Carrie Gunn, a member of the Women's Missionary Society of the Presbyterian Church, began to visit Chinese families in Victoria, trying to preach to the Chinese women—but she met with little success. By 1922, she was teaching a class of seventeen women and a children's class of twenty-four.

Vancouver's Chinese Christian Church was established in March 1913 in Chinatown. This mission both promoted Christianity to the Chinese and conducted fundraising campaigns. On February 26, 1916, the church held a performance of an opera called *Meng Hui Tou* to raise money to hire a teacher for Chinese students.

The first Chinese residents of Winnipeg arrived from the United States in November 1877, and Baptist, Methodist, and Presbyterian missionaries immediately began to visit Chinese labourers at laundries and cafés, inviting them to Sunday school and bible classes. A Chinese Sunday school run by the Women's Foreign Missionary Society of Winnipeg opened in 1886 with five students; membership had risen above thirty by the 1890s, but only seven of the members actually converted to Christianity. A Chinese YMCA branch established in 1913 also offered affordable housing to Winnipeg's Chinese bachelors, opened its doors to rotating credit association meetings, and organized a soccer team that played in a league against the Kuomintang and the Chinese Benevolent Association. In 1917, Reverend Mar Sheung, with the support of the Presbyterian and Methodist missions, opened a Chinese Christian Association on Logan Avenue.

In Toronto, the Chinese Presbyterian Church opened in 1905, although Protestant missionaries had been active in Toronto's Chinese community since the 1880s. Beginning in 1920, all Canadian missionary work east of Manitoba was administered by the Eastern Canada Mission, led by

W. D. Noyes and A. E. Armstrong and headquartered in Toronto. Chinese Christians in Toronto benefited from this centralization, which attracted a high calibre of church leaders to the city.

In time, Chinese Canadians began to act as missionaries in their own communities. Edward Gung and Philip Chu were trained as physicians at the University of Toronto and assigned to British Columbia as medical missionaries. There were also young Chinese individuals who graduated from mission schools in China and came to Canada to carry out missionary work among the Chinese in Canada. Tso Chow Mak (T. C. Mark) came from China to Toronto in 1914. He founded the Toronto Chinese School and worked closely with the Reverend Ma T. K. Wou, who had come from China to Victoria some years earlier. T. C. Mark and a group of young Chinese founders of the Chinese Christian Association in Toronto advocated for the community interests of Toronto's Chinese population.

BONES SHIPMENTS AND BURIALS

Many Chinese wanted to be buried in their home village in China if they died in Canada. They believed that their souls would be unable to rest until their bones were shipped back to China and reburied in their home village beside their ancestors. In addition, the Manchu government required agents who hired Chinese workers to work abroad to return them safely to China, or to return their bones if they had died. This requirement developed into a bone retrieval tradition among Chinese communities in the US and Canada.

Bone retrieval was an important service provided by Chinese associations. It was expensive, if not impossible, to ship a body back to China; instead the deceased person would be buried for seven years to allow for decomposition. In the seventh year, the grave would be opened and the bones removed. They would be cleaned and spread out on the ground to dry under the sun, then packed into a wooden crate on which the name, birthplace, and date of death of the deceased were clearly marked. Crates of bones from Chinese communities across Canada were sent to Victoria and stored in a wooden "bone house" in the Harling Point Chinese Cemetery until there were enough to warrant a shipment to Tung Wah Hospital in Hong Kong. That hospital would inform county representatives, who would collect the bones from Hong Kong and return them for permanent burial in their home counties. In 1907, the CCBA built a brick house in the Chinese Cemetery to store the bones and a wooden hut nearby for a caretaker to look after them. Before 1909, each clan or county association organized its own shipment of bones. To reduce shipping costs, in 1909 the CCBA entrusted the Taishan County association with the responsibility for collecting all the crates of bones across Canada, storing them in the brick house, and shipping them to China once every seven years.

In Vancouver, some county associations continued to arrange their own bone shipments. The Chong How Tong signed a contract with Vancouver's municipal government and retrieved the bones of more than five hundred Chinese people buried in Mountain View Cemetery. In 1919, the Hong Fook Tong retrieved the bones of seventy-six deceased people, including individuals from Vancouver, Victoria, Nanaimo, New Westminster, Kamloops, and Montreal. In October that year, their bones were shipped to the Tung Wah Hospital in Hong Kong. The practice of shipping bones from Canada to Hong Kong continued until the outbreak of the Second Sino-Japanese War in 1937.

During the gold rush, some Chinatowns in the mining districts—for example, Barkerville—had Chinese burial grounds. There were also scattered individual Chinese graves. The Quadra Street Cemetery, which occupied what is now Pioneer Square, was the first cemetery in Victoria, in use from 1858 to 1873. The northeast corner of the cemetery was set aside for Chinese people and became the first Chinese cemetery in Victoria. When the Quadra Street Cemetery became overcrowded, the bones of the Chinese people buried there were shipped back to China. The Ross Bay Cemetery was then opened and the Chinese were then buried there. The first Chinese person was interred in the Ross Bay Cemetery on March 18, 1873, listed only as "Chinaman No. 1." The Chinese who were buried after him were recorded similarly as Chinaman No. 2, Chinaman No. 3, and so on. Probably the caretaker found it difficult to spell Chinese names and did not bother to try to record them. It was not until October 1880 that Chinese names were included in the burial records. Between 1873 and 1909, a total of 1,178 Chinese people were buried in the Ross Bay Cemetery. The bones of these individuals were returned to China for permanent burial and the grave sites reused.

This cemetery was built on a slope, and the western section, where the Chinese graves were segregated, was low-lying, almost at sea level. The Chinese graves were often flooded after a heavy rainstorm and lashed by high waves when the sea was rough. Wind and waves eroded a few waterfront graves and swept away the Chinese remains. As a result, Victoria's CCBA decided to establish its own cemetery. In 1891, it purchased a piece of land north of Swan Lake for $2,200 to use as a cemetery. The site was on the southern slope of Lake Hill (now called Christmas Hill) in Saanich. The property faced the lake and was flanked on both sides by ridges. According to feng shui, water was an emblem of wealth and mountain ranges represented the life-giving earth, so this site had good feng shui. However, nearby farmers did not want a Chinese cemetery next to their farmland. When the first Chinese funeral procession reached the site, the farmers fired their guns at the Chinese and prevented the funeral from taking place. The CCBA dared not use the site as a cemetery and left it empty for over ten years, continuing to bury the dead in the Ross Bay Cemetery until the CCBA finally sold the Swan Lake lot for $925 in June 1902. The following year the association bought another suitable piece of property at Foul Point (now called Harling Point) in Victoria and used it as a Chinese cemetery.[†] It also had good feng shui.

Although the Chinese were assured by the city that they could use the property as a cemetery, they were worried that nearby residents, like those in Swan Lake, might oppose this use. To test local reaction, a mock funeral was arranged in the fall of 1903. As expected, a white resident fired a shotgun to interrupt the "funeral" and threatened the "mourners." The police were called and they arrested the man. After this incident, the Chinese were able to use the cemetery without further harassment from nearby white residents. In March 1909, the CCBA moved the Chinese graves in the Ross Bay Cemetery to the new Chinese cemetery. After that, very few Chinese people were buried in the Ross Bay Cemetery.

Many of the railway workers lived in campsites around Kamloops during the construction of the CPR and in Chinatown in Kamloops after it was completed. Deceased labourers were buried on the mountainside on the south side of the railway. This Chinese burial ground was set up in the mid-1880s on a piece of land owned by the Hudson's Bay Company, with the first report of a burial in an 1887 issue of the *Inland Sentinel*. Chinese graves remained unmarked until the 1920s, but when the Chinese Exclusion Act was passed in 1923, the Chinese who had decided to remain in Canada enclosed the cemetery with a fence and placed a stone altar and burner at the base of the slope.

Chinese cemeteries were also established in Vancouver, New Westminster, and other towns and cities in British Columbia. Vancouver's Chinese burial ground has the most complete records among the Chinese cemeteries. These records show how the Chinese population in Vancouver in the late nineteenth and early twentieth centuries increased and became stable. Mountain View Cemetery, the first cemetery in Vancouver, was built in 1886. Hundreds of Chinese people were buried there. The first was Ah Yee, a married Chinese man who died of tuberculosis when he was only thirty-seven years old. He was buried at Lot 3-01 on July 26, 1888. Most of the Chinese buried here were listed either as "Chinaman" or "Ah..." in the cemetery register book. The Chinese held a tomb-sweeping ceremony there each spring.

---

† The Chinese cemetery at Harling Point was named a national historic site in 1996, to recognize its cultural and historic importance to the Chinese community.

Chinese mourners praying at Mountain View Cemetery. Built in 1886, Mountain View was the first cemetery in Vancouver and hundreds of Chinese people were buried there. City of Vancouver Archives, CVA 371-1914.

Beechwood Cemetery in Ottawa was established in 1873. The first Chinese man to be buried there was Ching Kan Fook, a cook who died of tuberculosis on February 24, 1903, at the age of thirty. He was buried a week later. Another Chinese man buried in Beechwood Cemetery was Chung Lung, a laundryman who died in 1905. In 1916, his bones were exhumed and shipped back to China for burial in his hometown.

Within Chinese society in Canada, there was a wide gap in wealth between Chinese labourers and merchants, reflected not only in their daily lives but also in their funerals. The funerals of wealthy Chinese merchants were an opportunity to display their wealth and power, and they drew crowds of spectators. In the 1870s, the extravagant funeral of a wealthy merchant named Yip Jack took place in Victoria. Over a thousand Chinese people attended the funeral. The deceased was carried in a hearse down the main street by men wearing white and yellow robes and carrying soul-recalling flags (the Chinese believed that the flags would recall the soul back to the body). Yip Jack was then honoured with a feast of roast pork, mutton, and chicken and buried in the Chinese burial ground in Ross Bay Cemetery. The funerals of Chinese labourers, on the other hand, were extremely simple. Their tombs were merely mounds of earth, and only their name, place of origin, and date of death were carved on a simple headstone.

An altar was built in some graveyards for relatives and friends to pay their respects to the dead. The Chinese in Canada continued to observe the traditional Qing Ming Festival (Tomb-Sweeping Day) and Chongyang Festival (Double Ninth Festival), during which they went to cemeteries to visit graves and pray for their ancestors or pay respect to deceased family members. They tidied the graves, lit sticks of incense and candles, burned paper money and ingots of silver and golden foil, and offered gifts of fruit, wine, roast pigs, and steamed chickens to the spirits of the dead.

Mr. James Chu, a Vancouver Chinese community leader and president of the Chinese Benevolent Association of Vancouver, described a commemorative service:

> Early Chinese immigrants left their homeland and came to Canada in search of a better life. Because of their sentimental and cultural values, they wish to have their remains returned to their birthplace for proper burial after death. Clan associations raised funds and acquired land in local cemeteries. The overseas Chinese would initially be buried at these cemeteries and after a few years, the remains of the deceased would be dug up and returned to China. Many early overseas Chinese were buried at Vancouver's Mountain View Cemetery. A public [altar] was erected at this cemetery in 1901. Every year during the Qing Ming and the Chongyang festivals, the Chinese Benevolent Association of Vancouver would visit this public [altar] to make offerings and pay their respects to their early overseas Chinese forefathers.

CHINESE MEDICINE

Chinese people who became ill could not communicate with Western doctors because they could not speak English. Furthermore, many of them had no knowledge of or faith in Western medicine. Instead, the Chinese sought treatment from Chinese herbalists and took herbal medicines when they were ill. The large Chinese stores in Chinatown imported dried Chinese herbal medicines along with other Chinese products. *Codonopsis* (Dang Shen) is a Chinese herb that stimulates the body and inhibits fatigue; *Angelica sinensis* (Dang Gui) helps prevent and treat some forms of cardiovascular disease; and *Paeoniae alba* (Bai Shao) decreases blood pressure.

In Victoria, the Chinese Consolidated Benevolent Association rented a small wooden hut in 1885 to use as a *Taipingfang* (peaceful room) for very sick and poor single Chinese men. If a patient had no relatives or friends to provide food for him in the Taipingfang, and if two reputable guarantors confirmed that he was genuinely poor, the CCBA would pay his herbal medical expenses and provide him with two meals a day. Female patients were not sent to the hospital because housewives or maids were cared for at home by their families.

The Taipingfang functioned as a hospice, where patients could spend their final days and die in peace. A caretaker was on duty day and night. He cleaned and tidied the Taipingfang, prepared meals and herbal medicines for the patients, feeding them in bed if necessary, and removed dead bodies to the mortuary and arranged for their burial. Because the workload was too heavy for one caretaker to manage, the Taipingfang was poorly maintained. A reporter who visited it in February 1893 described the scene he witnessed:

> Lying on the floor of the filthy apartment was the body of the unknown Celestial, with mouth wide open, tongue protruding, and eyes aglare. In the corner of the room lay another dead body, covered up with a lot of repulsive looking rags. This was a man who had been removed to the hospital the previous day.... Two other dead bodies lay on benches similarly covered while the poor paralytic [patient] crouched upon a piece of matting, groaned in his torment of mind and body, and shivered for the want of sufficient bed clothing. The room was miserably cold, and no doubt the knowledge of being in a dead house added to the miseries of the already miserable man.

Although the reporter portrayed the Taipingfang as a house of horrors, to the impoverished Chinese patients, it was the only hospital they had. Without it, the homeless and poverty-stricken patients might have died of hunger and cold on the street much more quickly.

All the expenses of the Taipingfang were covered by the CCBA, without any financial support from the local government. The CCBA required each Chinese person who returned to China to pay a departure fee of two dollars, which it used as a fund to maintain the Taipingfang and, later, the Chinese Hospital.[†] (Destitute and elderly Chinese were exempted from the fee.)

As was the case in general, the white medical community discriminated against the Chinese. In March 1891, five Chinese people with leprosy were found living in Victoria's Chinatown. The city wished to send them to the federal government's lazaretto in Tracadie, Nova Scotia, but the Tracadie lazaretto would not accept the Chinese because "they would have a polluting influence on the noble Acadian lepers." The city built a hut on isolated D'Arcy Island in Haro Strait to house these Chinese lepers. The city and the Chinese community shared the costs of delivering food by boat every three

---

† A boat ticket to China would be sold to a Chinese person only upon presentation of a donation receipt. The CCBA archive contains 6,155 donation receipt stubs dated 1892–1915, stating the donors' names and counties of origin.

months. The lepers received no medical care and were simply left on the island till they died. This lazaretto remained in use until 1921.

The Taipingfang in Victoria failed to meet Chinese people's increasing needs for medical care. In June 1899, the CCBA raised enough funds to purchase a lot and build the Chinese Hospital, which opened later that year. The hospital did not have a resident doctor; instead, Chinese herbalists came to visit the patients and prescribed Chinese herbal medicines. It had twenty beds and accepted male patients not only from Victoria but also from other cities in British Columbia. The CCBA relied on voluntary donations and the compulsory departure fees to run the hospital.

As hospitals were built in the Chinese communities of other cities, the revenues of Victoria's Chinese Hospital declined steeply because it was no longer the sole hospital that could issue departure permits. The CCBA's practice of imposing a compulsory donation for the Chinese Hospital in Victoria was strongly opposed by Chinese associations in other Chinatowns. And Chinese people who left Canada no longer had to depart only from Victoria. Therefore the departure fees paid to the CCBA declined, and by 1922, Victoria's Chinese Hospital was badly in need of repair. In January 1922, the CCBA established the first Hospital Committee to administer the hospital and co-ordinate fundraising. The following spring, the first large-scale fundraising campaign for the renovation of the Chinese Hospital was launched. Funds were raised from the Chinese shops in Chinatown and from Chinese laundries and grocery stores outside Chinatown. A group of women sought donations from Chinese housewives. Within eight days, over $5,000 had been raised. Other donations were solicited from the Chinese communities in Cumberland, Nanaimo, and other northern towns. Within about a week, another $2,500 had been raised. These represented significant contributions at this time.

The renovation of the hospital began in August and was completed two months later. A celebration of the renovation was held in November 1922. But despite such efforts, the hospital continued to be plagued by financial problems, and eventually the CCBA turned to the owners of Chinese gambling houses to contribute, even though in general it tried to dissociate itself from gambling establishments.

As the Chinese population increased in Vancouver, its Chinese Benevolent Association considered whether to build a Taipingfang in Vancouver's Chinatown. On March 27, 1897, it requested assistance from the directors of the Chinese Hospital in Victoria in a letter co-signed by fifteen Chinatown merchants. However, their request was declined by Victoria's CCBA. As a result, a few years later, Vancouver's CBA informed the CCBA that the donations collected in Vancouver were needed for the purchase of a hospital property in that city's Chinatown, and if the CCBA insisted on claiming the donations, then the money would be considered a loan to the CBA of Vancouver.

The Vancouver CBA started planning a hospital in 1908 and raised enough funds to build the Chinese Hospital in 1910. Later, the CBA called on the Chinese to contribute to the construction of Mount St. Joseph Hospital in East Vancouver. After it was built, it incorporated the Chinese Hospital and absorbed all the Chinese patients. Thereafter, when the Chinese referred to the Chinese Hospital in Vancouver, they meant Mount St. Joseph Hospital.

In October 1918 in Montreal, the Chinese community was affected by the worldwide epidemic influenza. There was no Chinese hospital in Montreal at the time, and some Chinese community leaders rented two houses to serve as a temporary hospital. By 1920, they had raised sufficient funds to buy a building for the Montreal Chinese Hospital.

In addition to the Chinese hospitals in Victoria, Vancouver, and Montreal, there were also Chinese hospitals in New Westminster and Nelson, BC.

GAMBLING, PROSTITUTION, AND OPIUM IN CHINATOWN

Gambling—an ancient social pastime in China—was the most popular social activity in the early Chinese communities in Canada, a time when there were limited options for entertainment. There were gambling houses in every Chinatown and most Chinese shops also housed small-scale gambling facilities. Liang Qichao, who had travelled in North America, described Chinese gambling in his book, Overseas Colony Reports. He wrote that almost every Chinese family gambled. Some gambled at gambling houses, but gambling was also a popular part of social gatherings, banquets, weddings, and even meetings.

In the 1910s, the most famous gambling clubs were found on Fan Tan Alley in Victoria. Large clubs could accommodate more than a hundred people, and there were booths and peddlers walking through the crowds selling cigarettes and snacks. Singers, acrobats, and even opera singers from San Francisco put on shows in the gambling houses of Fan Tan Alley, and their performances attracted a wider clientele, including non-Chinese gamblers.

Gambling was very profitable. In the late nineteenth and early twentieth centuries, the Chinese in Vancouver alone spent as much as three hundred thousand dolllars a year gambling and, in the whole province of BC, as much as a million dollars.

Although most gambling was a social activity, some individuals became addicted to it and gambled away all their money, leading a few to commit robberies and even murder; others wandered in the streets, destitute. The social problems created by these few Chinese gamblers attracted the attention of the larger community, and newspaper reports exaggerated the extent of the problem, reinforcing a negative stereotype of the Chinese in the minds of the Canadian public and leading to discriminatory application of anti-gambling laws.

Gambling was one of the most popular activities for Chinese Canadians and gambling houses could be found in every Chinatown throughout the country. Vancouver Public Library, 416132. Photo by the *Province* newspaper. Circa 1950.

The relatively large number of prostitutes in Chinese society in North America was primarily a result of the demographic structure. The high ratio of men to women promoted prostitution, and huge demand and high profits fuelled the trafficking of women and girls, but it was also due to the custom in China, where women were often viewed as commodities and could be sold as concubines by their families.

A few merchants and some secret society members controlled prostitution in Chinatowns. Lee Mong Kow, a Chinese translator, testified to the Royal Commission on Chinese and Japanese Immigration that Chinese women made arrangements with merchants who would pay their head tax, their fare, and their living expenses. In return, a woman would work as a prostitute until her debt was repaid. He cited the example of Woon Ho, who borrowed $311.00 and worked as a prostitute until she earned enough to pay back $373.50 (including interest), at which time she became free. According to Lee Mong Kow, such arrangements constituted a sale, granting these merchants the rights to these women's bodies until their debts were repaid.

Some women were sold into prostitution not to facilitate immigration but as a source of income for impoverished families. At first, many of these women came to Canada from San Francisco. After the anti-Chinese act was implemented in the US in 1882, merchants brought these women from China directly to the ports in Vancouver and Victoria, and the price merchants paid for Chinese prostitutes rose from $500 to $2,500. Because the Chinese Immigration Act forbade Chinese prostitutes from immigrating to Canada, they pretended to be the wives or daughters of overseas Chinese upon entry.

Prostitutes in Vancouver's Chinatown were protected by white policemen. Chinese prostitutes working in Vancouver's red light district paid the police eight dollars a week in protection money to avoid arrest. In Victoria, however, Chinese brothels were constantly being raided by police in 1886–87. White prostitutes also worked in Chinatowns. In 1922, Emily F. Murphy, the first female judge in Canada, called sexual relations between white women and Chinese men "the ultimate in human degradation."

When John Endicott Gardiner arrived in Victoria in 1885, he was shocked by the young Chinese girls working as prostitutes. To help them, he set up a temporary refuge for child prostitutes who had been removed from brothels by the police, which he maintained at his own expense. In December 1887, he established the Chinese Girls' Rescue Home. The home also provided shelter for battered concubines or maids who had been abused by their employers. Local Chinese merchants resented Gardiner's involvement with their maids and concubines. They did not consider it an offence to purchase a girl for such purposes or to beat them if they were disobedient. Gardiner often confronted infuriated masters in court. As the number of rescued girls and women increased—and came to include Japanese prostitutes and mistreated Japanese women—the Chinese Girls' Rescue Home was renamed the Oriental Home and School in 1908 and officially opened at a new brick building on Cormorant Street.

Toronto's Chinatown also served as the city's secondary red-light district as a result of the sizable bachelor population. Chinese and non-Chinese women in the sex trade could more easily integrate into communities in Chinatown, where prostitution was accepted as a fact of life, than in Toronto's white neighbourhoods. However, politicians and commentators used public perception that Chinatowns were sites of prostitution and white slavery to oppose Chinese immigration to Canada in the early part of the twentieth century, contributing to the passage of the Chinese Exclusion Act of 1923.

Another activity in Chinese communities that attracted a lot of negative attention among the non-Chinese population was opium smoking. Towards the end of the nineteenth century, as Victoria became a hub for smuggling opium into the US, progressively increasing demand and rising prices fuelled a boom in the opium business. The high profits attracted Chinese merchants and secret society members who manufactured and sold opium, and opium use drained many labourers' hard-earned money.

Two men at the Richmond, BC, cannery, smoking opium, 1913. The 1908 Opium Act made it an offence to import, manufacture, possess or sell opium in Canada, but because it was not an imprisonable offence, it was hard to enforce. Courtesy of the Royal BC Museum and Archives, image E-05065.

Mainstream society became concerned that the opium habit was spreading from the Chinese population to white Canadians, and these anxieties increased amid lurid tales of white women lured into prostitution by Chinese opium pushers.

The opium problem attracted the attention of international governments. The Manchu government introduced an anti-opium initiative in September 1906. In 1908, it was followed by a resolution passed by the British House of Commons aimed at reducing the sale of opium for export and taking steps to terminate the licensing of opium dens in all British colonies.

When Mackenzie King was assessing losses sustained by the Chinese after the Vancouver riot of 1907, he was surprised to discover that the manufacture of opium was legal. Two opium manufacturers entered claims of six hundred dollars, and further investigation showed that large amounts of crude opium were imported annually into Canada. The amount of opium imported in the fiscal year 1905–06 was valued at $251,943; the value increased to $262,818 in the first nine months of 1906–07. There were at least seven opium factories in Vancouver, Victoria, and New Westminster, and their annual gross receipts amounted to about $650,000 in 1907. The prepared opium was consumed in Canada by Chinese and non-Chinese alike, but Mackenzie King found reason to believe that much of what was produced by these factories was smuggled into China and the coastal cities of the United States.

King rejected the Chinese opium merchants' claims and submitted a report in July 1908 to Governor General Lord Grey recommending a ban on the importation, manufacture, and sale of opium in Canada. The effect on the Chinese opium business in Victoria was disastrous. The legislation introduced penalties for any person who imported, manufactured, or sold opium of three years' imprisonment or a fine of fifty to one thousand dollars. In a social climate where opium was opposed by the Manchu government, the British Empire, and Canada, T. T. York and other Chinese community leaders established an Anti-Opium League in Vancouver on March 28, 1908. Soon, branches of the league were set up in New Westminster, Victoria, and other cities in BC. Legal and social forces worked in tandem to discourage the sale and use of opium in Canada.

However, opium addicts and suppliers were willing to circumvent the law. As the illegal opium trade was still profitable, some Chinese merchants took the risk and sold narcotics such as opium at a higher price. The police launched more raids and enhanced drug control. In 1920, the Royal Canadian Mounted Police assumed responsibility for enforcing drug laws in British Columbia, replacing the provincial police. Two years later, the federal government strengthened its narcotics legislation by giving itself the power to deport any alien found guilty of a drug offence. Immigration records of the mid-1920s show that during that decade, there was a small but steady flow of Chinese deportees under this law, the number averaging seventy-eight per year. Hence, in an overall anti-opium climate, and with a boycott led by Chinese society, opium selling and smoking gradually declined.

THE OVERSEAS CHINESE
AND CHINA

The Chinese people in Canada maintained close bonds with their home country, in part because so many of them had families left behind in China while they went to Canada to seek their fortunes, and also because they were excluded by the mainstream society there. These bonds were social, political, and economic, and were encouraged by successive Chinese governments.

THE CHINESE OVERSEAS AND DIPLOMATIC PROTECTION

Before 1860, China prohibited its citizens from leaving the country. Although it was illegal to leave China, a growing stream of people emigrated illegally, seeking to escape a life of poverty in Chinese villages. By and large, China turned a blind eye to this situation. In 1860, China was forced to sign treaties with both Britain and France. One of the terms of these treaties was that Chinese workers would be permitted to leave China with or without their families to work in the territories these countries controlled, including Canada. After this, the number of Chinese going abroad to work increased rapidly.

The status of Chinese citizens living overseas was unclear, since China had no legislation dealing with citizenship. In 1868, China signed an amendment to the *Treaty of Tientsin* (also called the *Burlingame Treaty* after the former US envoy to China) that stated that citizens and subjects of both the US and China would be granted the privilege of naturalization. It was not until 1909, though, that China clarified the citizenship status of overseas Chinese. The previous year, the government of the Dutch East Indies (now Indonesia) had forced the Chinese living there to become Dutch citizens. In response, the Qing government enacted the Chinese Nationality Law—the first nationality law in China. This law adopted the principle of bloodline, rather than birthplace, and ruled that all Chinese people, no matter where their birthplace or residence was, were Chinese citizens. Even Chinese people who had become naturalized citizens of their country of residence would remain Chinese citizens. This was the first time that China had legally clarified the status of overseas Chinese and also the first law in Chinese history that recognized dual citizenship.

With an increasing number of Chinese people going abroad, the Manchu government became more active in protecting its overseas citizens by establishing consulates to protect and govern its overseas subjects and to take diplomatic measures to protect Chinese workers abroad. In 1876, it appointed Guo Song-tao as ambassador to Britain—the first modern ambassador sent by China to a Western nation. When the British Columbia legislature passed the Chinese Tax Act in 1878, stipulating that every Chinese person over twelve years of age would pay ten dollars for a residency licence every three months, Chinese merchants appealed to Ambassador Guo for help. He protested to the British government, who forwarded the protest to the Canadian federal government, which disallowed the act.

The Chinese consulate in San Francisco, which had close ties with the Chinese community in BC dating from the gold rush days, advocated for the Chinese in Canada and resolved many problems that emerged. Huang Tsim Hsim, consul general in the 1880s, reprimanded labour contracting companies that ignored the plight of laid-off railway workers and asked the Chinese Consolidated Benevolent Association to help them. Huang Tsim Hsim also testified to the Royal Commission on Chinese Immigration in 1885:

> It is charged that the Chinese do not emigrate to foreign countries to remain, but only to earn a sum of money and return to their homes in China.... This [of] course depends wholly upon their treatment in any country they emigrate to.... You must recollect that the Chinese immigrants coming to this country are denied all the rights and privileges extended to others in the way of citizenship; the laws compel them to remain aliens. I know a great many Chinese will be glad to remain here permanently with their families, if they are allowed to be naturalized and can enjoy privileges and rights.

In 1891, Xue Fucheng was appointed China's ambassador to the UK, accompanied by Huang Tsim Hsim, who served as his counsellor. The CCBA, knowing of Huang's sympathy for his fellow Chinese in Canada, asked him to encourage Xue to negotiate with the British to counteract the discriminatory legislation passed in Canada. Xue accepted this suggestion and wrote to the British Ministry of Foreign Affairs, requesting that the British government repeal anti-Chinese legislation in Canada and try "not to hinder the growing amity between the peoples of the two countries."

In 1896, Li Hongzhang, a leading statesman and viceroy of China's capital province, visited Canada. He was warmly received by the local Chinese communities in Toronto, Winnipeg, Calgary, and Vancouver. During his stay in British Columbia, the CCBA asked him to negotiate with the government regarding the head tax. Li's negotiations may have delayed the tax increase, which was then under discussion, for a time.

In 1908, the Manchu government approved the establishment of a consulate general in Ottawa, and it was established in 1909. The Chinese in Canada finally had a representative from their home country to advocate on their behalf.

Auctions of Honorary Titles

The Manchu government auctioned honorary titles to overseas Chinese in exchange for donations. Although these titles carried no real power, they were a status symbol and many Chinese merchants in Canada actively sought to obtain them. On June 25, 1885, Huang Sic Chen, secretary of the consul general in San Francisco, acknowledged a four-hundred-dollar contribution from the CCBA towards the military expenses incurred in Guangdong Province in a war against France. On August 15, he again acknowledged the contributions of the Chinese in Victoria and asked for the names of the donors and the titles and ranks they wanted, based on established conventions for the sale of official ranks and titles. Since most of the Chinese merchants overseas had originally come from poor families, such titles were very satisfying and enhanced their prestige in local Chinese communities. The distribution of honorary titles was one way the Manchu government retained loyalty among its overseas citizens, as well as attracting donations and financial support from Chinese people abroad. Most of the overseas donations to domestic public welfare were driven by this honour system.

On December 20, 1897, two honourable titles of *liupin dingdai* (milky-white crystal button of the sixth rank worn on headdress) were put up for auction to provide relief funds for the Chinese community in Cuba. The two successful bidders in Victoria were Jiang Jingke, who paid $159.50, and Lee Kam Tao (also known as Lee Dye or Lee Kum Chow), who paid $125.00. On April 8, 1898, the Manchu government tried to raise more relief funds for the Chinese community in Cuba by offering three honourable titles of *wupin dingdai* (transparent white crystal button of the fifth rank worn on headdress). These titles were bid on and won by Lin Bangxi, Huang Fukang, and Lee Kam Tao.

Several CCBA board members also received honorary titles from the Manchu government. Li Hongqia (also known as Li Runhua) had the imperial-awarded first class sub-prefect of the fifth rank; Loo Yang Kiu had the single-eyed peacock feather intendant; Huang Fukang had a Military Merit Award of the white crystal button of the fifth rank worn on headdress; Huang Zhenwei had the title of collegian of the Imperial Academy of Learning; Liu Tongchun had the title of sub-district magistrate of Guangxi; and Huang Yulin was awarded the title of lieutenant.

Lee Mong Kow, an interpreter, became an important liaison official between the Chinese community and the government. His granddaughter, Dorothy Yung, recalled that when Chinese diplomat Li Hongzhang visited Canada in 1896, he wanted to meet her grandfather. Lee Mong Kow submitted a report on the situation of the Chinese in Canada, Sino-Canadian trade, and Chinese demographics to him. Li was very pleased with the report, and, in recognition of his contributions, the Manchu government conferred on Lee Mong Kow the imperial-awarded first class sub-prefect of the first rank of the privilege of wearing peacock feather in 1897.

FINANCIAL AND ECONOMIC CONTRIBUTIONS TO CHINA

The overseas Chinese maintained and strengthened contact with their hometowns by sending home money they earned abroad. Some were able to visit their families and purchase land and build houses for them in China. The money they sent home also provided financial support for economic and social development in these communities. Some returned to China with money earned in Canada to start enterprises and make donations that contributed to public service.

In comparison to the Chinese people in Southeast Asia, who gradually gained control of the local mainstream economy, the Chinese in Canada, in particular successful first-generation merchants, encountered cultural and language barriers that prevented them from expanding their economic horizons in Canada. Therefore they turned to China and their hometowns as a place to invest surplus funds. By doing so, they also satisfied their own psychological need for self-fulfillment and enhanced family status.

The overseas Chinese also contributed to disaster relief in their home country. In May 1907, a famine threatened Guangdong and it was expected that the price of rice would rise sharply. A charitable society in Guangzhou sent a telegram to the CCBA in Victoria asking for donations to purchase in advance rice that could be stored and sold at a low price when needed. The CCBA launched a fundraising campaign in Victoria and other communities in British Columbia, raising almost three thousand dollars in Victoria alone. In the summer of 1908, Taishan, Kaiping, Xinhui, and nearby counties on the Zhujiang delta were devastated by flooding. Within a few weeks, the CCBA had raised seven thousand dollars from individual donors in Victoria and remitted the relief money to China. In 1915, Guangdong also flooded, and relief money was raised by the Montreal and Vancouver CBAs.

The Canadian Chinese were also concerned about disaster relief in other areas of China besides their hometowns and provided assistance when needed. In 1889, the CCBA raised funds in Victoria and Vancouver to help ease famines in a number of Chinese provinces. Again, in 1918, Chinese businesses, associations, and individuals in Victoria donated money for flood relief in Fengtian and Zhili provinces. In 1921, drought afflicted five northern provinces of China. The Chinese communities in Vancouver and Montreal responded with generous donations collected locally.

The Canadian Chinese were also willing to assist the overseas Chinese in other parts of the world. For instance, the CCBA in Victoria donated a large amount of money to assist the Chinese in Cuba during the Cuban people's struggle for independence from Spain between 1870 and 1898. After an unsuccessful revolution in 1895, the Spanish military commander, Valeriano Weyler y Nicolau, instituted the *reconcentrado* system in the following year. He confined Cuba's rural population, which included many Chinese people, to centrally located garrison towns, where thousands died from disease, starvation, and exposure. Lai Wing Yiu, the Chinese consul general in Cuba, appealed to the association for relief aid in 1897, offering five honourable official titles for sale by auction in Victoria. The CCBA in Victoria also donated funds for Cuban Chinese relief and were thanked by the CBA in Cuba. In another instance, the CCBA in Victoria sent four thousand dollars to help Chinese victims in San Francisco after that city was devastated by an earthquake on April 18, 1906.

The Chinese in Canada contributed funds to help China militarily and to support the political parties they favoured. In 1884, the Hall of Sustaining Love, a benevolent society in Guangzhou, wrote to the CCBA acknowledging receipt of a donation of over three hundred dollars from the Chinese in Victoria to the Chinese coastal defence fund. The Chinese in Canada also donated money during the Sino-French War of 1885. Huang Sic Chen, secretary of the consul general in San Francisco, sent two letters to the CCBA acknowledging its donations towards the military needs of Guangdong.

After the Republic of China was established, the new government appealed to the Chinese in Canada for donations to help pay foreign debts. The republican government asked the CCBA in Victoria and the Chee Kung Tong (CKT) in Vancouver to establish a National Subscription Bureau (*guomin juanju*) to collect donations from the Chinese in Canada.

The republican government followed the Manchu government's practice of giving awards to donors. A Certificate of National Subscription Award was given to an individual who either donated one hundred dollars or less, or solicited one thousand dollars or less from other donors. Within three years, total donations in Victoria alone amounted to $35,840.

After defeating China in the First Sino-Japanese War in 1895 and Russia in the Russo-Japanese War in 1905, Japan gained considerable power in northern China and Manchuria. Japan continued to expand its control within China, and on January 8, 1915, it sent a list called the Twenty-one Demands to the weak Chinese government. These demands would greatly extend Japanese control of China. Yuan Shih Kai, president of the Republic of China, did not dare offend Japan and initiate a war. He accepted the demands after Japan slightly reduced some of their requirements. Japan's aggression angered the Chinese, and there soon appeared widespread "save-the-nation" campaigns in China and in overseas Chinese communities. In Canada, the well-known Chinese community leader Lee Mong Kow sent a telegram to the Chinese foreign ministry asking the minister to inform President Yuan that if war was declared against Japan, the CCBA in Victoria would donate two hundred thousand dollars towards military costs. Chinese communities in Cumberland, Vancouver, and New Westminster responded with donations to this cause. When Yu Junzhong and Yu Tongxin of China's foreign ministry came to Canada to promote the sale of government bonds, the Chinese in both Victoria and Vancouver enthusiastically bought the bonds to support their homeland.

The overseas Chinese also contributed to construction projects in China. In 1905, Chen Yixi, a successful merchant in Seattle, planned to build the Sunning Railway to connect Siyi, his home region, with Canton. He was aware that Victoria had a large population of Siyi natives with more financial resources than the Chinese in Seattle. He travelled to Victoria to raise funds for the construction of the railway by issuing shares. In May 1905, the Ningyang Yee Hing Tong, a Siyi association, bought two hundred shares. Siyi merchants such as Li Yiheng, Li Yingsan, and Lin Dachu bought shares worth tens of thousands of dollars. With the enthusiastic support of the Siyi people, the railway was built and opened to rail traffic in 1908. This was the first railway built in China to be financed by private investment. When the Sunning Railway started operating, the CCBA in Victoria congratulated Chen Yixi and awarded him a special gold medal and a commemorative plaque.

In 1908, Xu Qin and Mui Liu Shiji, who were members of the Chinese Empire Reform Association, formed the Zhen Hua Company (Zhen Hua meaning "vigorously to develop China") to develop mining in Guangxi Province. The Chinese in Canada subscribed for a million dollars' worth of shares in this company.

There were also factories and companies in China that were organized by overseas Chinese. Examples include the Jiangmen Paper Mill established in 1912, the Guangzhou Bus Company in 1922, and the Shanghai Chinese Merchants Automobile Company in 1929.

In addition to their contributions to China's economy, the overseas Chinese also contributed to charitable societies, hospitals, schools, and temples, especially in their home counties. In 1895, the CCBA donated $870 to the Hall of Sustaining Love benevolent society in Guangzhou and $1,216 to the Tung Wah Hospital in Hong Kong. In 1920, the Taishan Association in Victoria launched a fundraising campaign to build a middle school in Taishan and succeeded in raising twenty-five thousand dollars from the Chinese communities across Canada. The Taishan Middle School building opened in 1926. Over a hundred Chinese people in Cumberland, New Westminster, Victoria, Vancouver, and Chemainus made donations to support the Wuzuci (Five Ancestor Temple) in Canton.

In 1921, Cai Yuanpei, the president of Peking University (now known as Beijing University), came to Canada to raise funds to buy books for the library, and fifty-one Chinese in Vancouver donated money for this purpose. After this, Zhi Xin High School in Canton, the Guangdong Provincial Museum, and the True Light Middle School of Hong Kong sent representatives one after the other to raise funds from the Chinese in Canada.

During this period, China was plagued by armed bandits who raided villages. The wealthiest villagers built fortified watchtowers called *diaolou* to protect their villages. The Siyi Chinese overseas contributed funds to build diaolou to protect their home villages.

During these years, the overseas Chinese were deeply concerned with their home villages and country, even after they had emigrated to other countries. They did not hesitate to make donations to support charitable relief, business enterprises, and cultural and educational institutions in China whenever they were called upon to do so.

CHINESE CANADIANS AND THE TRANSFORMATION OF CHINA

❦

The late nineteenth and early twentieth centuries were a turbulent time in China. There was conflict between European nations and China, and between Japan and China. The ancient Chinese empire came to an end and was replaced by a republican government. The Chinese in Canada actively participated in the transformation of China during the early decades of the twentieth century.

THE CHINESE EMPIRE REFORM ASSOCIATION

China was defeated by Japan in the first Sino-Japanese War in 1894–95. It ceded Taiwan Island to Japan and transferred control of Korea to Japan as well. The balance of power in Asia shifted from China to Japan for the first time, due to Japan's military superiority. Emperor Guangxu recognized the need to modernize China, including its military, and to adopt a parliamentary system like Britain's. With advice from two prominent scholars, Kang Yuwei and Liang Qichao, the emperor issued a series of reform edicts on June 11, 1898, that introduced radical social, political, and institutional changes.

The reforms proposed by the emperor would negatively affect the interests of the Manchu nobles and the entire bureaucracy of the Chinese empire. On September 21, 1898, the powerful Empress Dowager Cixi placed Emperor Guangxu, her adopted son, under house arrest, revoked his reform edicts, and executed most of the reformers. This period of reform, which lasted for only 103 days, became known as the "Hundred Days' Reform." After the reform movement failed, Kang and Liang escaped and fled to Japan, and a bounty was placed on Kang's head.

Unable to enter the United States because of the Chinese Exclusion Act, Kang travelled to Canada from Japan, arriving in Victoria on April 7, 1899. Kang's reform ideology was supported by the British government, which asked Canada to provide Kang with protection. W. Fiffe, a member of the Northwest Mounted Police, was assigned as his bodyguard.

Kang was warmly received by the local Chinese community in Victoria. Wealthy merchant and community leader Lee Mong Kow introduced him to other prominent local Chinese merchants such as Lee Folk Gay, Lee Yick Wei,

Huang Xuanlin, and Lin Lihuang. While in Victoria, Kang launched a campaign to inform the Chinese in Canada about the Empress Dowager's coup of 1898, the imprisonment of Emperor Guangxu, and the reform platform that he had developed. Gradually, he won sympathy for the empire reform movement from the Victoria merchants, who regarded him as a patriot and a hero. In July, after returning to Victoria from a trip to London where he lobbied the British government for support, Kang mobilized the Chinese community to form a new political party whose goal was to save the empire and the emperor. On July 20, the Chinese Empire Reform Association (CERA) was founded in Victoria.

CERA's main objectives were to establish a constitutional monarchy in China, to protect Emperor Guangxu from persecution by the conservative faction led by the Empress Dowager Cixi, and to protect the overseas Chinese from racial discrimination. The membership fee of two dollars was to be used for publicity, communications, and a newspaper, as well as industrial and commercial development in China. Most of the founding members of the CERA were Chinese merchants and educated Chinese individuals, who were the main strength of the county and clan associations. The CERA membership grew and the party quickly developed into the most powerful political group among the Chinese in Canada.

On August 13, 1899, a memorial day was held to honour the six reformers who had been executed by Empress Dowager Cixi. Kang prepared *san sheng* (a dish of chicken, pork, and fish), served wine, and wrote a condolence letter that formed part of the memorial service held in the Palace of All Sages in the CCBA building in Victoria. On Empress Dowager Cixi's birthday, November 6, 1899, the CERA sent her a backhanded compliment. The telegram read: "Birthday congratulations. We request your abdication. Restore power of Quang Sui Emperor, to whom our compliments."

Kang next went to Vancouver to promote the empire reform movement. He helped establish a branch of the CERA in Vancouver on July 24, 1899. The complete Chinese name was Baojiu Daqing Guangxu Huangdi Hui (Protecting and Saving the Great Manchu Guangxu Emperor Association). Many individual Chinese people made donations ranging from fifty to five hundred dollars to the new party, adding up to a large sum of money. Soon, branches of the CERA had been established in many Canadian cities.

Western Canada was the originator of the worldwide empire reform movement. After his success founding the CERA in Victoria, Kang sent his followers worldwide. They organized branches of the party in more than 150 cities across the Americas and in Asia, Australia, and Africa. It is thought that at its peak there were as many as a million members around the world. The CERA in Canada was regarded as exemplary, and a number of the other branches adopted the same constitution as that of the Vancouver branch.

In 1902, the CERA established a corporation to develop transnational businesses. Their enterprises included banks in New York and Hong Kong and a streetcar company in Mexico. The banks and the streetcar company attracted investment of over US$100 million from overseas Chinese. These commercial concerns were controlled by Lee Folk Gay of Victoria. In 1903, the CERA in Vancouver began to publish the *Chinese Reform Gazette* (*Jih Hsin Pao*), the first Chinese newspaper in Canada, which promoted Kang's ideology of a constitutional monarchy.

Kang Tongbi, Kang Yuwei's daughter, followed in her father's footsteps. In 1903, she established the Chinese Ladies Empire Reform Association in Victoria. After leaving the city, she established similar organizations in Vancouver, New Westminster, and a dozen American cities, modelled after the Victoria association. This was the first Chinese women's political organization, both in China and among Chinese women overseas.

In 1904, Kang visited Canada for a third time. He travelled from Montreal to Vancouver and met with foreign dignitaries, including the American and Japanese consuls in Canada. By this time, the CERA had branches in twelve cities across Canada, with a membership of seven thousand people, most of them middle-aged and older people who supported the empire. Inside the CERA's headquarters in Victoria (located at 1715 Government Street), there is a stone plaque engraved with the year 1907 and the names of several hundred donors from thirty-seven Canadian cities.

LIANG QICHAO IN CANADA

Liang Qichao, who was a journalist and had been a student of Kang Yuwei, adhered closely to his teacher's ideas. He participated in the Hundred Days' Reform. After it failed, he fled to Japan with Kang. In March 1903, he travelled from Japan to Vancouver, where he was warmly received by both Chinese and Western politicians and wealthy merchants. He was the guest of business and political leaders from British Columbia and Washington State, and he tried to establish closer relations between the Chinese in North America and Chinese reformers. Later, he visited Ottawa and Montreal, where he continued to promote his reform ideology.

During his stay in Canada, Liang Qichao inquired into the living conditions of the overseas Chinese. Through his investigations, he learned about the discrimination that the Chinese experienced in Canada. He also discovered that although the Chinese found it difficult to find jobs in Canada, there was still a stream of immigrants coming into Canada. Some of these came first to Canada with the intention of surreptitiously crossing the border into the United States, assisted by certain Chinese merchants, who earned illegal money through this practice. Liang also found that many Chinese gambled, smoked opium, or patronized houses of prostitution, which he deeply regretted. After returning to Japan, he wrote *New World Travels* (*Xindalu Youji*), in which he described the situation of the Chinese living in Canada. He found them generally to be hard-working, diligent, and thrifty. He also argued that Chinese unity in Canada was hobbled because it existed only among clan members or people from the same home county. He felt that since the overseas Chinese were often involved in internal conflicts, they did not present a united front in their dealings with the mainstream society.

In 1906, the Manchu government announced a plan to establish a constitutional monarchy. In response, Kang Yuwei and Liang Qichao renamed the CERA the Constitutional Party (Diguo Xianzhengdang or Xianzhengdang) and continued to support the Manchu government's plan for constitutional reform.

SUN YAT-SEN'S REPUBLICAN PARTY IN CANADA

Meanwhile, a movement to abolish the empire had been emerging in China, led by Sun Yat-sen. Sun was born in Zhongsan County. In 1878, when he was twelve, he went to live in Honolulu, where his elder brother Sun Mei worked. After attending school in Honolulu for five years, he returned to China to study medicine. In 1892, he graduated as a medical doctor from the Hong Kong College of Medicine for Chinese, and practised medicine in Macao and Canton. In Hong Kong, Sun was associated with a group of reform-minded thinkers who saw the need to modernize China so that it was more like the Western democracies. In June 1894, he sent a detailed proposal for reforming and modernizing China to Li Hongzhang, Viceroy of the Qing government, but his proposal was rejected. The defeat of China in the first Sino-Japanese War in 1895 led Sun to decide that the only way to revive China was to overthrow the weak and corrupt Manchu government and establish a republic.

In 1894, Sun returned to Honolulu where he founded the Reviving China Society (Xing-Zhong Hui), whose goal was to overthrow the Manchu government and replace it with a republic. The next year, in February 1895, he set up the head office of the Xing-Zhong Hui in Hong Kong and established branches in Canton and other places. He planned to start an uprising in Canton in October, but news of his plan was leaked. Guns that had been delivered to Canton were confiscated by the Manchu government and the leaders of the planned uprising were arrested. Sun fled overseas, first to Japan and then to England. In October 1896, he was arrested by the Chinese legation in London but was rescued by British supporters, and then returned to Asia by way of Canada. Sun arrived in Montreal on July 11, 1897, where he registered himself as Y. S. Sims at his hotel to conceal his identity. Nevertheless, he was tailed across Canada by a private detective from Slater's Detective Association, hired by the Manchu government and accompanied by Zeng Guangquan, a Manchu official.

Sun stayed very briefly in Montreal, Vancouver, and Nanaimo, and concluded his visit with a thirteen-day stay in Victoria before boarding the *Empress of India* bound for Yokohama, Japan. The surveillance limited Sun's activities among the Chinese in Canada. Very few Chinese leaders and wealthy merchants entertained him since local Chinese people did not know him and they either did not understand, or feared, his revolutionary agenda.

During this tour of Canada, Sun learned that the Chee Kung Tong, a lodge of the Hongmen Society, was very influential in the Chinese communities across Canada. Lodges of the Hongmen Society had been established in North American Chinese communities under a variety of names, including Chee Kong Tong, Hip Sing Tong, and Bing Kung Tong, among others. The Chee Kung Tong was the largest and most powerful lodge of the Hongmen Society in the US and the only Hongmen lodge in Canada. Although the Chee Kung Tong shared Sun's objective of overthrowing the Manchu government, it paid no attention to Dr. Sun's tour across Canada because he was not a member of the Hongmen Society.

After his tour across Canada, Sun realized that he needed to enlist the support of the Hongmen Society for his revolutionary agenda. Zhen Shao Bai, a revolutionary, joined the Hongmen Society and went to Hong Kong in 1899 to unite the revolutionaries and the Hongmen in the Xing-Zhong Hui (Reviving China Society). He recommended that Dr. Sun become the society's chair, which marked the beginning of Sun's relationship with the Hongmen Society, although he was not yet a member.

In 1903, Sun went to Honolulu, where he became a member of the Hongmen Society. He was appointed to the rank of Hong Gun, the third rank in the society's leadership. After that, members of the Hongmen Society enthusiastically supported Sun's uprisings against the Manchu government.

Sun went to San Francisco in 1904, where he met with Wong San Tak, leader of the Chee Kung Tong in that city. He recommended that Wong change the CKT's policy from overthrowing the Manchu dynasty and restoring the Ming dynasty to overthrowing the Manchu dynasty, restoring Zhonghua (Chinese rule), establishing Menguo (the people's country), and equalizing land rights.

Since the Hongmen Society contained many different lodges under a variety of names, Sun toured with Wong to cities across the United States, asking the Hongmen members to recognize the CKT in San Francisco as the leader of the Hongmen Society and to pay three dollars to register as members. Sun estimated that there were about seventy thousand overseas Chinese in the United States and that if everyone joined the Chee Kung Tong as members and paid the fee, he could raise over two hundred thousand dollars, an amount sufficient to fund a major uprising against the Manchus. However, he was unable to realize this dream and subsequently left the US.

In July 1905, Sun went to Tokyo, where he united several anti-Manchu student groups and reviving China societies into the China Alliance Society (Zhongguo Dongmeng Hua) with the same goals he suggested earlier to the CKT. In February 1910, Sun returned to the US and established branches of the China Alliance Society in San Francisco, Chicago, New York, and other cities. In June the following year, members of the China Alliance Society joined the Chee Kung Tong as Hongmen members as well.

Rivalry between the Chinese Empire Reform Association and the China Alliance Society

After Sun Yat-sen joined the Hongmen, he significantly influenced the political position held by the Chinese in Canada. As Sun's political campaigns gathered momentum, Kang Yuwei, still a staunch advocate of reforming the empire, launched an attack on Sun and his party. Sun counterattacked by emphasizing the founding principle of the Hongmen: to remove the Qing dynasty from power. He also stressed how ineffective the plan to protect the emperor and reform the empire had proved, and he declared that the only effective solution to China's problems was to overthrow the Manchu government and transform China into a modern republic.

In 1907, some young revolutionaries in Victoria established the Jijishe (Striking Oar Society) to support revolution against the Manchus and to contest the CERA. Members helped distribute the China Alliance Society's newspaper, *Min Pao*, to promote Sun's ideas to merchants and residents of Chinatowns and denounce the CERA's advocacy of Manchu rule in China. Jijishe members were opposed to holding a memorial service for the deaths of Empress Dowager Cixi and Emperor Guangxu. Their activities gradually weakened the CERA's influence. The Jijishe was dissolved two years later after its organizers left Victoria, and its members then joined Sun's China Alliance Society.

Revolutionaries also actively opposed the CERA in other Canadian cities. In the election of directors for Vancouver's Chinese Benevolent Association in 1911, many China Alliance Society members were elected, and the CBA became an important supporter of the revolution and opponent of the CERA in Vancouver.

The Vancouver-based *Chinese Daily News* was also influential in attracting support for the revolutionary party at this time. The newspaper of the CERA, the *Chinese Reform Gazette*, challenged the positions promoted by the *Chinese Daily News*. An intense debate between the two parties occurred in the pages of these newspapers, with more than two hundred articles appearing. Over the course of this long debate, many overseas Chinese were enlightened and inspired, and eventually the revolutionary party gained the support of the Chee Kung Tong, which dissolved its alliance with the CERA.

Sun Yat-sen's Fundraising Campaign in Canada, 1911

In November 1910, Sun Yat-sen met with revolutionaries in Penang, Malaysia, and planned another uprising in Canton in 1911. At this time, the colonial governments of Britain, the Netherlands, and France did not permit funds to be raised to oppose the Manchu government. As a result, Sun had to seek donations from the overseas Chinese in North America, especially among Hongmen Society members.

When Sun arrived in Vancouver on February 6, 1911, he was warmly received by CKT members, and the next day, a reception was held at the Ko Shing Theatre in Chinatown, where Sun made a speech calling for the overthrow of the Qing Dynasty. With the help of Zhen Wen Xi, a Hongmen leader, Sun established the Hongmen Fundraising Company (Hongmen Chou Xiang Ju). The Vancouver branch of the CKT made an initial donation of three thousand dollars, and CKT branches in other Canadian cities followed suit; more than thirteen thousand dollars was raised, a large sum at that time.

Sun Yat-sen also travelled to Victoria to raise funds. He gave a speech at the China Theatre in which he described each of the uprisings in China and analyzed the reasons for their failure. He claimed that if overseas Hongmen could raise three hundred thousand dollars to buy ammunition and food for the revolutionary troops, they would be able to overthrow the Manchu government. He suggested that if the CKT in Victoria mortgaged its building on Fisgard Street, it could raise enough money to support the upcoming Canton Uprising. The CKT proceeded to mortgage its building to the British Columbia Land and Investment Agency for twelve thousand dollars. Sun promised that after he succeeded in overthrowing the Manchu dynasty, the new government would redeem the building. (He did not carry out this promise, and the Hongmen members in Canada eventually raised the funds needed to redeem their building in November 1919.)

Sun Yat-sen travelled to various communities in British Columbia to raise money in February and March. In every place, Chee Kung Tong members looked after him and assisted his fundraising efforts. On March 31, Sun left BC for Calgary, where he raised over eight hundred dollars with the help of the local Hongmen members. Next, he visited Winnipeg, where he raised three thousand dollars, and then travelled to Toronto, arriving on April 25.

Meanwhile, Huang Xing, a revolutionary leader, bought enough ammunition with funds sent from Canada to start the uprising. On April 27, he led revolutionary troops in an attack on the head offices of the Guangdong and Guangxi governments. That evening, Sun received a telegram from Huang Xing notifying him that the uprising had failed. Over seventy revolutionaries died; about two hundred managed to escape to Hong Kong. Sun received a request for funds to help the revolutionaries leave Hong Kong for safety in southeast Asia. The Chee Kung Tong in Toronto immediately sold its society building and sent the money to Hong Kong to help the evacuation.

After leaving Toronto, Sun went to Montreal where he raised another six thousand dollars with the help of the CKT there. In his three-month fundraising campaign in Canada, Sun Yat-sen, with the help of CKT members across Canada, succeeded in raising over $112,000 for the Canton Uprising on April 27, 1911.

TWO GOVERNMENTS IN CHINA

Although the uprising in Canton in Guangdong Province failed, the uprising in Wuchang, Wubei Province, on October 10 was successful. The revolutionaries continued moving eastward to take Nanjing in Jiangxi Province. Sun's successes encouraged military governors in other provinces to declare independence. As a result, the Manchu government in Beijing assigned high-ranking officials to carry out governmental reforms and appointed Yuan Shih Kai, a powerful northern military leader, to lead the army to suppress the revolutions.

After the revolutionaries occupied Nanjing on January 1, 1912, the Republic of China was established, Sun becoming its interim president. Sun also reorganized the China Alliance Society, which became the political party known as the Kuomintang (KMT).

Yuan Shih Kai accepted Sun's plea for peace and forced the Manchu emperor to abdicate, and he became the president of the Republic of China. On April 8, 1913, the Republic of China was officially declared in Beijing and Parliament opened, including representatives of the Kuomintang, the Gonghetang, and other political parties. Soon Yuan turned against the Kuomintang because its members opposed his efforts to raise a loan of twenty-five million pounds from Britain, France, Germany, Russia, and Japan. Song Jiao Ren, a KMT Member of Parliament, was murdered. This caused Sun to start the Second Revolution against the Yuan government and set up a southern government in South China.

In January 1914, Yuan Shih Kai dissolved the Chinese Parliament and demanded that Canada and other foreign countries ban KMT activities within their borders. The Canadian government recognized Yuan's government and closed the KMT office, banning its activities in Canada. Nevertheless, the KMT continued to exist in Canada, carrying out its public activities in the name of the Chinese Benevolent Association and other associations. In Victoria, the Minsheng Reading Room and the Zhonghua Qingnianhui were actually organized by Victoria's KMT branch. The ban of the KMT did not affect the party's efforts to oppose the Yuan government. In China, Sun Yat-sen formed a new party known as the Chinese Revolutionary Party (Zhonghua Gemingtang) to fight against the Northern Government.

In December 1915, Yuan Shih Kai proclaimed himself emperor. The Canadian Chinese were furious at this announcement and organized military groups to fight against him in China. A new army underwent training in Vancouver, Edmonton, Saskatoon, Lethbridge, and Victoria, and aviation fleets were formed in Esquimalt (part of Victoria) and Saskatoon. The Huaqiao Gansi Xianfengdui (Overseas Chinese Dare-to-Die Vanguard Corps) was formed in Vancouver, with Li Yimin as instructor and Xia Zhongmin as the corps captain. In March, the corps was renamed Huaqiao Yiyongjun (Overseas Chinese Volunteer Army). More than two hundred army troops left for Japan in two batches. In the first half of April, the whole army arrived at Yokohama and was summoned by Sun Yat-sen. In late May, just as the army was preparing to head for Qingdao, Yuan Shih Kai died. Sun Yat-sen went to Yokohama from Tokyo and summoned a plenary meeting of the army. He instructed the army to move quickly to Shandong to eliminate the remnants of Yuan Shih Kai's support. In mid-June, the Volunteer Army joined Qu Tongfeng's army in Wei County.

When Sun Yat-sen established the southern government in Guangzhou in September 1917, some soldiers in the Canadian Volunteer Army remained in China while the rest returned to Canada. Some of the former were even incorporated into Sun's guard. This demonstrated Sun's deep trust in the Canadian Chinese. Among these guards, the best known were Huang Huilong and Ma Xiang. They were successively Sun's adjutant attendant and guard captain. In 1922, Chen Jiongming, a warlord in Canton, mutinied and attacked Sun's headquarters. Even though he was seriously wounded, Huang Huilong fought heroically and escorted Sun to the *Yongfeng* warship. Ma Xiang carried Sun's wife, Soong Ching Ling, on his back, breaking through a hail of bullets. After this event, Huang Huilong and Ma Xiang were each rewarded with a "Southern Warrior" silk banner.

SUN YAT-SEN'S RELATIONSHIP WITH THE HONGMEN

After the establishment of the Republic of China in 1912, the Chee Kung Tong in North America wished to participate in Chinese affairs and applied to become a political party in China. Sun turned down the request because he felt that since the goal of the Chee Kung Tong had been to overthrow the Manchu government, which was now achieved, there was no longer any need for it to exist. He suggested that members of the Chee Kung Tong join the Kuomintang, but the CKT in Canada was infuriated by this suggestion and accused Sun of disloyalty to the Hongmen society.

Rivalry between the CKT and the KMT evolved into a serious and lasting confrontation and competition for party members. The confrontation intensified internal conflicts within Chinese society, and some conflicts even developed into tong wars. Sixty-nine key Hongmen members formed the

Dart Coon Club in Victoria on November 12, 1915, to fulfill the objective of "have one's own public right." The club accepted only Chee Kung Tong members who were not also members of the KMT and who were dedicated to Hongmen ideals.

On October 8, 1916, Loo Gee Guia (Liu Zikui), alias Charlie Bo, and his Chee Kong Tong members were attacked by Hoo Hee and other members of the KMT (the Nationalist League.) This sparked off the tong wars between the two parties throughout the late 1910s not only in Victoria but also in other cities across Canada.

Thereafter, the Hongmen society in Canada allied itself with the Constitutional Party to strengthen its power to oppose Sun's Kuomintang in Canada. On April 1, 1918, the Chee Kung Tong in North America adopted Chinese Freemasons as its English name.

On October 10, 1919, Sun Yat-sen renamed the Chinese Revolutionary Party the Zhongguo Kuomintang. In Canada, it was registered as the Chinese Nationalist League of Canada, and a total of twelve branches were set up in Victoria, Vancouver, Edmonton, Calgary, Lethbridge, Winnipeg, Ottawa, Toronto, Thunder Bay, Hamilton, Montreal, and Quebec City.

While China was governed by the Northern Government, the KMT's development in Canada faced a crisis, mainly because of different political positions held by the Canadian Chinese. Some Canadian Chinese supported the Northern Government; many CKT members felt betrayed by the KMT and thus had an adversarial relationship with the KMT.

In early 1917, China entered World War I on the side of the Western Allies against Germany. The northern government ordered Chinese consulates to mobilize the Chinese across Canada to launch campaigns that demonstrated Sino-Canada friendship and to participate in Canadian war actions. Chinese Benevolent Associations, the Chee Kung Tong, and the Constitutional Party that had evolved from the China Empire Reform Association in Canada, followed the order, except for the Kuomintang. The KMT opposed the northern government and all of its policies. The Chinese consulates sent another reminder notifying the Canadian government of the KMT's possible collusion with Germany.

Although the Canadian government did not discover any such conspiracies, it eventually banned the KMT on the grounds of the Chinese consulates' intelligence. In 1918, the Kuomintang, three related organizations (the *New Republic* newspaper, the Min Sing Reading Room, and the Kwong Chow Min Kuun Association), and the Chinese Labour Association (Zhonghua Gongdang) were all banned by the Canadian government, and some of their leaders were imprisoned. In fact, the southern government also declared on Germany, although Sun's government was not recognized by the Western powers.

PART III

THE EXCLUSION ERA, 1923–46

Onlookers in Vancouver's Chinatown waiting for
a funeral procession. City of Vancouver Archives,
CVA 260-1008. Photographer James Crookall.

THE CHINESE EXCLUSION ACT
❀

Anti-Chinese legislation passed by both federal and provincial governments prevented the Chinese from participating fully in Canadian economic, social, and political life. In 1923, the Canadian government passed legislation that prohibited Chinese immigrants from entering Canada entirely.

CHANGING IMMIGRATION PATTERNS AND POLICIES

After World War I ended, economic depression gripped Europe, and thousands of Europeans, even from former enemy states like Germany and Italy, emigrated to North America in search of a better life. The influx of European immigrants in the postwar period, compounded by the return of thousands of Canadian veterans seeking work, aggravated Canada's financial difficulties. As had been the case after the railway was completed in 1885, the Chinese were thought to be taking jobs away from white people, and veterans' organizations and trade unions once again complained vigorously that "Orientals" were taking jobs that should belong to their members. White veterans demanded that they replace Asian workers, and labour leaders called for an end to immigration from Asia. Politicians in British Columbia supported the demand for a ban on Chinese immigration, and Premier Richard McBride was quoted saying, "We stand for a white British Columbia, a white land, and a white Empire."

Not only were there calls for an end to Chinese immigration, but the Chinese already in Canada were also denied the right to vote. In 1920, in response to pressure from BC, Canada's electoral law was revised and a new clause was inserted into the Dominion Elections Act stating that people disenfranchised by a province "for reasons of race" would also be unable to vote federally. This clause primarily affected the large Chinese population in British Columbia, where they were prohibited from voting provincially and municipally. Saskatchewan also denied voting rights to the Chinese, but there was only a small population of Chinese people in Saskatchewan at that time. Thus, because of the distribution of the population, the Chinese were effectively prevented from voting federally after 1920.

During the federal election campaign of 1921, Chinese immigration was a major issue. The Conservatives and Liberals each accused the other of being pro-Chinese. In BC, virtually every candidate pledged to reduce or eliminate Chinese immigration. And in Toronto, labour organizations declared that Asian immigrants not only had lower living standards but also lower ideals, and they supported the proposal made by their BC colleagues that the immigration law be changed.

The Liberal Party defeated the Conservatives in this election, and Mackenzie King became prime minister. In spring 1922, H. H. Stevens, a Vancouver MP, and W. G. McQuarrie, the MP for New Westminster, introduced a resolution in Parliament requesting that the federal government "take immediate action with a view to securing the exclusion of future immigration" of "the wily Chinese." The resolution was unanimously supported by all thirteen MPs from British Columbia, as well as some MPs from other provinces.

While the resolution was being discussed in Parliament, Mackenzie King, interested in developing trade ties with China, opened negotiations with the Chinese government in summer 1922. He suggested that two treaties be signed, one for immigration and one for trade. Chinese communities and associations across Canada organized meetings to determine what a new treaty should include. In September 1922, the Chinese Labour Association of Vancouver, the Chinese Shingle Workers Federation, and the Chinese Produce Sellers Groups presented several requests: for example, that Chinese labourers, like other foreign labourers, have unrestricted opportunity to visit China; that the Chinese be permitted to bring their families to Canada; and so on. In January 1923, a Vancouver Study Group, headed by Seto Ying Shek, presented a proposal requesting the abolition of the head tax and the removal of various restrictions in order to give the Chinese in Canada the same rights as other foreign residents. Consul General Chilien Tsur met with the white Canadian groups and suggested that improvement of Canada-China trade relations would follow if Canada would accept Chinese immigration. Having received input from various associations, Tsur presented a proposal to Mackenzie King in March 1923 requesting the abolition of the head tax and that Chinese individuals be able to bring their families to Canada, among other points.

Meanwhile, in the House of Commons, parliamentarians continued to discuss the Chinese immigration bill, which had finally been introduced in March 1923. It contained the following provisions: that the head tax be abolished; that students below university level no longer be admitted to Canada; and that only four classes of immigrants from China thenceforth be admitted—university students, merchants, diplomatic personnel, and Canadian-born Chinese.

In April 1923, the editor of the *Tai Hon Kong Bo* (the *Chinese Times*), a Chinese Freemasons newspaper, stated that a weak country such as China had no foreign policy, and that it was up to the Chinese in Canada to lodge a protest. The paper suggested that telegrams be sent to influential business and educational groups in China pointing out how the proposed bill was an insult to China.

When the Chinese government proved itself unable to contend with anti-Chinese policy in Canada, the Chinese in Canada mobilized to try to defeat the passage of the exclusion act, or to amend it to be less prejudicial. On April 14, Lau Kwong Joo, president of the Chinese Consolidated Benevolent Association in Victoria, went to Vancouver to meet with the directors of the Vancouver Benevolent Association to discuss the issue. The two associations decided to hold a convention on April 19, to which representatives of many Chinese associations and societies in Vancouver were invited. At the convention, it was decided to found the Vancouver Regulation Refutation Bureau to protest the bill. Similar bureaus were later formed in other communities, such as Cumberland and New Westminster. Community leaders in Toronto felt that it would be more effective if all the bureaus were united in an organization that represented all the Chinese across Canada. Accordingly, the Pan-Canada Overseas Chinese Regulation Refutation Bureau (POCRRB) was established in Toronto with representatives from major Chinese communities across Canada. On April 29, the POCRRB held a convention in Toronto and over a thousand representatives from cities across Canada attended. After the convention, the POCRRB formed a committee that would go to Ottawa to lobby against the bill.

Nevertheless, despite the efforts of the Chinese, the House of Commons passed the Chinese Exclusion Act in May 1923. Although the POCRRB tried to influence the Senate to amend it, it did not meet with much success, and the act entered into law on July 1, 1923.

THE CHINESE IMMIGRATION ACT OF 1923

The new Chinese Immigration Act came into effect on Dominion Day (now called Canada Day) in 1923. The act consisted of forty-three clauses that discriminated against the Chinese—including Chinese people with British citizenship. The Chinese called the act "the 43 Harsh Regulations on Chinese Immigration," or the Chinese Exclusion Act. According to this act, no person of Chinese descent would be permitted to enter Canada except five exempted groups: members of the diplomatic corps; Canadian-born Chinese children; merchants; students coming to Canada for the purpose of attending a Canadian university; and returning Chinese residents who, before leaving Canada, had registered with the immigration office. (Registered Chinese residents had to return to Canada within two years of the date of registration.)

Even the Chinese wives of Canadian citizens, if they had not landed in Canada before, would not be admitted to Canada because they were not citizens themselves. Those Chinese who had the right to live in Canada but who left temporarily and failed to fully observe the re-entry regulations in the new act would be denied re-entry. The act effectively stopped Chinese immigration to Canada. Only about fifteen Chinese immigrants entered Canada from the time the act was passed till it was finally repealed in 1947.

If the head tax had been a serious financial blow that specifically targeted the Chinese, the total ban on Chinese immigration was worse: it separated husbands and wives, parents and children, grandparents and grandchildren in thousands of Chinese families. Many people were never reunited with their families in their lifetimes.

July 1: Humiliation Day

Soon after the Exclusion Act was passed, Consul General Chilien Tsur telegraphed Chinese communities across Canada, suggesting that they organize a protest demonstration on July 14, 1923. But it was soon realized that such a march was technically impossible, since it would require permission from the police forces in the various communities. After several meetings with representatives from six local Chinese associations and societies, the Chinese Consolidated Benevolent Association in Victoria instead decided that July 1, Canada's Dominion Day and the anniversary of the passage of the Chinese Exclusion Act, would be commemorated every year by Chinese communities across Canada as Humiliation Day. The CCBA told the Chinese community not to forget that Canada despised China; that Canada treated the Chinese in Canada inhumanely; and that the Chinese in Canada received unequal treatment compared to other ethnicities.

The association sent out a notice asking that on Humiliation Day the Chinese community take the following actions:

- All Chinese stores and businesses should remain closed.
- Chinese stores and organizations should not fly Canadian flags.
- Chinese people should not attend or participate in Dominion Day parades.
- Mass meetings should be held in Chinese theatres at which community leaders would speak about the Chinese Immigration Act of 1923 and its harmful impacts on the Chinese in Canada. Speeches should be delivered condemning the act and the harsh regulations it imposed on the Chinese.
- English articles about the impacts of the Exclusion Act would be written and submitted for publication in local English newspapers.
- Chinese people should design and wear Humiliation Day badges.
- They should cover their cars with signs illustrating the damage the act caused the Chinese community and drive past the Parliament buildings and through white neighbourhoods, honking to draw the attention of the public.

The CCBA's notice was received enthusiastically by the Chinese across Canada. On July 1, 1924, Chinese Canadians in Vancouver held an assembly at the Shengping Theatre in which Chinese community leaders spoke to a full house. On the same day in Cumberland, BC, representatives of Chinese associations gathered at the Benevolence Hospital to protest the Chinese Immigration Act. A few weeks later, on July 15, the Chinese Consolidated Benevolent Association launched the "July 1 Commemoration" movement and solicited poems and essays for a book titled *The Miserable History of the Chinese in Canada.*

The next year, on July 1, 1925, the City of Vancouver held an exuberant event to celebrate Dominion Day, with a marching honour guard and a brass band. The celebration drew large crowds—but not a single Chinese Canadian. At one o'clock in the afternoon, the Chinese Benevolent Association of Vancouver began to hand out leaflets printed in Chinese characters that said "Never Forget National Humiliation." Meanwhile, Ye Maojun, the chairman of Vancouver's CBA, chaired a meeting held at the Shengping Theatre, speaking about the Exclusion Act to a large audience. In Montreal, the Montreal Chinese Neighbourhood Society encouraged the Chinese to shut down their shops, restaurants, laundries, and other businesses on Humiliation Day as an act of protest. In Victoria, the CCBA sent out circulars to Chinese associations and stores in Victoria instructing them to observe Humiliation Day every year on July 1.

Chinese communities organized elaborate observances of Humiliation Day for a few years, but after the late 1920s, it began to be observed less and less rigorously. The Chinese, especially the younger members of the community, gradually became more integrated into mainstream society, and the white community became less hostile to the Chinese. Humiliation Day memorial activities virtually ceased after the early 1930s, as the Chinese community became more concerned about the conflict between China and Japan.

CHINESE COMMUNITIES DURING THE EXCLUSION ERA

After the Chinese Exclusion Act of 1923 was passed, the flow of newcomers ceased with just a few exceptions. The immigration of Chinese people that had begun over fifty years earlier was halted by legislation that would not be repealed for a quarter of a century. Chinese communities came under huge pressure, and their survival and development were threatened.

CHANGES IN THE CHINESE POPULATION

The Chinese Exclusion Act significantly reduced the Chinese population in Canada. According to the 1931 census, there were 46,519 Chinese people in Canada, 0.45 per cent of the country's total population. By 1941, that number had dwindled to 34,627, or 0.3 per cent of the national total. The Chinese population in large cities was greatly reduced. Between 1931 and 1941, the Chinese population in Vancouver declined by 44.9 per cent, while Winnipeg's population dropped by 30.4 per cent, and Calgary's by 24 per cent. The depopulation of the Chinatowns in many smaller towns led to their extinction, and in some places the entire Chinese community disappeared.

The exclusion era was a period of exodus for the Chinese in Canada. Many single men returned to their hometowns in China to marry and start a family, since they knew that no women could now come to Canada. Others who were already married left Canada to be reunited with their families in China. Some went home to take care of aged parents.

The Great Depression of the 1930s also had an impact. To encourage hungry, unemployed Chinese to return to China, the Canadian government passed Order-in-Council PC 3173 in December 1931, allowing registered Chinese to be absent from Canada for four years instead of two. Furthermore, those who were willing to return to China permanently would be repatriated at the expense of the Canadian government, a sixty-five-dollar one-way fare. The white public endorsed this policy because they saw it as a way to ease the unemployment in Canada and reduce the number of Chinese applying for relief. In 1934-35, nearly a thousand Chinese residents returned to their homeland, while 889 Chinese did not bother to register before their departure because they had no intention of coming back to Canada. In all, a total of 61,213 Chinese left Canada during the exclusion era.

Other factors contributed to the declining population. The persistent gender imbalance in Chinese communities depressed the birth rate and prevented the natural growth of the population. And during the Great Depression, an undetermined number of Chinese people died from starvation or malnutrition-related illnesses.

The Chinese Exclusion Act also led to significant changes in the distribution of the Chinese population. British Columbia, in particular, saw a large-scale migration of the Chinese to other provinces and cities where there were better chances of finding work, not to mention less hostility. The demographic shift caused the Chinese population to gradually decrease as a percentage of the total population in BC but increase in other provinces. BC's Chinese population had represented 59.4 per cent of the total Chinese population in Canada in 1921, but by 1941, it had dropped to 53.8 per cent. In Ontario, meanwhile, the ratio climbed from 14.2 per cent to 17.1 per cent. Quebec also saw an increase to 6.9 per cent.

Although some Chinese residents began to leave Chinatowns and city centres to live in better neighbourhoods in suburban areas—partly because they could afford better accommodations and partly because discriminatory attitudes had abated somewhat—most still lived in downtown neighbourhoods. According to the 1941 census, half the 34,627 Chinese Canadians lived in the ten largest Canadian cities and their suburbs, and over 90 per cent of these city dwellers lived near the centre of the city. In Toronto, 91 per cent of the Chinese lived in the City of Toronto, and 9 per cent lived in suburban areas like York or Etobicoke. The situation was similar in Montreal, where 91 per cent of the Chinese lived in the City of Montreal, and the other 9 per cent were scattered in outlying communities like Verdun.

OCCUPATIONS AND LIVING CONDITIONS

During the exclusion era, most of the Chinese continued to work at low-paying, labour-intensive jobs, although that gradually changed as the composition of the Chinese population evolved. A small number managed to find white-collar work, but still, in 1931, the majority of Chinese Canadians worked as cooks and in restaurants, on farms and in market gardens, in retail jobs, and as domestic servants. The Dominion Elections Act of 1920 also reinforced employment discrimination that had been in effect for decades: many professions would only accept members who were registered voters, so disenfranchisement of the Chinese prevented them from working in certain fields, such as law or medicine.

After the 1920s, many Canadian-born Chinese women entered the workforce. Many of these women worked alongside their husbands in family-owned businesses like laundries, restaurants, and grocery stores. Chinese family businesses often relied on the labour provided by wives and children. Like many Chinese men, Chinese women often worked at unskilled jobs for meagre wages.

In 1925, the provincial government conducted a survey of Asian activities in BC. The survey revealed that of 341 trading licences issued to Chinese business owners in Victoria, about half operated businesses outside Chinatown, showing how the Chinese economy was expanding beyond the confines of Chinatown because of the declining Chinese customer base. That same year, twenty-one Chinese people owned 206 greenhouses in British Columbia. The provincial minister of agriculture, E. D. Barrow, reported that 90 per cent of the produce sold in the Vancouver market was grown by Chinese market gardeners and more than 55 per cent of the potatoes grown in BC were grown by the Chinese. They leased thousands of hectares of agricultural land and, in the Victoria area, all but two greenhouses were owned by Chinese growers.

However, during the exclusion era, a second generation of Chinese Canadians, born and educated in Canada, began to emerge. Having been educated with white students in public schools, these Canadian-born Chinese had a better grasp of Western traditions and culture and were fluent in both Chinese and English. Some became professionals and tradespeople, working as teachers, mechanics, draftsmen, financial workers, real estate agents, and so on. Together with a few first-generation Chinese immigrants who had learned fluent English, the Canadian-born Chinese gradually changed the landscape of the Chinese job market. They emerged as the leaders of the Chinese community during the first half of the twentieth century.

With the exception of a wealthy few, most Chinese people led a very modest life during the exclusion era. Their meagre wages not only had to meet basic subsistence needs—many also needed to send money to their families in China and to make payments on loans they had taken out to pay the head tax. Many Chinese labourers continued to accept the lowest wages in order to find employment. But after November 1, 1926, when BC introduced a trial implementation of a minimum wage of 40 cents an hour, many Chinese labourers either lost their jobs in companies that had paid them less than the new minimum, or had to accept less than the minimum wage. The unemployed had to survive on an extremely slender relief fund, a situation that made things worse for the aging bachelors that had now become commonplace in Chinatown.

Unlike most labourers, Chinese merchants and business owners had managed to bring their families to Canada before the Chinese Exclusion Act was passed, so they did not experience the pain of family separation.

Some of them could read and speak English, and understood local laws and cultural norms, and were therefore able to connect more readily with the mainstream community. As employers, they tended to offer less pay and subordinate positions to their fellow countrymen than did white employers, knowing all too well that no resistance would be met. As patrons to the Chinese associations, many were celebrities within their communities. But their status in Chinatown did not exempt them from discrimination by the white community: equality remained as elusive as ever, even for the most privileged Chinese.

IMPACTS ON CHINATOWNS

The exclusion era saw Chinatowns across Canada struggling to survive the compounded difficulties imposed by anti-Chinese sentiments, the Great Depression, depopulation, and disruptions in some industries caused by mechanization. Adapting as best they could to their reduced circumstances, Chinese immigrants proved themselves to be tenacious and self-reliant. Even though many small-town Chinatowns became extinct during the exclusion era, their spirit and heritage were carried on in major cities by Chinese people who had migrated there from small towns. With increased diversification and inclusiveness, metropolitan Chinatowns survived the hardships imposed by the severe social and economic climate.

Vancouver's Chinatown had for some decades served as the weather vane of the Canadian Chinese community. Its status as the gateway city for Asian immigrants caused it to feel the effects of the Chinese Exclusion Act strongly. In 1931, there were 13,011 Chinese residents and a dozen overseas Chinese associations in Vancouver. A decade later, the Chinese population had dropped to 7,174. Such rapid depopulation inevitably sapped the vitality of businesses there, and once-thriving streets became lifeless. The Great Depression of the 1930s further exacerbated the situation. Although Chinatown was looked at as a filthy, overcrowded slum by the surrounding community, Vancouver's municipal government made no effort to improve it. Instead it merely condemned buildings in Chinatown and evicted tenants. In August 1944, over three hundred Chinese tenants were evicted from several tenement buildings on Shanghai Alley after the structures were declared unsanitary. After 1945, some of the Chinese began to move into the formerly Japanese neighbourhood on Powell Street, but most still preferred living in their crowded Chinatown.

During the exclusion era, particularly during the Great Depression of the 1930s, many Chinese property owners lost their properties because they defaulted on loans and tax arrears. In Victoria, several Chinese association buildings were sold at tax sales. The Chinese Hospital owned by the Chinese Consolidated Benevolent Association was acquired by the City of Victoria due to tax arrears. In the 1910s, Chinese associations and individuals owned over thirty city lots in Chinatown, but by 1939, they owned only fifteen, because their properties had either been taken over by the mortgagees or sold by the city tax collector at public auction. Many Chinese merchants closed their businesses due to lack of customers. Victoria's Chinatown had more than 150 businesses operating in 1911, but the number had fallen to 85 by 1934-1935.

New Westminster's Chinatown, once the second-largest Chinatown in British Columbia, began to decline as well. By 1938, it had fewer than three hundred residents and only two hand laundries, two grocery stores, and a barber shop. Eventually, New Westminster's Chinatown became extinct after most of its residents moved to Vancouver and other cities. Kamloops's Chinatown, once a large Chinatown in the Interior of BC, also declined. By 1927, most of its three hundred Chinese residents lived outside Chinatown in a variety of neighbourhoods within the city. Meanwhile, half the city's forty-one Chinese businesses were located in the white community and no longer depended solely on Chinese patrons.

Many Chinatowns in gold- and coal-mining communities became extinct after the mineral resources were exhausted. Although gold fever began to lose its momentum after the 1890s, mining operations continued until the late 1920s. Small Chinatowns such as those in Lillooet, Quesnel, and

Newspapers such as the *Chinese Times* (Vancouver) and the *New Republic Chinese Daily News* (Victoria) were a major source of information for the Chinese community. City of Vancouver Archives, CVA 260-246. Photographer James Crookhall.

Keithley were abandoned once the gold was depleted, and the Chinese miners left. Barkerville's Chinatown, once the largest in the mining area, had few Chinese residents left in the 1930s and was virtually deserted by the 1940s.

Chinatowns in BC's coal-mining towns had a similar fate. From the mid-1920s, as the Great Depression unfolded, dropping productivity and coal output and resultant massive lay-offs of Chinese miners led to shrinking

The Ladysmith Bakery and Hop Lee Grocery. Courtesy of the Royal BC Museum and Archives, image D-07239.

Chinatowns in Ladysmith and Extension. The Extension mines were finally closed in April 1931, its Chinatown deserted; by 1931, Ladysmith's China-town no longer existed either. After half of Cumberland's Chinatown was destroyed by fire in 1936, nearly all the Chinese community left, leaving it virtually extinct except for a few old miners who stayed on in their wooden huts. Nanaimo's Chinatown entered its withering stage during the exclu-sion era. Towards the end of the 1920s, hundreds of Chinese coal miners were laid off and several Chinatown merchants went bankrupt. With dimin-ishing rental incomes, the Land Yick Land Company, the largest local real estate agent, also faced bankruptcy. To save the local Chinatown, Chinese merchants established a non-profit company known as the Wah Hing Land Company and appealed to Chinese people across Canada to buy shares in the company. Eventually, four thousand shares were sold. When Wah Hing pooled enough capital in 1929, it bought up the lands owned by the Land Yick Land Company. Though successful in preserving their own property, these Chinese merchants were unable to reverse the depopulation trend in Chinatown. Only 298 Chinese people remained in Nanaimo's Chinatown by 1941, about two-thirds of the 1921 population.

Chinatowns on the prairies formed later and on a smaller scale than those in Vancouver and Victoria, so the Chinese Exclusion Act had less of an im-pact on them. In Calgary, many of the Chinese laundries and grocery stores were located outside Chinatown to cater to white customers and were there-fore able to stay afloat. But as was the case in other Chinatowns, Calgary's Chinese population declined during the exclusion era. In 1931, there were 1,054 Chinese people in the city and a few Chinese associations. By 1941, the population had dropped to about eight hundred, less than half of whom still lived in Chinatown.

Lethbridge had very few Chinese people and thus its Chinatown was tiny. About 230 Chinese people lived there in 1931; by 1941, there had been a tiny increase of 18 to reach 248. Most of the Chinese community in Le-thbridge were surnamed Leong and came from Kaiping County. The Liang Zhongxiaotang and Hoy Ping Huiguan were the largest clan and county associations in Chinatown, and lodges of the Kuomintang and Hongmen Society were also located there.

Edmonton's Chinatown developed slowly and declined after the ex-clusion era began. In 1929, the Chinese Benevolent Association set up a branch in the city's Chinatown, thus expanding its service to northern Alber-ta. There were also a few clan associations, such as the Wong's Association. However, the prosperity of Edmonton's Chinese associations didn't reverse the downward trend of its Chinese population, which declined from 467 in

1931 to 384 in 1941. Its Chinatown became a skid row in the Boyle Street area, where there were already many cheap hotels, rooming houses, shabby theatres, taverns, dance halls, and second-hand stores.

During the exclusion era, the precarious existence of some Chinatowns was further threatened by other factors. In Moose Jaw's Chinatown, as in other Chinese communities, the introduction of steam laundry and the 1930s depression put many Chinese laundries out of business. The local Chinese population dropped from 320 in 1921 to 260 by 1941. It is fair to say that Moose Jaw's small Chinatown was extinct by the 1940s.

The most highly populated city in Saskatchewan, Saskatoon, had only a few Chinese people, so the exclusion act did not have much of an impact. In 1921, the city had 228 Chinese and that increased to 308 by 1931. At the same time, a tiny Chinatown was established but its lifespan was short, less than ten years. By the late 1930s, it no longer existed.

Winnipeg's Chinatown began to wither in the 1930s. In the 1920s, there had been over three hundred Chinese laundries, but by 1938, only 125 were left, because inexpensive Chinese labour had lost its competitive edge as the laundry business became mechanized. Chinese restaurants and grocery stores fared no better, many closing down as customers disappeared. A few overseas Chinese associations managed to stay active, such as the local office of the Kuomintang. A sluggish Chinatown triggered a series of other problems. Unable to pay property taxes, some Chinese landowners lost their property and were forced to move into rented premises. But it was difficult to rent a place outside Chinatown; rental agents for the James Street properties on the southern border of Winnipeg's Chinatown warned their white tenants that their leases would be endangered should they sublet to Chinese tenants. For Chinese immigrants, therefore, even accommodation became a problem.

Chinatown took shape comparatively late in Toronto. Many Chinese people there had migrated from western Canada. During the 1920s, Toronto's Chinatown expanded rapidly northward along Elizabeth Street to Dundas Street West. There were 2,635 Chinese in 1931, but that number had decreased to 2,326 by 1941. By the 1940s, Toronto's Chinatown had expanded, becoming the third largest in Canada. But it still looked dilapidated when compared to the metropolitan city surrounding it. Such disparity to some extent reflected Chinatown's plight during the exclusion era. After World War II, the municipal government of Toronto decorated and expanded the city's downtown area. Since Chinatown was adjacent to that area, it attracted many real estate agents who bought up shabby buildings in the Chinatown and resold them to the municipal government.

Ottawa's Chinatown also formed comparatively late. In 1911, Ottawa had a Chinese population of about 170, but there was no Chinatown. The population slowly grew to three hundred by 1931. That same year, a small Chinatown, consisting of three grocery stores, two laundries, two recreation clubs, and one gift shop, developed on Albert Street between Kent and O'Connor streets. In ten years, by 1941, the Chinese businesses in Ottawa's Chinatown had increased to twelve: four restaurants, three laundries, two grocery stores, and three other shops. In addition, it had four associations: the Oriental Club of Ottawa, the Dai Lou Club, the Moo Chung Chinese Club, and the Chinese Nationalist League. An anti-Japanese organization also formed in Chinatown after Japan invaded China in the 1930s. It was renamed the Chinese Charity Association during the late 1940s.

During the 1930s, Hamilton's Chinatown began to decline, partly because the hand-laundry business was being phased out and partly because of depopulation. Many Chinese residents in Hamilton moved to Toronto where there were more job opportunities. By 1941, fewer than two hundred Chinese people remained in Hamilton. By the end of the 1940s, the city's Chinatown was virtually extinct.

Montreal's Chinatown seemed able to maintain its population level at the beginning of the exclusion era, but over time, with no fresh inflow of immigrants and a depressed economy, its population began to decrease. In 1921, Montreal's Chinatown had a population of 1,735, the fourth largest in Canada; by 1931, the thriving community had grown to 1,982 people; but by 1941, it had shrunk to 1,708. Montreal's Chinatown was bounded by Dorchester (now René Lévesque Boulevard), Clark, Vitre, and Chenneville streets. As in other metropolitan Chinatowns, a large number of Chinese businesses and institutions were centred here, including the Chee Kung Tong, the Chinese Hospital, and the Chinese Methodist Church, all located on De la Gauchetière Street West, the commercial spine of Montreal's Chinatown.

Quebec City's Chinatown was situated in the St. Roch neighbourhood. It was very small, with a few shops and laundries and only a few associations. Reaching a peak population of 140 in 1941, it was eclipsed by Montreal's Chinatown.

THE VOLUNTARY ASSOCIATIONS

During the exclusion era, Chinese voluntary associations, large and small, began to develop more formal rules and regulations and to establish permanent offices. They organized events to fight for the rights and interests of the Chinese, and led protests against anti-Chinese attitudes and the harsh regulations imposed on the Chinese. They also spearheaded fundraising campaigns for a variety of causes; after the Sino-Japanese War began in 1937, many of the Chinese associations mobilized Chinese communities to donate funds to support the war against Japan.

The Chinese Benevolent Associations (Zhong Hua Hui Suo) in different communities continued to function as umbrella associations of all the Chinese associations in a Chinatown. The basic tenet of these associations was expressed at the inauguration ceremony for the Chinese Benevolent Association of Windsor, Ontario, founded on May 18, 1924: *Survival is only possible when we are united; since we are striving to live in a foreign land, solidarity is a must for our self-preservation.* Other Chinese Benevolent Associations were founded in communities ranging from Edmonton (1929) to Cumberland (1932).

The social role the CBA played can be seen in an example from Regina, where, in the late 1920s, many Chinese living there lost their jobs and consequently no longer had a place to socialize. The local Chinese Benevolent Association rented a tented house on Broad Street so the jobless could meet. During the Great Depression of the 1930s, many solitary Chinese seniors died with no relatives nearby to take care of their burial. In Halifax, the local CBA (known in Chinese as Zhonghua Gongsuo), established in February 1934, donated money to procure a small piece of land in the city's cemetery to bury those who passed away.

Besides their many charitable acts in the Chinese community, the top priority for all the Chinese Benevolent Associations was to lead the Chinese protest against the Chinese Exclusion Act. On July 1, 1928, Vancouver's Chinese Benevolent Association held a special meeting for this purpose. Many stepped up to the podium to condemn the act to an audience of over six hundred people. All the speakers expressed the wish for a united Chinese community. In August 1933, the 5th Pacific International Academic Conference convened in Banff. The Chinese Consolidated Benevolent Association of Victoria (CCBA) sent delegates to the conference with brochures protesting the "43 Harsh Regulations." The Chinese Benevolent Association's second-most vital task during the 1930s was to support China's anti-Japanese war.

Besides their high-profile activities in the community at large, local branches of the Chinese Benevolent Association sometimes experienced internal struggles, especially regarding finances and the assignment of positions in the governing structure of the organizations. The Chinese Benevolent Association of Vancouver, one of the oldest CBAs, suspended operations several times due to internal conflicts. At one point, conflict among members became so irreconcilable that the association's registration as a non-profit organization with the BC government expired because it was not renewed in time. It was only three years later, in June 1933, that the association managed to renew its registration under the management of Chow Baoshan. And like many of its fellow associations elsewhere, the Chinese Benevolent Association of Vancouver had financial difficulties. In early 1938, it had to solicit donations from the local Chinese community to pay local taxes and pay off arrears owed to the Chinese Hospital.

It is evident, therefore, that as a leading group boasting a broad network of members, the Chinese Benevolent Association was able to rally wide support within the Chinese Canadian community for a variety of causes. However, since the local CBAs were composed of a mix of people with varied opinions, they were also exposed to disputes and disorder. This weakness stubbornly dogged the associations throughout their history.

Besides the dominant Chinese Benevolent Associations, clan associations continued to play an important role in the Chinese community. In Vancouver, the Lim Sei Hor Tong, the Wong Kong Har Tong, and the Wong Won Shan Association were still in operation. New clan associations were also formed. The Lam Kuo Mo Kong Association was established in 1924 by a group of Lam clan members, the Cheng Wing Yang Association was established in 1928 by the Cheng clan, and the Sam Duck Association was established in 1933 by the Wu, Cai, and Yong clan members.

In other cities, clan associations were also very active. In Calgary, members of the Wong Association, the Mah Association, the Chan Association, the Lam Association, the Leung Association, and other clan associations participated in the repair and beautification of the Chinese cemetery in 1935, and worked together to support the war against Japan in China.

Many county associations continued to function in Chinatowns and, even though there were no new immigrants from China, some new ones were founded. In Vancouver, the Kaiping Association was established in 1925, the Zhongshan County Association and the Yushan Association in 1939, and the Enping Association in 1946.

Like the clan associations, county associations had busy agendas. In July 1930, as the Ning Yung Yee Hing Tong of Victoria prepared to collect and ship the bones of deceased Chinese to Hong Kong, it advertised in newspapers appealing to those Chinese who had close ties with local officials to help facilitate the undertaking.

One of the most famous county associations was the Shon Yee Benevolent Association. When introducing the association, Fred Louie, chairman of its branch in Calgary, said:

> Our association was established in the autumn of 1922. At that time, many immigrants from ZhongShan county moved from Vancouver to Calgary and a dozen of them founded the Shon Yee Benevolent Association. Since its inception, our members have worked hard for our association's development. We organize

ancestor worship ceremonies, celebrations of Chinese festivals, and association anniversary events. At the Spring Festival, members usually get together to celebrate and dine. Occasionally we would [organize] a celebration parade, but we are a small number, so there was no lion dance or dragon dance. We have many charity programs. For example, we send condolences and a wreath when an old compatriot passes away. Each year we would have a plenary memorial ceremony for early immigrants. The anniversary celebration is our major activity in the year. There are three associations of us across Canada—the other two are the general association in Vancouver and an affiliate association in Victoria. Both would send delegates when we held anniversary celebrations in Calgary. Our forefathers made some donations when Dr. Sun Yat-sen visited Calgary years ago. One member, named Lin Sanhe, who is also a member of the Hongmen Society, used to be Dr. Sun's bodyguard. Compared with our Vancouver association, ours in Calgary is smaller and has fewer members. But all of us, including the one in Victoria, have the same constitution, keep up regular correspondence, and help each other. A few decades ago, we bought the building at 109 2nd Ave as our office lodge and built the Shon Yee Building at 114 3rd Ave Southeast. We rent out the first and second floors as well as some units on the fourth floor of the latter to fund our daily operations.

During the exclusion era, Chinese businessmen established associations to promote their businesses, provide resources for their members, and defend their economic interests. The Overseas Chinese Farmers and Merchants Association, the Zhenhua Trade Association, and the Zhenhua Overseas Chinese Students Association were united in April 1926 to form the Overseas Chinese Workers and Merchants Association. The Zhenhua Students Association was included because many of its members were descendants of Zhenhua Trade Association members or were active members in the trade association themselves.

Other new business associations in Vancouver were the Chinese Agricultural Association, founded in 1927, and the Vancouver Melon and Vegetable Growers Association, established in 1934. The China and Canada Association was set up in 1944 to promote friendship and business relationships between the two countries.

Business associations appeared in other cities as well. In Victoria, the Chinese Agricultural Cooperative and the Greenhouse United Association were formed. In Kamloops, there was the Overseas Chinese Agriculture Association. Chinese business owners in cities outside British Columbia also established associations for promoting Chinese trade and commerce.

Like students in China, Chinese students in Chinatowns did not have sports teams. However, after the 1920s, Canadian-born Chinese youths began to adopt Western sports. In 1920, the senior Chinese students in Vancouver established the Chinese High School Students Soccer Team. This team won many games. The match with a Western soccer team on May 25, 1926, drew a large crowd of nine thousand spectators, both Chinese and white, including the Chinese Consul and directors of the Chinese Benevolent Association. The two teams were well matched and the competition fierce, and the Chinese team won the match, 5 to 3. A few years later, in 1933, this team beat the University of British Columbia team 4 to 3, winning the BC Mainland Cup.

In 1929, the Philippines Chinese Basketball Team played the first game of a North American tour in Victoria. This inspired local Chinese youths in Victoria to found the Chinese Students' Basketball Club in 1931, which soon became well known because it regularly won championships. In the 1940s, the club was renamed the Chinese Students Athletic Club and branched out to include table tennis, softball, and tennis.

Chinese athletic clubs were also formed in Calgary, Toronto, and other cities. In addition to training in Western sports and games, these clubs also taught traditional Chinese martial arts, the lion dance, and the dragon dance. The Hon Hsing Athletic Association of Vancouver was founded during this period and still exists today. It was organized by the Wong's Benevolent Association in 1937 to offer martial arts training for all Chinese and was named for a great warrior in Chinese history. It also raised funds to aid China through performances of traditional Chinese lion dancing.

During the exclusion era, Canadian-born Chinese began to form their own organization, which gradually came to play a prominent role in the Chinese community. The second generation, eager to improve their community, wanted to change the biased impression the society at large held about the Chinese. They also wished to introduce elements of Western culture into Chinatowns to modify some Chinese cultural practices that were becoming increasingly problematic. Women's associations were active in this regard and challenged the traditional view of male superiority, strengthened women's sense of independence, and helped children from poor families. These new associations gradually distinguished themselves from traditional voluntary associations. The Chinese Youth Association of Victoria, established in 1939, organized fundraising campaigns in Chinatowns to support the Sino-Japanese War.

The Chinese Young Girls' Patriotic Society of Victoria, founded in 1940, performed operas to raise money to assist refugees and children in China. In 1929, a group of local-born young people founded the Youth Group of the Chinese Canadian Club in Victoria (the Chinese name, Tong Yuan Hui, means that members shared the same origins).

Across Canada, Canadian-born Chinese founded associations such as the Chinese Health Association, the Student Council of Mon Keang School, the Victoria Qiaosheng Shaonian Tuan, the Chinese Women's Club of Vancouver (formerly known as the Chinese Women's Club), the Chinese Aid Association of Canada, the Chinese Military Club, the Chinese Women's Association of Winnipeg, and the Confucius Society in Montreal, Ottawa, and other cities.

POLITICAL PARTIES

Political divisions in China led to the disunity of Chinese communities in Canada. In the early 1900s, they had been divided into two factions, one supporting reform of the empire, the other supporting Sun Yat-sen's revolution. By the 1930s, the empire reform party was virtually defunct. After that date, there were only two political groups in Chinese communities: the Kuomintang (formerly called the China Alliance Society) and the Chee Kung Tong.

During the revolution that overthrew the Manchu government, the China Alliance Society had allied with the Chee Kong Tong, but after the empire fell in 1912, the alliance broke down. Sun's suggestion that CKT members join the Kuomintang angered them and they formed the Dart Coon Club in 1915 to lead the CKT members. Only CKT members who were not also Kuomintang members would be admitted to the club. On October 8, 1916, the KMT directors of the Chinese Consolidated Benevolent Association in Victoria attacked the CKT directors, and several CKT directors were sent to hospital. On January 18, 1928, Fook Luk Sou, a CKT gambling house, was robbed of four hundred dollars by two KMT members, Lee Lim and Lee Sing. After the two were arrested, they were bailed out by Lee Chee, the Kuomintang's secretary. Lee Chee was later attacked by Yip Tai, owner of the gambling house, while walking in Chinatown. Police learned that over eighty Chinese men armed with pistols and knives had come to Victoria from Vancouver, Nanaimo, and other cities, and anticipated an outbreak of violence. On February 5, three Kuomintang members ambushed Huang Lin, a Hongmen member, near Herald Street and shot him in retaliation for the assault on their party secretary. Since gambling establishments were a major source of income for the CKT, some KMT members petitioned the city police to close all the gambling houses in Victoria's Chinatown, claiming that they were the source of all the fights. Accordingly, on February 9, the police commission ordered John Fry, chief of police, to shut down Chinese gambling houses to restore order in Chinatown.

These conflicts in Victoria led to more altercations between the KMT and CKT members in Chinatowns across Canada for over thirty years. On December 8, 1929, two KMT members were beaten by CKT members in Toronto. The KMT identified Hong Zhaozhi as the instigator and Lin Henian as the major assailant. On December 20, police apprehended Hong and Lin and the CKT hired a barrister to argue in their defence, claiming that neither Hong nor Lin was present when the assault occurred. Both sides clung firmly to their own story. In the end, the defendants were acquitted by the jury, drawing the incident to a close.

Conflicts between the two rival parties broke out in other cities as well. On December 14, 1933, several CKT members quarrelled with several KMT members while having a midnight snack at a restaurant in Montreal's Chinatown. What began as a squabble soon escalated into a full-blown brawl as both sides called in reinforcements. When police eventually quelled the chaos, three CKT members were seriously wounded. Since both sides acted as plaintiff and defendant simultaneously, this case became unusually complicated. The first court hearing was held on January 12, 1934. As other hearings followed, the police inspected restaurants, clubs, and laundries in Chinatown and arrested twenty Chinese people, charging them with possessing handguns and narcotics. Concerned community leaders in Montreal called for a reconciliation meeting to be held in the Chinese Hospital between the parties, but the meeting ended in another violent exchange. Eleven people, including some of the mediators, were wounded. Over ninety people were arrested, and numerous sabres, iron rods, and wood sticks were confiscated by the police.

SOCIAL PROBLEMS IN CHINATOWN

Despite the business successes and growth of their associations during the exclusion era, life in a Chinatown was far from perfectly harmonious. Certain activities that had originated in the early days of Chinatowns, including illegal immigration, opium use, and gambling, continued to interrupt the peace.

Illegal immigration and the falsification of documents to gain entry to Canada had been a perennial headache for Canadian immigration authorities. This continued during the exclusion era since many Chinese were desperate to leave the turmoil in China behind. Banning the entry of Chinese immigrants only fuelled illegal entry into Canada, and many resorted to unlawful means to help their relatives and friends come to Canada and to reunify families separated by the exclusion policy.

As had been the case in the head tax era, some Chinese who left Canada with permission but no intention to return sold their re-entry papers to friends and relatives in China. Other fraudulent documents were used to gain entry, such as falsified Canadian birth certificates or authentic birth certificates sold by Canadian-born Chinese.

A few high-profile cases involving fraudulent papers attracted attention in Canada. On October 10, 1924, twelve Chinese men were detained in Victoria by immigration officials for using counterfeit re-entry permits. Before they could stand trial, nine other Chinese men were caught trying to enter Canada with similarly counterfeited documents. The close proximity of the two cases spurred the government to call for an early hearing for all twenty-one men, partly to deter further potential offenders and partly to pacify disgruntled Canadians. Each offender was sentenced to six months in prison and deportation upon release, but all twenty-one refused to admit their guilt, claiming themselves to be victims of duplicitous immigration sponsors. After a debate between the defence lawyer and the immigration officer, the judge ruled that these Chinese would be spared imprisonment because they had not officially landed in Canada when they were detained. They were then sent back to China.

Chinese immigrants continued to falsify documents and stow away on ships during most of the exclusion era. When World War II expanded into the Pacific theatre, however, illegal immigration came to a halt, since it had become too dangerous to travel across the ocean.

Illegal opium smuggling was another ongoing problem in Chinatown. Using the importation of legal goods as a front, smugglers brought opium into Canada in large volumes. In July 1928, a shipment of opium worth $120,000 was captured in a joint operation by the anti-smuggling team of Nanaimo Customs and the BC provincial police. Split into sixty-six packages and labelled as peanut oil, the opium was carried by the steamer *Empress of Russia* to a consignee Chinese store called Hua Shang Lian Mao. In early December 1930, the Victoria police arrested two Chinese men, Huang Xiao and Li Zhen, in the city's Chinatown and charged them with smoking opium. Both were released on bail for one hundred dollars each. In a later court trial, Huang Xiao pleaded guilty and was fined fifty dollars; Li Zhen did not appear for his trial and his bail was forfeited. In April 1934, a seventy-five-year-old Chinese man named Huang Long was captured in a sting operation conducted by the Royal Canadian Mounted Police. He was accused of selling five cans of opium. On April 6, Huang pleaded guilty and was sentenced to a twenty-three-month imprisonment, a three-hundred-dollar fine, and repatriation to China upon his release. His lawyer pleaded for a reduced sentence because of Huang's advanced age and because he was a first-time offender, and the judge shortened his imprisonment to six months. Others continued to be charged with opium-related offences. In November 1946, Li An, a Vancouver man, was accused of illegal opium possession and sentenced to a one-year imprisonment and a two-hundred-dollar fine.

During the exclusion era, few married Chinese men were able to bring their wives to Canada and single men were unlikely to marry because of the shortage of Chinese women in Canada. This unfortunate situation contributed to the continued prominence of prostitution in Chinatowns, and arrests and trials concerning prostitution were not uncommon. In November 1930, Tan Hau was arrested and charged with procuring Caucasian women for prostitution in New Westminster, for which he was fined. There were also incidents reported in the media of white women arrested for working as prostitutes in Chinatown.

Although many businesses in Chinatown struggled during the exclusion era, gambling thrived as much as ever. Gamblers in Chinatown were a mix of people from different walks of life, including laundry workers, farm labourers, and small shop owners.

Gambling varied in form and scale among Chinatowns. There were large gambling clubs that could cater to over a hundred people, and small-scale gambling with fewer than a dozen participants. The hard-earned money of gamblers was quickly turned into ample profits for gambling house owners.

In October 1924, the Vancouver Police Department launched a sweeping campaign against gambling and narcotic sales in Chinatown after a murder in Chinatown was triggered by fighting between two gambling establishments. This campaign achieved considerable results. In a raid on a club on East Pender Street, over a dozen gamblers and the club owner, Liang Jiang, were arrested. Each was fined fifty dollars. At another club just a few blocks away, thirty-five Chinese patrons and the club owner, Liu Jiu, were charged and each was fined fifty dollars. In the evening of October 3, 1924, twenty-one Chinese gamblers were captured and held in custody pending trial. The next day, the gambling organizers were fined fifty dollars, the participants ten dollars, and the fifteen-dollar bail posted by those who failed to attend the trial was confiscated.

Police raids on gambling houses were also carried out in other Chinatowns. In January 1931, ninety-seven Chinese individuals were arrested in Montreal's Chinatown and charged with operating gambling houses and taking part in gambling.

During the exclusion era, police raids on brothels and gambling establishments in Chinatowns across Canada were reported in the media and thus familiar to members of Canadian society. However, there were very few reports of police raids on brothels and gambling clubs owned by white people: another example of discriminatory use of legislation against the Chinese.

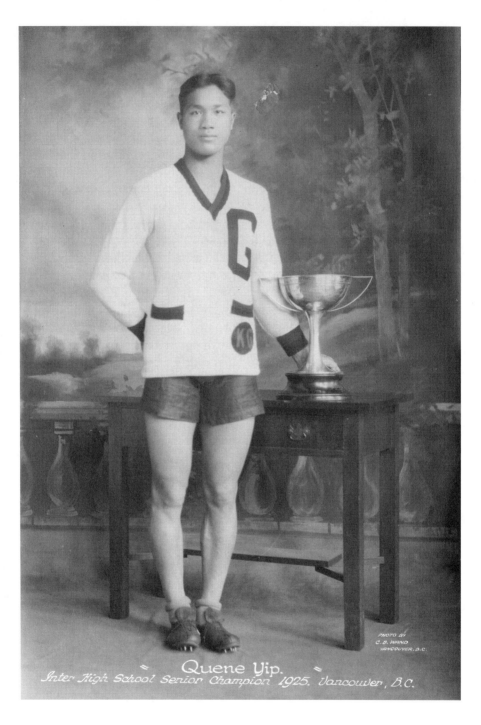

Quene Yip was the Inter high school senior champion 1925, Vancouver, BC. City of Vancouver Archives, CVA 689-67.

CHINESE EDUCATION
AND CULTURE
❧

CHINESE SCHOOLS DURING THE EXCLUSION ERA

Throughout the history of Chinatowns, Chinese education played a crucial role in preserving traditional culture. Chinese schools taught Confucian studies, classical poetry, and the ancient legal traditions of China. Overseas Chinese schools attached special importance to the Confucius memorial ceremony, in which the great philosopher and his teachings were commemorated. Some schools held their graduation ceremonies on that date. The Pei Ying School in Winnipeg celebrated its Confucius memorial day on October 14, 1925. At the celebration, all the participants bowed down three times on their knees before a statue of Confucius before singing an ode to him. A member of the Lim clan told historical stories of the sage, while someone from the Lai clan explained Confucian philosophy. Such reverence in Canada contrasted sharply with the sweeping criticism of Confucius that was occurring in China at this time.

School openings and graduations were also celebrated at Chinese schools on China's National Day. Such events were usually honoured by the attendance of Chinese community leaders. These leaders would, as a token of the community's commitment to education, encourage the students through speeches, prizes, or even performances by various troupes. These occasions were usually widely reported in the Chinese press.

During the exclusion era, Chinese schools built by various Chinese associations sprang up in Chinatowns across Canada. In March 1923, for example, the Qinge Xuexiao was established in New Westminster, BC. This school received significant support from the Chee Kung Tong. On January 11, 1925, the Mon Keang School, founded by the Wong Kong Har Tong of Vancouver, held an elaborate opening ceremony. A dozen Chinese associations and representatives of the Chinese government attended the event or sent congratulations. The Mon Keang School was one of the first schools in Vancouver's Chinatown and the only Chinese school at the time to be established by a single clan. It was located on the third floor of the Wong's Benevolent Association building. Because of limited classroom space, only seventy-five students were admitted in the school's first semester. All the students that year performed well academically. The school initially offered tutoring and primary classes; after World War II, it raised sufficient funds to add senior classes. The Mon Keang School attracted many Chinese students with its advanced teaching techniques and dynamic teachers.

In January 1927, through the pioneering efforts of Huang Kongzhao, a Chinese man who had lived in Vancouver for two decades, the Minglun School set up a Chinese correspondence course. Its purpose was to allow working Chinese individuals an opportunity to learn about Chinese culture. Students learned the four genres of ancient Chinese masterpieces: analects, essays, letters, and poems. This course was endorsed by the consulate of the Chinese Nationalist Government.

The Chinese Public School of Vancouver was founded in 1917 as the Vancouver Chinese School. It was managed by members of the Chinese Benevolent Association and the Kuomintang. By 1922, as support from the Chinese Benevolent Association dwindled, the school was short of funds. After opening and closing several times, the school suspended operations. In August 1932, it was taken over by the Kuomintang and other concerned Chinese people and reopened. Its location was moved from the Vancouver Chinese Benevolent Association's building to the premises of the Kuomintang. The number of students enrolled recovered and increased as school operations resumed. In 1941, the school was registered with the Overseas Chinese Education Design Committee of the Nationalist Government and renamed the Overseas Chinese Public School of Vancouver.[†] By 1942, the school had over two hundred students. Founded to offer universal education, the school charged no tuition fees, but budgets were tight and the school relied heavily on donations from Chinese associations to survive.

The Yuren School in Vancouver had been closed for some years, after its teacher had left. In 1935, the school reopened when Xu Zile, a highly regarded educator, was hired to manage it. It offered classes for junior and senior primary students (grades 1 to 7), charging $1.50 and $2.00 per student respectively for a semester. In 1936, the Correspondence School of Traditional Chinese Studies hired Xu as a senior teacher. He taught three classes on a

---

† In 1929, the Ministry of Education of China's Nationalist Government set up the Overseas Chinese Education Design Committee because the government realized that without Chinese education programs, the Chinese overseas would not be familiar with Chinese traditions. To be able to register with the committee, a school had to have sufficient operating funds, complete facilities, more than one full-time teacher, and a Chinese principal.

monthly basis, and he distributed lecture notes every week; the charge was $3.00 per student.

Vancouver's Zhonghua School, founded by businessman Zhu Guangwei in 1936, had only one classroom and one teacher—Zhu himself. Its curriculum, however, covered various subjects, including history, geography, composition, calligraphy, and so on. It offered day and night classes on classic Chinese ideas and texts. Day classes in modern language writing were offered to school-aged children and included vernacular Chinese classes. Night classes were for individuals no longer in school and had no age limit.

Aside from the regular full-time schools, to help Chinese adults adapt to life in Canada, some Chinese associations set up free day and/or night schools that taught in both English and Chinese and charged no fees to attend. The Tai Kung Free School was set up in 1941 in Vancouver's Chinatown. Over seventy students had enrolled three days after it opened, and its quota of a hundred students was reached in less than a week—many potential students were left disappointed. The free schools typically were sustained by donations from the Chinese community.

The Guangzhi School was one of the biggest schools at this time. Set up by the En Ping Tong Fu's Benevolent Association, the school's principal was Xu Yueru, a highly regarded member of the Chinese community. The school offered classes for senior primary school and junior middle school students. It also offered night classes in English. Xu personally taught health classes, and a member of the school's academic committee, Wu Yushu, taught physical education and singing.

When new schools opened in Chinatowns, the number of teachers became a concern that persisted throughout the exclusion era. Many schools had to hire teachers or administrators from China, sometimes with the assistance of the Kuomintang government or the Hongmen Society. In 1928, the Vancouver Mandarin School hired Li Junshi from China as a teacher. Li taught at the Qinge Xuexiao in Victoria, the Chinese Public School in Vancouver, and the Holy Spirit School of Montreal. Another teacher, Zhu Shuocun, who had returned to China after working at the Mandarin School as dean of studies, returned to Vancouver in 1929 to assume a new post at the school.

All the teachers hired from China were forced to return to China once their visas expired. Farewell celebrations were usually held for the departing teachers. For instance, a send-off attended by admiring community members was held on November 17, 1929, for Wen Shulei, a teacher from the Calgary Chinese School who was returning to China.

Many experienced teachers and administrators, after working in Canada for some years, had to return to China before re-entering Canada on a new visa. Zhu Shuocun's case was just one example. Despite this barrier, teachers hired from China at that time were well paid, and many were able to bring their families with them to Canada.

Because the Chinese schools were not part of the provincially funded education system, they relied on the Chinese community for support. Although the Great Depression negatively affected businesses in Chinatown, it did not dampen support for traditional Chinese education. Donations to support Chinese schools continued throughout the exclusion era, unhindered by clan loyalties and political differences.

The case of the Calgary Chinese Public School was typical. In 1927, in debt as a result of purchasing a school property, the school asked for donations from the Chinese living in Calgary and nearby towns. Donations flooded in. The school expressed its gratitude in a letter reprinted in the *Chinese Times*, saying, "All the debt has been repaid and now the school owns a property where it can permanently serve Chinese education. We owe this to our compatriots."

Individuals who declined to donate were publically taken to task: an article in the *Chinese Times* with the title "Surging Donations to Education from Overseas Chinese in Calgary" wrote, "All our compatriots donated except two, Zhang and Deng, both of whom have stable income from work yet still refused to contribute..." Such reports show that some of the donations may not have been voluntary; even the most legitimate cause had its rough edges!

Schools often combined performances with requests for donations. In 1930, Qinge Xuexiao, founded by Victoria's General Benevolent Association of the Chee Kung Tong, staged four dramas performed by its students, with gymnastics displays during the intermissions.

Chinese associations also sold raffle tickets to raise funds for schools. Twenty-five per cent of the revenue from the sale of raffle tickets was distributed to sales agents, 37.5 per cent was spent purchasing lucky draw prizes, and 37.5 per cent went to schools. The first prize could amount to several thousands of dollars, which encouraged robust sales.

Some schools in Chinatowns also required monthly donations from their students both to finance their own operations and to raise funds to assist needy individuals in China. Starting in August 1925, the Vancouver Mandarin School required its students to make regular monthly donations, provided by their parents. Each student in the senior classes was required to donate twenty cents a month, and those from junior classes, ten cents.

Student drama performances were a popular way for the Chinese schools to raise funds. Not only did they enrich the lives of the students and cultivate their sense of social responsibility, it also brought them enormous satisfaction when large sums were collected due to their direct efforts. Students also suggested innovative ideas to raise funds. At Qinge Xiaoxue in Vancouver and Victoria, for instance, students held a Charity Tea Party on January 1 and 2, 1938, to solicit donations for refugees and wounded soldiers in China. The two-day event was enlivened by singing and dancing by both Chinese and white students, and bustled with Chinese and Western donors from dawn till dusk.

The younger generation of Chinese Canadians attended mainstream institutions of higher education, such as the University of British Columbia, with their white peers. These universities began to incorporate programs in Chinese history, culture, and language, in part to interest second-generation Chinese Canadians in the ancient culture of their motherland. On October 2, 1930, McGill University announced that the well-known scholar and politician Dr. Jiang Kanghu would become a professor of Chinese language and teach courses in the university's department of liberal arts. McGill was already renowned in North America among the Chinese. With an enormous collection of 110,000 Chinese texts, including major classical Chinese works, the university boasted a Chinese library unparalleled in North America at the time.

Many Chinese parents encouraged their children to take technical training that complemented traditional Chinese education, since it made their children more competitive in a discriminatory labour market. At that time, many technical schools actively recruited Chinese students by advertising in newspapers such as the *Chinese Times*. The Trade and Engineering School of British Columbia, for instance, advertised in 1933 for its new classes on bicycle and aviation mechanics, promising to turn its students into skilled mechanics.

CHINESE ARTS AND MEDIA

Traditional Chinese opera, especially Cantonese opera, continued to be the major entertainment for the Chinese in Canada during the exclusion era, although during the Great Depression there were fewer performances and the opera tradition was also interrupted by World War II. From the 1920s to the early 1930s, most Chinese operas staged in Chinatowns concerned romantic love; after the Sino-Japanese conflict began, many operas with nationalist themes appeared. A change from earlier times was that women now performed the women's roles; another change was the improving status of opera performers, some of whom now became famous stars.

Among the Chinese communities in Canada, Vancouver's Chinatown was the hub of traditional Cantonese opera, and touring opera troupes from Guangzhou and Hong Kong competed with each other to attract audiences. In the 1920s, many famous opera troupes, such as the Da Wu Tai Troupe and the Qiao Sheng Troupe, had performance runs in Vancouver. Famous operas staged by those troupes included *General Yang Secretively Leaving the Three*

Passes, Incredible Injustice in the Struggle for the Throne, The Decapitation of Wu Sangui, The Sly Woman, Enraged Zhou Yu, and *Winning the Beauty Queen.* The Zhu Min An Troupe, which toured the Chinatowns of New York, Seattle, and Vancouver in 1924, boasted a cast of thirty prestigious Chinese actors and an orchestra of six. This was a mixed troupe with both male and female stars.

Vancouver's resident troupe, the Jin Wah Sing Troupe, was founded in April 1934 by members of the Chinese Freemasons and staged its much-acclaimed inaugural performance in the Far East Theatre.† Among the long list of operas performed by this troupe were *Gorgeous Touch, Real Brother and Sister, Three Battles at Huang Po Dong, Chastising the Princess on a Drunk, Dou Fu Xi Shi,* and *The Trial of Shui Bing Xin.* The opera *Story of the Wronged Wife* was such a massive hit that the *Chinese Times* reported in October 1935 that "crowds had to elbow their way into the theatre, and those who arrived late had to stand in the aisles."

This troupe was also a keen contributor to public causes. Not only did it perform voluntarily to raise funds for major community activities, it also created new operas with themes that reflected contemporary events. In November 1934, for example, upon hearing the news that General Cai Ting Kai would be visiting Vancouver, the troupe specifically created a Beijing-style opera titled *A Sudden Clap of Thunder* to raise funds for the welcoming ceremony organized by local Chinese associations.

Another contemporary opera club, the Shin Kiu Opera Company, was founded in 1935 and specialized in gong-and-drum Cantonese operas—that is, operas with a focus on percussion. At its first performance, it staged two operas, *Butterfly Beauty* and *A Perfect Match.* The former was described in the *Chinese Times* as "mournful yet romantic" while the latter was "elegant and humorous." This troupe performed a large repertoire of operas, including the opera series of *Fan Lihua Punishing Her Son* and the modern satirical opera *A Humiliated Puller's Speech to the Police.* The Qiao Sheng Troupe was another well-known troupe in Vancouver. Its representative works were contemporary operas such as *The Quarreling Son-in-Law* and *A Murder in Hong Kong* as well as operas protesting the Japanese occupation of China, such as *No Home for the Countryless.* But not all troupes in Vancouver's Chinatown prospered. The Guo Zhong Xing Troupe was dissolved in May 1926 due to performers' resignations and other reasons, a demise much regretted by opera lovers in Vancouver.

---

† The Jin Wah Sing Troupe, now called the Jin Wah Sing Musical Association, still exists and celebrated its eightieth anniversary in 2014. The Ching Won Musical Society, founded in 1935, is a second troupe founded in the exclusion era that still exists in contemporary Vancouver.

Chinese musicians playing during VJ day celebrations in Vancouver's Chinatown.
City of Vancouver Archives, CVA 1184-3053. Photographer Jack Lindsay.

Toronto's Chinatown, though formed much later than Vancouver's, boasted traditional Cantonese opera troupes that were equally successful. The Zhen Hong Sheng Troupe was founded between the 1920s and 1930s with support from the Hongmen Society. Its repertoire included an original opera created by the troupe, *The Budding Red Flowers,* and the erotic opera *Peony in Jiangnan,* which was performed frequently in China and overseas. The troupe later incoporated more traditional operas into its repertoire, including *The Filial Grandson* and *The Flooding of Jinshan Temple.* This troupe was also known for its lavish spending on elaborate costumes made in China.

Other famous troupes in Toronto were the She Qu Yuan Troupe, founded in 1932, and the Toronto Chinese United Dramatic Society, which was formed in 1933. The latter dedicated itself to three tasks: organizing Cantonese opera performances; inviting performers and musicians from Hong Kong and Guangzhou to Toronto to train local amateur performers; and providing affordable boarding and food to jobless and impoverished overseas Chinese.

Records of ticket sales provide a glimpse into the popularity of Chinese opera at the time. When the Zhu Min An Troupe performed *Shih-lin Worships Leifeng Pagoda* as a fundraiser, 1,300 tickets were sold for 1,060 seats, earning an impressive income of $1,300.

Many Cantonese opera performers in Asia visited Canada on temporary visas during the exclusion era, including Tuey Ping Lee-Hum, who came to Canada in 1936 with her troupe to tour Canada and the United States before eventually settling in Canada. In wartime, the Shin Kiu Opera Company invited Gui Mingyang, Wen Huamei, Gui Dingxiang, and other renowned performers to Canada to entertain the Chinese community. In the 1930s, the trans-Pacific passenger liners owned by the Canadian Pacific Railway Company—the *Empress of Asia,* the *Empress of Russia,* the *Empress of Canada,* and the *Empress of Britain*—all had Cantonese opera troupes on board, but the performers were prohibited by the Chinese Exclusion Act from disembarking to entertain local people when they were in port. The restriction was later eliminated when the directors of the Jin Wah Sing Troupe vouched for the performers. The ships' performers proved equally wonderful when ashore, and their performances became a routine for several years when the ocean liners docked every two or three weeks.

Besides these professional troupes, amateur troupes formed by schools and associations also put on shows. The performers were a combination of retired actors, senior amateurs, and young students. Big schools such as the Ginge Xuexiao often boasted student troupes that were capable of presenting full-length operas for fundraising occasions. Student troupes were also unique in their transformation of traditional operas into modern satires, bringing the older-generation immigrants in the audience up to date on social issues. For example, the student troupe of the Ginge Xuexiao staged an opera called *The Jade Dragon Case* at Vancouver's Global Theatre in late 1930. With a narrative woven around a jade dragon stolen at a private school in Nanjing, the opera told a moving story of how the villain's conscience caused him to regret his crime and confess, thereby clearing the name of a wronged innocent. This opera was much acclaimed in the Chinese community.

The Qing Yun Musical Club was popular in Vancouver's Chinatown. Set up in 1936, this theatrical troupe had over forty employees. It aimed to support China during the Sino-Japanese war and promote traditional Chinese music by performing Cantonese operas and other songs. Their anti-Japanese opera, *The Pulpit*, received thunderous applause in the local Chinese community. In Victoria, the Yang Yang Musical Club also raised considerable funds to help the war effort in China through its performances. On one occasion, it raised a sum of $112,800, which it wired to Kung Hsiang-hsi, the finance minister of the Nationalist Government.

Overseas Chinese needed the entertainment of Chinese operas to brighten their sometimes dreary lives. Thus opera troupes were invited, much to the delight of fans, to fundraising events, school openings, corporate events, the annual festivals of the clan associations, Confucius memorial ceremonies, and other community events. While enjoyed purely as entertainment, the operas also became a powerful tool used to arouse patriotism and motivate individuals to make donations during the Sino-Japanese War.

Guest appearances by famed performers and exchange visits by master performers from China added to the glamour of this sweeping theatrical style. For example, when Mei Lanfang, a much-revered opera master in China, stopped in Victoria in January 1931 while en route to the United States to perform at the upcoming presidential inauguration, he was invited ashore by the Chinese Consolidated Benevolent Association for a meeting with the local Chinese community. Travelling a long distance to promote Chinese traditional art, Mei provided much encouragement to his overseas compatriots.

The same period also saw purely musical concerts coming into fashion in Chinatowns. Popular music brought Westerners and Chinese together as an audience. At Vancouver's Pantages Theatre, for example, a concert by Zhou Ruxue, a famous Chinese singer, was advertised to all. When the Chinese-Western Touring Art Troupe performed at the Jin Wah Sing Theatre (the Far East Theatre) in 1937, tickets were sold out and one of the performers, Ms. Gong Yue Qiao, greatly impressed both Chinese and Western audience members.

Large musical ensembles thrived within the Chinese community. Besides the Qing Yun Musical Club mentioned above, another well-known group was the Overseas Chinese Choir established in Vancouver in 1938. Its first concert, performed at the Jin Wah Sing Theatre, had over five hundred singers, almost all the students in Vancouver's Chinese schools. They sang China's national anthem, then the "March of the Volunteers," the "Fengyang Flower Drum Song," and the "Hoeing Song," among others.

As electricity was installed in buildings, cinema soon became a leisure-time activity for Chinese Canadians. Many Chinese films were imported and screened in Chinatowns. They revealed a rich vein of critical realism. *Eternal Regret for Drunkenness*, for example, a movie shown by the Xin Han Movie Corporation in late 1926, depicted a sad family story full of educational elements. From early morning to late night, the film ran non-stop for three days. Advertisements claimed it was essential viewing for parents, sons, and daughters. Its ticket price was above average: fifty cents for an adult seat on the first floor, and thirty-five cents for an adult or twenty cents for a child on the second floor. In 1941, the Jin Wah Sing Theatre projected a sound film, *The Light of Overseas Chinese*, preceded by a short promotional film about the "One Bowl of Rice" movement in Los Angeles. Ticket prices were usually very affordable, averaging ten cents per adult and five cents per child.

It became common during the Sino-Japanese War for musical troupes to screen anti-Japanese war films and to collect donations to support the war, especially in its final stages when a wave of such films appeared. Examples include *The Battle of Ti'erzhuang* and *100,000 Miles* screened by the Qing Yun Musical Club. The Strand Theatre in Vancouver's Chinatown was the first to screen the film *Americans on the Burma Road*, a story about the drivers delivering supplies on the Burma Road under heavy fire from Japanese troops. The Orpheum Theatre dedicated a whole week to screening Chinese movies on the Sino-Japanese war. It is clear that after the attack on Pearl Harbor, mainstream society in Canada became much more attentive to the war in China, which constituted a major front in the Pacific War.

The China-Canada Association also sponsored the screening of two films at the Far East theatre to raise funds. One was *Life in China*, which compared life in the feudal age and in the current age; the other, *Motherland Continues to Fight*, depicted resistance efforts by the Chinese military and citizens against the Japanese invasion.

Besides movies, art exhibitions also emerged in Chinatowns and provided a window into China for mainstream society. The most celebrated event was the Vancouver Chinatown's fiftieth anniversary exhibition, which opened on July 8, 1936. A grand display with diverse content, it impressed visitors with Chinese artistic works as well as the architecture and decorative arts of rural China. Adding to its attractions were lively performances of Beijing opera, kung fu performances, Chinese fashion shows, and flower parades.

During the exclusion era, and especially during wartime, Chinatowns in Canada began to enjoy diversified entertainment that integrated Western elements into Chinese art forms and provided varied entertainment for all tastes.

During the exclusion era, Chinese newspapers established their role as the mouthpiece of the Chinese community. Major papers such as the *Chinese Times* (Vancouver), the *New Republic Chinese Daily News* (Victoria), and *Shing Wah News* (Toronto) continued to dominate the Chinese media as few new newspapers emerged at a time when the Chinese population was shrinking.

Of the few new publications—some of them short-lived—one worth mentioning was *Chung Pao*, founded on February 21, 1928, in Toronto. Started jointly by the Chinese Freemasons and the Chinese Constitutionalist Party, it was later independently operated by the Chinese Freemasons once the Constitutionalist Party had dissolved. Competing with the *Shing Wah News* in eastern Canada, *Chung Pao* soon gained a firm foothold among readers. It was originally established as a weekly newspaper, but the warm response from investors in the community caused it to become a daily publication instead.

During this era, Chinese newspapers concentrated on three major issues. The first was comprehensive criticism of the Chinese Exclusion Act of 1923. In their editorials, Chinese newspapers denounced the law, called for organized protests by the Chinese community, and demanded that the law be repealed. The second was reporting on and criticism of Japanese aggression in China. Updating readers with every detail of the Sino-Japanese War, the overseas Chinese newspapers informed and aroused the support of the overseas Chinese community. The third was detailed reporting of Canada's part in the Pacific theatre of World War II. These latter reports helped Chinese Canadians strengthen their identification with Canada. Of the three major issues, reporting on the Sino-Japanese War exceeded the other two in terms of time span, number of articles, and the level of detail included.

Although national interests became the focus of most overseas Chinese newspapers in Canada at that time, the battles between newspapers on behalf of their patron parties or clans only died down as the community grew less tolerant of such sparring during wartime. For example, from 1929 to 1931, *Hung Chung She Bo*, the mouthpiece of the Chee Kung Tong, and *Shing Wah News*, the voice of the Kuomintang, engaged in a two-year war of words which only ended through mediation by the Chinese Benevolent Association of Montreal.

Pre-eminent among the various Chinese newspapers and magazines was the *Chinese Times*. Covering politics, history, education, business, entertainment, leisure time, weddings, and funerals, the back issues of this newspaper are virtually an encyclopedia and historical database recording life in Chinatowns during the exclusion era.

In 1933, the *Chinese Times* published a report on the annual conference of the Institute of Pacific Relations that provides a precious historical record of China-Canada relationships at that time.[†] The conference had been held in August 1933 in Banff, Alberta, and the newspaper report covered three aspects. First was the activities at the conference of the Chinese and Canadian delegations. The Chinese delegation was led by Dr. Hu Shi, a prominent Chinese scholar. The Chinese communities in Canada expressed their grievances over the exclusion law to the Chinese delegation and requested that it lodge a complaint on their behalf to the Canadian delegation to the conference.

Second was the united appeal by both the Chinese and Japanese delegations to the Canadian delegation protesting the discriminatory limitations applied to Asian immigrants. Both the Chinese and Japanese delegations blamed the low pay and miserable living conditions of East Asian immigrants for their slow integration into the host society. The Canadian delegation replied that with so many Canadians (meaning white Canadians) jobless, it would be difficult to allow more East Asians to enter Canada, and that even if conditions did improve in the future, those of British nationality would be preferred. A detailed report was made of the speeches delivered by Dr. Hu as well as his criticisms of the Japanese Manchuria-Mongolian Policy. He stressed that Japan's intended restoration of Puyi, the dethroned Qing emperor, would eliminate any chance of peace between China and Japan, and that lasting peace would only be possible in East Asia if Japan reined in its militaristic policies.

In addition to conventional newspapers, some of the voluntary associations published journals. And besides news media, there were also general publications. One publication, the *Pacific Weekly*, published beginning May 9, 1936, released a new issue every Saturday. It assembled articles on current events, political reviews, health care tips, anecdotes, essays, and theatre and novel reviews. Also noteworthy is that late in the exclusion era, the newspapers peddled in the streets of Chinatowns were not limited to Chinese publications from Canada or the United States but also included publications from Hong Kong. These included daily papers like *Circulation News Daily, Industry and Commerce Daily, Sing Tao Daily, Overseas Chinese Daily, Sing Pao, Shin Sheng Daily News, National Daily,* and *Hua Shang Daily,* and tabloids such as *Chun Qiu, Sao Dang, Zhong Hua,* and *Min Sheng*.

---

† The Institute of Pacific Relations was an international organization founded in 1925 to enable the discussion of problems and relationships among the countries of the Pacific Rim. It was dissolved in 1960 and its journal, *Pacific Affairs*, was published thereafter at the University of British Columbia.

RELIGION

Confucianism remained by far the most prevalent doctrine in the daily life of the overseas Chinese during the exclusion era. Confucian philosophy was observed both at home and in the classroom. Taoism, with its emphasis on simplicity and humility, was woven into the traditional thinking pattern of Chinese and helped ameliorate the harsh living conditions they experienced in Chinatown. Buddhism had numerous followers despite the absence of any Buddhist temples, which were not allowed at that time.

However, Christian churches continued their efforts to convert the Chinese. By establishing schools and holding fundraisers and other church activities, the Christian churches all found ways to involve themselves in the daily life of the Chinese community and attract new members. Although only a relatively small number of Chinese people became members of Christian congregations, there was a steep increase in the number of people participating in various church activities. Some of the Chinese who interacted with or even joined Christian churches likely did so to gain acceptance in mainstream society. Many Chinese businessmen and association leaders began to hold Christian ceremonies at the weddings of their children and funerals of their elders; they also began to celebrate Christmas. More of the second and third generation of Chinese embraced Christianity than did their elders. Religious organizations established by the younger generations, such as the Chinese Young Men's Christian Association, were active in public welfare events in Chinatowns.

Western Christian churches opened churches in Chinatowns where Western ministers held services. In Canada, only Zhonghua Christian churches were founded by the Chinese themselves and run by priests from China. Community services were among the benefits offered by Chinese churches. The Chinese Christian Church, for instance, offered Chinese language classes after school. When daytime classes were full, night classes were added that were open to young people for a small fee and to children free of charge. The Presbyterian Church also had affiliated schools in the Chinese communities in Vancouver, Toronto, and Winnipeg.

The United Church operated affiliated schools in various Chinatowns.[†] The Union Schools were open to primary-school-aged students at a charge of $1.50 per student per month, less than the average for elementary public and association schools, and the fee could be further reduced if multiple siblings from a single family enrolled. The schools had specific

---

[†]   The United Church was founded in 1925 when the Methodist church and two-thirds of the Presbyterian churches in Canada joined together to form a single church (also called the Union Church). The Chinese Methodist Church in Vancouver's Chinatown was renamed the Vancouver Chinese United Church.

Chinese language classes that taught the classic Confucian texts, as well as geography, writing, calligraphy, and other courses.

The Roman Catholic Church also actively preached to the Chinese. The Chinese Catholic Church of Victoria and the Chinese Catholic Church of Vancouver, which were founded in 1933, organized community goodwill events in addition to holding Sunday mass. For example, the Chinese Catholic Church in Vancouver staged a mini-opera called *Light Festival* on the evenings of June 17 and 19, 1937, to entertain both members and non-members. The performance was followed by a lucky draw in which the winner was awarded a tour of Alaska. This event featured Bao Junhao, the Chinese consul in Vancouver, who spoke to the audience and awarded prizes to graduates of the church's kindergarten.

It was very common for churches with Chinese congregations to invite prestigious religious figures to come to Canada and preach. For example, after Zheng Hefu, a renowned figure in both educational and religious circles in China, attended an Anglican conference in the United Kingdom in late 1938, he detoured to Canada where he was awarded an honorary doctorate. Invited by the Chinese community in Vancouver, he spoke on the development of Christianity in China to an audience of both Chinese and Westerners.

Unidentified group of Chinese men in front of an entrance to a church. City of Vancouver Archives CVA, 99-3486. Photographer Stuart Thompson.

During wartime, the Chinese churches, regardless of their denomination, supported the resistance effort against Japan in China and the Pacific war. When refugees began to flood China after war broke out, the Union of Chinese Christian Churches in Vancouver started relief efforts by collecting donations of clothes and appealing for financial aid from Western shops and wealthy individuals, and sent its priests door-to-door to raise money. In January 1938, the church shipped about twenty-five tons of clothing to China. In July 1938, the Vancouver Union Women's Association, an affiliate of the United Church, wired a substantial donation collected through charitable tea parties to China for refugee relief.

Although there had been few Chinese Christians in the head tax era, that number rose during the exclusion era. The 1931 census records the majority of Chinese Canadians as Confucian and Buddhist, but there were also now significant numbers identifying themselves as members of the United, Presbyterian, and Anglican churches, as well as smaller numbers belonging to the Roman Catholic and Baptist churches. Some either declined to identify a religion or were recorded as having no religion. In the 1941 census, although the total population of Chinese people had dropped by more than ten thousand individuals, the pattern of religious affiliation was quite similar.

There were significantly more Chinese Christians in Toronto than there were in BC. According to the 1931 census, while there were 3,165 Chinese attending a United, Presbyterian, or Anglican church in Toronto, in BC there were only 1,650. The number of Chinese who followed Confucianism or Buddhism in Toronto was 1,639, compared to 17,860 in BC. In other words, Chinese Christians outnumbered Chinese Buddhists and Confucians combined in Toronto, but were outnumbered in BC by a margin of over 90 per cent. By the time the 1941 census was recorded, the number of Chinese Christians had increased significantly in BC, but remained stable in Toronto. The number of Buddhists and Confucians declined in BC but grew in Toronto—but Toronto still had many more Chinese Christians than BC did. Such religious distribution profoundly influenced the postwar development of the Chinese community, because belonging to Christian churches allowed the Chinese to become integrated into mainstream Canadian society more easily.

HEALTH CARE

In the exclusion era, especially during the war years, it became difficult or impossible for elderly Chinese people to return to their hometowns in old age. Because of the growing number of elderly Chinese, hospital facilities in Chinatown were improved and fundraising for hospital construction and maintenance became more diversified.

Although the Chinese continued to solicit donations to help fund their hospitals, hospitals in Chinatowns began to use lotteries to raise money during the exclusion era, as was the practice in mainstream society. In 1931, the Chinese Hospital of Montreal held a lucky draw event that sold tickets to Chinese people both in and outside of Montreal. It awarded twelve thousand dollars to the first-prize winner, as well as four major prizes, four minor prizes, and two hundred miscellaneous award items. All the money generated from this event, less the cost of the prizes, went towards maintaining the hospital's operations. Such charity lotteries also helped fund the construction projects of the Chinese Benevolent Associations. The Chinese Consolidated Benevolent Association in Victoria, for example, held lotteries to raise money to pay hospital property taxes, as well as for revamping cemeteries and renovating its building.

It became more common for the Chinese to seek medical help in Western hospitals and from Western doctors during the exclusion era. Chinese associations, therefore, adopted a more supportive attitude towards fundraising campaigns for Western hospitals. In February 1924, the Chinese Benevolent Association of Vancouver requested that its member association purchase life insurance issued by the Vancouver General Hospital as a fundraiser because many Chinese patients had benefited from the hospital.

Not all Western hospitals were as welcoming to Asian patients as Vancouver General Hospital. Public hospitals in Chilliwack refused to accept Chinese patients even after the Chinese Hospital in Chinatown burned to the ground in 1934. An emergency meeting was consequently called in Chinatown to raise money to rebuild the Chinese Hospital.

The same period saw an increase in Chinese practitioners of Western medicine. By the late 1920s, there were many Chinese doctors who, having completed their training in Western medicine, were ready to practise. Dr. Xu Ruyue was just one example. Graduating from the school of medicine at the University of Toronto in spring 1925, he then completed post-graduate study and an internship in New York. After being issued a licence by the College of Physicians and Surgeons of British Columbia, he started treating patients in early 1926 at his own clinic in Vancouver's Chinatown. After eight years, Dr. Xu went to China to work as a training director at a branch of the Guangzhou Academy of Military Medical Sciences and concurrently as a first-class military doctor of the Fourth Army. He would return to Vancouver during his holidays and open his clinic for patients during his stays in Vancouver. Less than a block away from Dr. Xu's clinic was the clinic of Dr. David Huang, who earned his medical degree in the United States and his licence in Canada before opening a practice in November 1926.

Some of the Chinese doctors practising Western medicine provided pro bono service. Dr. Gong Bangyao, whose clinic was in Vancouver, made it a rule that from 10:00 a.m. to 2:00 p.m. every Tuesday he would offer patients a free examination and diagnosis.

For most of the Chinese, traditional Chinese herbal medicine remained their first choice to treat illnesses, and herbalists in Chinatown thrived. No place had as many stores selling traditional Chinese medicines as Vancouver. Sheng Long Zhan Drugstore, located on Pender Street, was one of the largest. This store made medical tinctures and external-use medicines in-house that were very popular treatments. Its unique balm with a lion mark was also a famous panacea that could be used both internally and externally. Many of the large Chinese drugstores also sold groceries such as various melons, seeds, and cereals imported from China that were considered to have high medicinal value. There were many such drugstore–grocery stores in Vancouver's Chinatown, including the Guang Yu Long Store. Yong An Drugstore on Pender Street was another big drugstore that boasted in the *Chinese Times* of its ability to "make authentic traditional cures from selected raw herbs bought from China." Its sesame seed candy was famous as a gift. This store also offered a mail-order service.

Drugstores located in the United States also sold their products to the Chinese in Canada, either through commissioned sales or mail orders delivered through the Huo Sheng Drugstore and other drugstores in Vancouver's Chinatown. The Cao Tong Xin Drugstore in Los Angeles, the Huang Lian Shi Drugstore in Boston, and many other drugstores in the United States made sales this way. Dr. Zheng Shoumin from Los Angles hired sales agents in Vancouver and Montreal to sell his various pills, a method also used by many Chinese herbalists from Toronto. Dr. Zhang Jingxian from Calgary had developed a large business distributing pills. Opening his Chinese drugstore in Calgary in 1932, he sold over a hundred types of herbal pills and balms and had agencies in nine cities across Canada including Vancouver, Toronto, and Montreal.

As some drugstore–grocery stores expanded, they began to employ inhouse herbalists to attract customers. The Lian Xing Company in Victoria advertised in June 1924 that they had hired the famous herbalist Liu Meng Yi as their in-house doctor. The Yu Chang Long Store even hired two herbalists, Rong Yuechi and Lin Hanyuan, to serve its customers.

Besides drugstores, many traditional Chinese herbalists opened their own clinical practices. Zhong Yuesheng, a doctor of traditional Chinese medicine who sold herbal medicines as well as seeing patients, opened his own clinic on Pender Street in Vancouver. But with only a meagre income possible from diagnostic services, most doctors had to trade in medicine as a sideline to keep their clinics afloat. There were a handful of exceptions: some prestigious doctors, like the general medical practitioner Huang Shenyu, would engage only in diagnosis.

Although it became more common for the Chinese to turn to Western doctors and medicines during the exclusion era, traditional Chinese medicine remained the first choice of most Chinese patients, especially for common and minor diseases, thanks to affordable and easy-to-use herbal medicines. Herb-selling drugstores sprang up across Canada, and competition among them intensified within Canada and across the border in the United States. It was overall a time of diversified development for both Western and traditional Chinese medicine.

CHINESE BURIAL PRACTICES

At the beginning of the exclusion era, most Chinese still wished to be buried in their hometowns in China. Elderly Chinese would either go back to China to live out their days or request in their will that their bones be shipped back to China for burial. Xue Sitong, who had come from Xinhui, Guangdong Province, was one of those who chose to return to China. Xue was ill and had little money but, with the help of donations from his countrymen, he was able to buy passage home on the *Asian Queen*. He sailed on November 29, 1923, having first published a notice in the *Chinese Times* expressing his gratitude to the Chinese community for its help. But many were unable to return to China as Xue did to live out their remaining days. The long journey back to China was physically demanding and expensive. As had been the case in earlier periods, most of the Chinese who died in Canada were buried temporarily and had their bones shipped back to China after seven years by their clan associations.

As bone retrieval increasingly became an economic burden, some members of the Chinese community advocated an end to the tradition. An article published in the *Chinese Times* on May 29, 1928, listed several reasons why the tradition should be abandoned: it was a heavy financial burden for the friends and relatives of the deceased; the exhuming, packing, and shipping of the bones was expensive and disturbed the spirits of the dead; and digging new graves in China encroached on scarce agricultural land, thereby harming the local economy. The article's position was not unfounded. A letter of complaint from Tung Wah Hospital in Hong Kong (which handled the distribution of the bones in China) to the Ning Yung Yee Hing Tong described how many of the bones fell out of the flimsy packing boxes used, became damaged during shipping, and arrived as a muddle of bones impossible to distinguish. As a result, most of these bones were buried in a pauper's graveyard.

In the 1930s, there was a backlog, and it could take as long as ten years before remains were returned to China. In October 1936, the Yu Shan Chong How Benevolent Association announced in the *Chinese Times* that it was launching a campaign to retrieve the backlog of bones that had accumulated since 1928. In July 1937, the Chinese Amalgamated Exhumation Board tried to recruit help to retrieve bones, offering payment of two dollars for each grave exhumed. Probably because there were few applicants, the board soon put up another notice that doubled the payment to four dollars. According to these notices, over 1,500 graves awaited bone retrieval in Chinatowns across Canada.

The tradition of bone retrieval lasted until the Sino-Japanese War erupted in 1937, followed by the Pacific War in 1941 and later the occupation of Hong Kong by Japan. War made civilian marine traffic impossible and marked an end to the bone retrieval tradition in Canada. After this time, most of the Chinese who died in Canada were buried permanently in local cemeteries. For example, many of the Chinese in Toronto were buried in Mount Pleasant Cemetery instead of having their bones shipped to China. Mount Pleasant Cemetery had been opened north of Toronto so that people who were not Christians could be buried; at that time, the only cemeteries in Toronto were attached to Christian churches.

Chinese burials of the wealthy during the exclusion era were notable for their extravagance. In particular, the funerals of elite members of the Hongmen Society were large-scale events with many prominent members of the Chinese community in attendance. Reflecting the influence of the Hongmen Society within the Chinese community in Canada, these funerals were also an occasion for Hongmen members to pay their respects to deceased members.

One example was the magnificent funeral of Mah Ben Zhao of Kamloops, BC, who died on January 22, 1924, at the age of 53. A dedicated member of the Hongmen Society and an English teacher at the Chee Kung Tong English School, his funeral was held in the Chee Kung Tong building. Attending were over three hundred people, including representatives of the Hongmen Society and other local associations. A procession of forty vehicles travelled to the grave site. Similarly, when Lin Liben, president of the Chee Kung Tong, passed away in Cumberland, his funeral was attended by over two hundred mourners in a procession of over forty vehicles that included drum corps and countless wreaths containing elegiac couplets. Many unable to attend in person called to express their condolences.

Chinese people who had become Christians incorporated Christian burial services into their funeral practices. In late 1946, Ma Lisui, a senior Hongmen member who had served in various crucial positions within the organization, passed away. His funeral service was conducted by a Christian priest after representatives from the Chinese community had delivered their condolences. Six people, friends or relatives of the deceased, served as pallbearers and carried the coffin to the Chinese graveyard.

One of the highest-profile funerals during the exclusion era was that of Lee Mong Kow. A prominent businessman in Victoria's Chinatown for nearly three decades, Lee Mong Kow was also a founder of the earliest Chinese hospital and Chinese schools. He was a devoted contributor to the Chinese Consolidated Benevolent Association and was appointed general manager of the Hong Kong branch of the Canadian Pacific Railway Company. He died on May 9, 1924, at the age of sixty-two. To honour him, Lee's Benevolent Long Sai Tong, Shi Shi Xuan, Yu Shan Chong How Benevolent Association, the Public School of Overseas Chinese, and other associations in Chinatown prepared for months, posting notices in the local newspaper requesting contributions to a eulogy. On August 24, the memorial ceremony was held in the building of the Chinese Consolidated Benevolent Association. The extraordinary ceremonies for Lee Mong Kow and other community leaders helped forge the tradition of expressing thankfulness to the pioneers and ancestors to whom the community owed its thriving present.

Ye Chuntian, a successful businessman, was well respected for his generous contributions to his community. He died at the age of eighty-five in 1927. Once a ticket agent for the Canadian Pacific Railway Company when the railway was under construction, he was one of the few Chinese known by his compatriots in both Canada and the United States. His sons were educated at the University of British Columbia; one of them, Ye Qiujun, was a football star on the local Chinese football team. The Ye family was well known in Vancouver. More than fifty relatives signed his obituary and three hundred condolence letters were received. His funeral procession comprised 150 bicycles, four of which carried wreaths, and six Chinese and six Western pallbearers. The funeral service was a Christian ceremony administered by Guan Yaonan. The descendants of Ye scattered across North America. By the late twentieth century, the Ye family had become an enormous clan with over a thousand members.

Funerals of clan leaders were comparable in scale with that of Ye. On October 11, 1946, Huang Qiachang, the patriarch of the Huang clan, died. His funeral was organized by the Wong Won Sun Association of Wong Kong Har Tong. Over six hundred friends and relatives, Chinese and non-Chinese alike, attended. A Christian funeral service was held, and the pallbearers were Chinese and Western celebrities, including Chen Shuren, director of the Overseas Chinese Affairs & Education Department of the Nanjing Nationalist Government, and Odlin, the Canadian ambassador to China. Huang's funeral procession marched through the streets of Chinatown, watched by a crowd of pedestrians, and then into the graveyard for the burial service. It was a spectacular farewell to a man who had lived with honour and died deeply mourned.

THE SINO-JAPANESE WAR AND WORLD WAR II

❧

The Chinese in Canada were involved in war from 1937, when they began supporting China in the Sino-Japanese War, until the end of World War II. After World War II expanded into the Pacific theatre, they supported Canada and its allies, which included China. These wars deeply affected the lives of Chinese Canadians. When World War II expanded into the Pacific theatre in 1941, young Chinese Canadians set aside the discrimination they faced in their own country and fought for Canada. Their participation, even though they did not enjoy full citizenship rights, laid the foundations for postwar changes in the unjust treatment of the Chinese in Canada.

THE SINO-JAPANESE WAR

China was a country at war during most of the exclusion era. In 1927, civil war broke out between the Kuomintang-led Republic of China and the Communist Party of China. This civil war continued intermittently until 1937, when the two sides united to fight the Japanese, and resumed after the end of World War II, ending in 1949 with the victory of the Communist Party and the retreat of the KMT government to Taiwan.

Concurrently, Japan and China were in intermittent conflict from 1931 onward as Japan tried to annex Chinese territory. As early as 1931, the CCBA in Victoria supported a ceasefire in the civil war so that a united front could be presented to the Japanese. Full-scale war broke out in 1937 when Japan invaded China, initiating a Sino-Japanese war that would not come to an end till World War II was over and the Emperor of Japan surrendered to the Allies on September 2, 1945, which became known as VJ day, for Victory over Japan. Overseas Chinese people around the world united to resist the Japanese and support the anti-Japanese war efforts in China. The Chinese in Canada were no exception.

Chinatowns were the hub of Chinese Canadian efforts, and the Chinese news media were the means through which fundraising requests and news were circulated. Chinese National Salvation Bureaus were founded, and other local organizations supporting the war effort emerged in Chinatowns across Canada. Chinese women actively contributed through women's caucuses of these organizations or through pre-existing women's groups such as the Chinese Women's Associations in Vancouver and Toronto. The contributions of the Chinese Canadian community were expressed in donations, both cash and in-kind, in boycotts of Japanese goods, and—in the case of a few—in direct participation in the conflict serving in the Chinese military.

Throughout the exclusion era, the Chinese in Canada continued to donate money to assist their fellow Chinese—including their relatives and friends in China—when natural disasters or political unrest rendered this necessary. An earthquake in 1923, famine in 1929, and massive flooding in 1935 all stimulated generous donations to help those in need. Labour unrest in Shanghai in 1925 threw many out of work, and in this case too, the Chinese community sent aid through the Chinese Consolidated Benevolent Association. Education remained of special interest to the overseas Chinese, and donations to support schools continued to flow from Canada to China. But during the exclusion era, the most important cause was the war against Japan.

The Chinese contributed both cash and in-kind donations to support the war effort. According to the *Chinese Times*, donations from the overseas Chinese in Canada between 1932 and 1945 added up to over a million dollars, an enormous amount at that time. A continuous series of campaigns raised funds through benefit performances by theatrical troupes, charity bazaars and parades, and charity teas. Drives to collect goods were also held. Thanks to the steady flow of donations, money, weapons, clothing, medicines, and food were sent both to the front lines and to civilian communities in China.

Chinese communities began to hold fundraising events as soon as Japanese aggression became apparent in northern China in the early 1930s. Daluotian, a famous Chinese opera troupe, staged a benefit performance in Vancouver to raise money for the Chinese army. This performance was supported by Vancouver's Hongmen National Salvation Association. The opera depicted the story of a beautiful woman striving to save China and showcased the patriotism of the overseas Chinese; it attracted a large audience.

Even though most overseas Chinese were labourers earning a low income, they scrimped and saved in order to donate as much of their hard-earned money as possible. One campaign that was very widespread among the overseas Chinese labourers was the "One Bowl of Rice" movement initiated by Sun Yat-sen's widow, Song Qingling, in 1939. Each person skipped one bowl of rice each day and donated its value to support the army fighting on the front lines.

The overseas Chinese were particularly keen to help China's air force acquire fighter planes because the Japanese had a superior air force at the start of the war, with more than twice as many war planes as the Chinese. Chinese Canadians set up the Chinese Aviation Research Society of Canada to find pilots for the Chinese army and raise funds to buy planes. The Chinese responded quickly when calls for such donations were made. The Shon Yee Benevolent Association of Vancouver, for instance, always made generous donations when help was requested for this purpose. In April 1945, the Chinese Aviation Association awarded the Shon Yee Benevolent Association a gold medal and a certificate of merit signed by Chiang Kai-shek.

Besides donating money, the Chinese in Canada also supported the war effort in China with material donations ranging from medical equipment to winter clothing. These donations were sent to soldiers on the front line as well as to aid wounded soldiers and refugees. The Chinese Women's Association of Vancouver used donated money to purchase a batch of antibiotics worth thousands of dollars and ship it to China to treat the wounded. Tons of donated clothing were also shipped to China.

The purchase of Chinese government bonds was another way in which the Chinese in Canada contributed to the war effort in China. To sustain the enormous military spending during the war, the national government in Nanjing sold several issues of government bonds, and Chinese Canadians bought them to help fund the war. In 1938, an elderly Chinese man living near Moose Jaw, Saskatchewan, used money scraped together from his social relief payments to buy government bonds. In 1943, the Vancouver branch of the Overseas Chinese Government Bond Promotion Office in Canada remitted 1,043,100 Chinese dollars to China and received a letter of thanks from Kung Hsiang-hsi, the finance minister of the Nanjing Nationalist Government.

Campaigns were organized to boycott Japanese goods in an effort to weaken Japan's economy. The boycott movement began in China and, from there, spread across the world to the overseas Chinese communities. In Canada, Chinese businessmen in Toronto initiated the first boycott in their shops, followed by a similar initiative in Vancouver. As usual, the Chinese media were key in circulating information about the boycott; a September 1937 issue of the *Chinese Times* reminded readers to boycott all Japanese goods. The Chinese hoped their boycotts would result in an embargo against Japan.

Related to this was a series of protests between 1937 and 1941 initiated in North America against sending shipments of scrap metal to Japan from Pacific coastal ports in both the US and Canada. Massive amounts of scrap metal were being sent to Japan, where it was reused in weapons manufacture. Demonstrations were organized at pier sites so that both Chinese and white people could protest these shipments, in the hope that the Canadian government would prohibit such shipments. The boycotts gradually expanded to the other provinces. Saskatoon, Moose Jaw, Regina, and other inland cities also established resistance associations and agitated against scrap metal shipments to Japan. The governments of Canada and the United States did stop such cargo shipments to Japan, and this became a major cause of Japan's attack on the United States and its invasion of Southeast Asian countries such as Malaysia to obtain the materials it was no longer receiving from North America.

A small number of Chinese youths in Canada returned to China to fight on the front lines in the Chinese air force both before and after the Pacific War began. For example, Mah Jianjin, the descendant of a Taishan family who grew up in Calgary, was an expert pilot and mechanic. He enlisted in the Republic of China Air Force, and in 1939, while on a bombing mission that targeted a Japanese airport in Yuncheng, Shanxin Province, he and his comrades-in-arms blew up more than thirty Japanese fighter planes, for which they were awarded military medals. He returned to Canada after the war ended, later moving to the US.

Another Chinese Canadian, Harold Chinn, was born in Vancouver and received his pilot's training in BC. He also enlisted in the Chinese air force, serving from 1933 to 1935. In 1937, he became a China National Aviation Corporation (CNAC) transport pilot flying between Chungking, Kweiyang, and Hong Kong, until that city fell to the Japanese in December 1941.[†] After 1941, CNAC moved its headquarters to India for the duration of the war. Chinn flew transport planes carrying supplies from India into southwestern China over the Himalayas, a dangerous route known as "the Hump," which was plagued with severe weather and where planes were targeted by the Japanese. He flew over six hundred flights on the Hump run, more than any other pilot in CNAC. Kuo Lim Mah, from Kelowna, BC, also joined the China National Aviation Corporation in 1942 as a transport pilot, flying the treacherous Hump. He was killed on August 1, 1944, when his aircraft failed to clear a cliff when taking off from Kunming, a city in southwestern China.

Zheng Zhaogen, born in Vancouver in 1911, joined the British Army Aid Group after he witnessed a Canadian soldier being killed by the Japanese in Hong Kong in December 1941. He worked in Japanese-occupied China as a secret agent and was known as Agent 50. Agent 50 undertook dangerous assignments such as spiriting medicine, messages, escaped prisoners,

---

†   The Chinese National Aviation Corporation was jointly owned by the Chinese Nationalist Government and Pan-American Airlines. During the war, it transported supplies into China.

and downed airmen back and forth through the Japanese lines. For his extraordinary services, he was the only Chinese Canadian to receive a British Empire medal.

World War II

Once World War II broke out and the Japanese bombed Pearl Harbor in 1941, the Sino-Japanese War merged with the larger war and became known as the Pacific War. Just as the Sino-Japanese War in China had aroused the Chinese community to take action, so did Canada's entry into World War II stir Chinese youths to action, in particular the second- and third-generation Chinese Canadian youths who had grown up in Canada. They readily volunteered to fight for a country that had not yet accepted them socially or politically. The motivation to enlist varied among Chinese youths. Some wanted to fight for democracy, some wished to explore a military career, and some, unhappy with the discrimination they faced in their host society, wanted to earn equal social and political status to that of white men by fighting side by side with them in the battlefield.

After war broke out and the Germans had won several important victories, the National Resources Mobilization Act (NRMA) was enacted on June 21, 1940. It empowered the federal government to conscript soldiers and deploy its military forces in and out of Canada. Many young Chinese applied, encouraged by the new act. But to their dismay, the Royal Canadian Air Force and the Royal Canadian Navy regulations stipulated that they could only enlist "pure Europeans" and "pure whites." And the Canadian Army, although it did not explicitly reject them, still shut the door on Asian applicants in practice.

Rejection of Chinese applicants was most conspicuous in BC, where anti-Chinese discrimination had deep roots. BC's premier, T. D. Pattullo, felt that it was more important to prevent the Chinese from becoming enfranchised than it was to win the war. He flatly admitted, "If they are called up for service, there will be demands that they be given the franchise, which we in the Province can never tolerate."

A few months after the National Resources Mobilization Act was enacted, the Chinese petitioned the minister of national war services in Ottawa, pointing out that Chinese Canadians would be more than willing "to give whatever service should be expected of Canadian citizens" in connection with compulsory military training. In return, they argued, they "should receive complete recognition as Canadian citizens and should have all the privileges of citizenship"—especially the right to vote. However, reality remained a far cry from what the Chinese wished, and both the Chinese and Japanese were banned from enlisting till later in the war. Within the army, the few Asian soldiers who had already enlisted were spared a purge.

On December 7, 1941, Japan attacked Pearl Harbor, ushering in the Pacific War. This attack changed the status of Asian Canadians, including that of Chinese Canadians, as Canada followed America—both countries allied with China—in declaring war against Japan. In the early stages of the Pacific War, Japanese aggression in Southeast Asia put Britain, then fighting a two-front war in Europe and Asia, in sore need of reinforcements. The British War Office consequently asked Canada to extend recruitment to Asian soldiers to serve in the Pacific theatre, in part because of their knowledge of Asian languages and their familiarity with the culture. Opinions on the advisedness of this change in policy varied at the top levels of the Royal Canadian Air Force, the Royal Canadian Navy, and the Canadian Army, but eventually all three branches of the military accepted Chinese recruits, and between five and six hundred Chinese Canadians served in the Canadian forces on land, at sea, and in the air.

The majority of these Chinese soldiers aspired to join the front lines, and in Europe, Southeast Asia, and the Pacific war zone, many established excellent military records. The Chinese at home in Canada also contributed to civil defence initiatives, including organizing air raid protection units, participating in wartime factory production, being trained in first aid and ambulance work, and developing other useful defensive skills.

The Chinese communities in Canada also contributed to the federal Victory Bond fundraising initiative. Victory Bonds were issued by the Canadian government to help fund Canada's military expenses during World War II. The War Finance Committee issued nine series of Victory Bonds between 1941 and 1945, promoting them broadly. In 1941, the committee issued posters in a variety of languages, including Chinese, to encourage immigrant groups to help finance Canada's war effort. When the second series of Victory Bonds was issued in 1942, a coalition of Chinatown associations in Vancouver, including the Chinese Benevolent Association and the Hongmen Society, held an event at the Xinhua Restaurant to promote the bonds to the Chinese community. In total, the Chinese across Canada bought Victory Bonds worth over ten million dollars, thereby earning respect from outside their community: in April 1943, the director of the War Finance Committee wrote a letter to the Chinese community, saying, "We appreciate the support provided by Chinese here in Canada and deeply admire the mighty generosity of your country and people."

Some individual Chinese Canadians had already enlisted in the Royal Canadian Air Force before October 1942, but they were excluded from the NRMA call-up. With the modifications that came into effect on December 9, 1942, the Royal Air Force began to accept Chinese recruits, and a few were later assigned to the British Commonwealth Air Training Plan. Part of the plan was to train new pilots at a base in St. Thomas, Ontario. Among the instructors engaged for this purpose were two Chinese brothers from Prince Rupert, BC, Albert and Cedric Mah. The Mah brothers were already trained commercial pilots when they tried to enlist in the Royal Canadian Air Force in 1940, but they were refused because they were Chinese. Both worked instead as instructors for the British Commonwealth Air Training Plan.

In 1943, Albert Mah went to China and joined the China National Aviation Corporation; Cedric Mah followed in his footsteps in 1944. Both flew supply transport flights over the dangerous Hump route. Under grim conditions, Albert Mah made 420 return trips over the Hump. His brother Cedric also successfully flew the Hump a few times. Both returned to Canada after the war.

Several Chinese RCAF pilots were killed in Europe. Joseph Hong was shot down over Alençon, France, on May 23, 1944, on his first flight. He was twenty-three. He was buried at the Bretteville-sur-Laize Canadian War Cemetery in France. Guan Jil Louie from Vancouver enlisted in November 1942. Mainly flying bomber flights, he was later dispatched to England and promoted from pilot officer to lieutenant. He fulfilled nearly thirty bombing missions over Europe. While on a bombing raid on January 16, 1945, Guan's aircraft was shot down by air defence artillery over Magdeburg, Germany. The whole crew, including Guan and four others, died. Guan was also only twenty-three years old.

Kam Len Douglas Sam from Victoria enlisted in the RCAF in 1942 and served in Europe in Bomber Command. He was on the Nuremberg raid in which ninety-four Allied bombers were shot down, but he was not. He was later shot down in France behind enemy lines, but he survived and was able to avoid capture. He worked for the French Resistance, for which the French government awarded him the Croix de Guerre, Silver Star. He returned to a hero's welcome in Victoria and continued his military career in the peacetime Canadian air force till 1967, eventually becoming a lieutenant colonel.

In addition to piloting fighter planes, some Chinese in the RCAF became military technicians, contributing to the war effort by maintaining the planes. Thomas Kwok Hung Wong, now ninety-five, was the first Chinese person to join the Royal Canadian Air Force. Recalling his military life, he said:

> I was born in Victoria in 1917. My father was a famous cook in the kitchen of Government House. We lived only one block away from the two best schools in Victoria (a boys' school and a girls'). But back then Chinese kids could not go to either of them, and we were forced to attend specific schools for the Chinese. One day my mother went to the local education office to ask why her children could not attend these schools. When she told one of the officers

there in fluent English that her two brothers had fought in World War I, the officer asked the names of her brothers and recognized that one of them had saved his life in the war. The grateful officer helped get all the kids in my family admitted to the two schools. I went to the Victoria Middle School after graduation from the boys' school. In 1935, I started a one-year special course in the Vancouver Technical School. It was for teacher training and included lessons on drawing and carpentry. After that, I helped my father in the kitchen for a while, but honestly, I wanted to be an engineer and I liked flying.

Thus, when World War II broke out in 1939, I applied to join the Royal Canadian Air Force. By then I was already a member of the Victoria Flying Club. The recruiter at the draft centre told me that I could not enlist because I was Chinese, but he said that my background might help me become a volunteer pilot in the future and to look out for notices asking for volunteers. Soon after the attack on Pearl Harbor by the Japanese, I received a letter from the government asking me to check in at the Vancouver draft station. At that time, the Royal Canadian Air Force was not publically enlisting Chinese yet, so I was the very first Chinese accepted.

At first, they put me in a mechanic's position. However, given my educational background, they later sent me to the 3rd Training Centre of Edmonton, and then to continue my studies at the St. Thomas Training Centre. At St. Thomas, I officially enlisted and received my uniform. Thereafter, I was sent to the 3rd Pilot Service Centre in Calgary for a one-year training session. They recommended me to a school in Malton to learn engine inspection. After that, I became an airplane inspector at the Jericho Beach Airplane Inspection Station near UBC, Vancouver, or what they called AID [Aeronautical Inspection District]. I was also inspecting airplanes at Sea Island. There were only seagoing planes on Jericho Beach, but Sea Island had fighter jets. Both belonged to the Royal Canadian Air Force. I had a good job and was paid over 100 bucks every month free of tax. I knew that Chinese were discriminated against in society, but in the military, I had a wonderful job and the whites were very friendly. I had no hard feelings and worked there until 1945.

Joining the navy was no easier for Chinese Canadians than joining the air force. With anti-Chinese sentiment remaining strong and the unfavourable recruitment terms of the military for Asians, few Chinese served in the navy.

One counter-example was William Lore, born in 1909 in Victoria. In 1939, Lore was employed by the navy as a technician. In January 1943, he joined the Royal Canadian Navy at the request of Vice-Admiral Percy F. Nelles, chief of naval staff, becoming the first Chinese Canadian to join the navy, and the first person of Chinese ancestry to serve in any of the British Commonwealth navies. After receiving officer's training, Lore served in various places in North America before being posted to the Pacific theatre. In September 1944, he received orders to proceed overseas on loan to the British Royal Navy, and by the end of March 1945, Lore was transferred to the British Pacific Fleet. After serving in various capacities for both the Americans and the British, he took part in the liberation of Hong Kong and Kowloon from the Japanese. He was sent with a detachment of marines to regain control of the British shore station, called HMS *Tamar*. The Japanese had occupied the base and were using it as a prisoner-of-war camp. On August 30, 1945, Lieutenant Lore and his men gained control of the base from the Japanese and found inside forty Canadian prisoners of war. This marked the beginning of the liberation of Hong Kong. Lore was promoted to Lieutenant Commander of the Royal Canadian Navy in 1952 and served until his retirement in 1969.

Besides William Lore, many other Chinese men served in the Canadian Merchant Navy, a fleet of ships that transported equipment, personnel, and supplies to military forces stationed in Europe and the Pacific theatre. Although the mariners of the merchant navy were not uniformed military personnel, they played an important role in the course of the war and were often the target of Axis aggression.

Unlike the Chinese who enlisted in the navy and the air force, the Chinese who joined the army were involved in the full spectrum of service. They were variously members of the Royal Canadian Army Medical Corps, the Royal Canadian Artillery, the Royal Canadian Electrical and Mechanical Engineers, the 1st Canadian Parachute Battalion, the Royal Canadian Corps of Signals, the Canadian Infantry Corps, the Canadian Armoured Corps, the Royal Canadian Army Service Corps, Home Defence, the Canadian Intelligence Corps, and the S-20 Japanese Language School. Like their compatriots serving at sea and in the air, Chinese soldiers in the land force were professional, courageous, and disciplined.

Many Chinese soldiers died serving Canada. Diamond Quon from Calgary served in the 1st Canadian Corps. On March 12, 1945, he was killed in an operation at the age of twenty-three and was buried in the Nederweert War Cemetery. Ivan G. Lee from Montreal served with the South Saskatchewan Regiment. He died in action on September 27, 1944, and was buried in Schoonselhof Cemetery. George Hong from Windsor served in the North Nova Scotia Regiment. He was killed in Italy on September 8, 1944, at the age of eighteen. He was buried at Ancona War Cemetery on the Adriatic Sea.

In addition to fighting on the front lines, many Chinese served in logistics operations. Harry Bing Mon Lim, from Victoria, enlisted in the 16th Canadian Scottish (Reserve) in February 1942. He became active on January 21, 1943, taking basic training in Vernon, BC, and advanced training in Calgary. In summer 1943, he was sent to Britain as a reinforcement, and from there to the Loyal Edmonton Regiment in Italy. On New Year's Day, 1944, Harry Lim arrived at Naples. From Naples he was sent on to Avellino, to the No. 1 Canadian Base Reinforcement Group, and later joined the Army Service Corps.

There were also Chinese musicians in the army band, such as Rifleman Robert Lee, who enlisted in the Queen's Own Rifles of Canada in Toronto in 1944. After basic training he was transferred to No. 2 Headquarters Department, Army Band. Bandsman Robert Lee was decommissioned in September 1946.

Not all Chinese Canadian soldiers were men. A few Chinese women joined the Canadian Women's Army Corps. Mary Laura Mah from Victoria enlisted in July 1942. She was employed as a teletype keyboard operator at 29 Admin. Corps from May 1944 to July 1945.

A few Chinese Canadians who were graduates of the S-20 Japanese Language School served in the intelligence corps. They and some Japanese Canadians volunteered to work as language specialists at the South East Asia Command (SEAC)—the command centre set up to oversee all operations of the Allies in Southeast Asia—upon graduation and were loaned to the British Army. They served as translators of Japanese documents for the South East Asia Translators and Interpreters Corps (SEATIC). Kwong Chee Lowe of Victoria was one of the best translators in this corps; some of the documents he translated were used as evidence in the war crimes trials that took place in the years following the war.

The Special Operations Executive (SOE) was a British agency founded to conduct espionage and sabotage in occupied areas of Europe and Southeast Asia during the war and to assist local resistance initiatives. In 1944, the SOE held a recruiting meeting at the Hotel Vancouver to recruit Chinese Canadian soldiers to serve as agents who could blend in with the enemies to infiltrate occupied areas. A dozen Chinese soldiers volunteered for Operation Oblivion, including Douglas Jung, who would go on to become the first Chinese Canadian elected to Parliament and later Canadian ambassador to the United Nations. The group of twelve soldiers, known as Force 136, attended a secret training camp where they learned to sabotage structures with explosives and jungle survival skills. They travelled to Southeast Asia to begin their mission but, in a control struggle between the United States and Britain, Operation Oblivion was cancelled.

Nevertheless, some of the members of Force 136 saw action, including Roger Kee Cheng and four of his men. Cheng was born in Lillooet in 1915, a third-generation Canadian. He studied electrical engineering at McGill University, graduating in 1938. He became the first Chinese commissioned officer in the Royal Canadian Corps of Signals, beginning in 1941 as a second lieutenant and finishing his military career as a captain. After joining the army, he served two years at the Ottawa Electronic Communications and Design Headquarters. His fluent Cantonese and subsequent training in commando and guerrilla warfare led him to be assigned to the British Secret Service Special Operations Executive from November 1944 to October 1945. Even though Operation Oblivion had been cancelled, he led a dangerous mission to Borneo during that time. He and his men were parachuted behind enemy lines to rescue prisoners of war held in remote jungle camps and to train resistance fighters. They repatriated hundreds of POWs while living among a headhunting tribe. He and his men were awarded British military medals for acts of bravery. In December 1945, Cheng boarded the SS *English Prince* to return home to Canada.

During World War II, about six hundred Chinese youths joined the military to fight for a country that had discriminated against them and their parents and grandparents for over half a century. Many of them sacrificed their lives even as they were denied citizenship and voting rights. The bravery and patriotism of these young Chinese individuals were widely known in Chinatown, deeply impressed the mainstream society, and brought honour to the Chinese community. The meritorious deeds by both civilian and enlisted Chinese Canadians thus contributed to the final victory that ended World War II. And the active and unified response of the overseas Chinese to Canada's needs during World War II helped shift the biased view of the Chinese held by mainstream society.

When the war ended, the surviving Chinese soldiers and pilots returned to Canada alongside their colleagues to begin a new life. Although the number of Chinese soldiers was perhaps insignificant in winning the war, their participation helped shift negative opinions about the Chinese to more positive territory, stimulating a move towards more equitable treatment of the Chinese in Canada in the postwar period.

PART IV

THE ERA OF
SELECTIVE ENTRY,
1947–66

Chinese Canadian soldiers fought courageous-
ly on behalf of Canada in World War II. In this
picture a Chinese Canadian soldier attends a
Victory Bond promotion. City of Vancouver
Archives, CVA 586-2672. Photographer Alfred
(Don) Coltman (Steffens-Colmer Studios Ltd).

Getting the news. City of Vancouver Archives, CVA 586-3960. Photographer Alfred (Don) Colman (Steffens-Colmer Studio Ltd).

CANADIAN GOVERNMENT POLICIES

❧

After the end of World War II, Chinese veterans and community leaders fought hard for equal treatment for the Chinese. In the process of a policy shift, Chinese Canadian veterans became a major force advocating for the abolition of anti-Chinese legislation. Eventually, the Canadian government repealed the Chinese Exclusion Act that had banned Chinese entry to Canada. However, various rules and policies that were selectively applied between the end of the war and 1967 continued to inhibit Chinese immigration.

THE STRUGGLE OF CHINESE CANADIAN VETERANS

The victory of the Allied forces in World War II stimulated appreciation for the veterans among the Canadian public. The relatively few Chinese Canadian soldiers had ignored the discrimination they and their forebears had experienced in Canada and fought courageously on behalf of all Canadians. They earned honour for themselves as well as respect for the whole Chinese community. The fact that China had allied with Canada enhanced this shift in public opinion. Chinese Canadian veterans, therefore, demanded equal treatment to that received by veterans of other ethnic backgrounds and the repeal of legislation that discriminated against them. The Chinese community supported the veterans and called for an end to the Chinese Exclusion Act.

Once an end to the war was in sight, Chinese veterans and voluntary associations began to prepare a campaign to pursue equal rights, especially citizenship rights. In early March 1945, the Chinese Canadian Club of Victoria, BC, sent representatives to attend a Chinese Canadian veterans' meeting with John Hart, the premier of British Columbia, to demand citizenship rights for Chinese immigrants to Canada.

British Columbia had been at the forefront of discrimination against the Chinese, and the appeal by Chinese associations and veterans put the provincial government under a great deal of pressure. Just as victory was impending in the Pacific theatre, and with the whole country standing behind its servicemen, the veterans' appeal forced the BC government to reflect on the fact that no serviceman of any other Allied country fighting in either Europe or Asia was a second-class citizen in his own country. As a result, on March 28, 1945, the BC government passed an amendment granting all Chinese Canadians who had served in either of the world wars the right to vote. This marked the first victory of both active and retired Chinese Canadian servicemen in their quest for full citizenship.

Not content with obtaining their own franchise, Chinese veterans continued to agitate on behalf of non-military Chinese through the Chinese Veterans Association, founded in May 1946. In October 1946, a Chinese veteran was forbidden to vote in Vancouver's municipal election that was to be held in December that year because of a municipal bylaw that prohibited the Chinese from voting. In response, the Chinese Veterans Association called an emergency meeting and later sent five representatives to the Vancouver Veteran Representative Conference requesting that the latter negotiate with the municipal government to lift the ban on Chinese voting rights. When the conference refused to oblige, the veterans' association sent two more representatives, He Rongchen and Ma Guoguan, to the Veteran Representative Conference of BC to seek its endorsement of the Chinese rights movement.

The Chinese veterans also appealed for citizenship rights for all Canadian-born Chinese youths. It was fully understood that even if all the Chinese veterans in Canada could vote, they still represented a tiny minority unable to gain equal treatments for all native Canadian Chinese simply by casting a ballot. Instead, the whole Chinese community needed to unite to achieve this goal. The veterans organized meetings to discuss possible action plans that would encourage the government to review and modify existing election rules. In addition, the Chinese Veterans Association reported on this subject to the Veteran Representative Congress of Canada, where the *Chinese Times* reported that it "won sympathy from the majority" and "received offers of assistance from many representatives."

While all Chinese Canadians faced discriminatory legislation, veterans had some special concerns. In particular, there were the so-called "war brides"— women whom Chinese soldiers had married. Though white Canadians who married European women were free to bring their wives home to Canada, Chinese veterans like Thomas Lock, who married a Chinese woman abroad, repeatedly appealed to their government to allow their wives to immigrate to Canada during the exclusion era. Keith Lock, the son of Thomas Lock, recalled his father's experiences:

> My father was born in Toronto in 1916. His full name was George Thomas Lock. Before he enlisted, he worked at the family laundry shop and part-time in a furniture store. In about 1941, he joined

the Canadian military. It was not easy for a Chinese to enlist back then. Many people in Chinatown applied but were not accepted.

My father was sent to study dentistry at the Royal Canadian Dental Corps. He was really lucky. When Japanese troops entered Southeast Asia, the British government decided to recruit some Chinese for operations in the enemy's rear.[†] My father was therefore summoned for special training. Then he was dispatched to Australia. Twelve men were sent there and he was one of them. They had decent payment and benefits.

Part of the training my father received in Australia was to work as an agent. He later talked about a simulated exercise during which they sneaked into a water plant. He had a suicide pill in his mouth that could help him commit suicide if the enemy captured him. Clearly Father and his comrades were prepared to sacrifice their lives for the country.

In about 1944 he met my mother. They spoke Chinese to each other and there was no language barrier. In May or June that year, they got married. After that my father retired from the army. But unfortunately the immigration law in Australia, much like that of Canada, excluded Chinese immigrants. So my father had to return to Canada alone. It was during the exclusion, so my mother couldn't join my father in Canada either. They were forcibly separated. But there were also some white soldiers who married Chinese women. They requested permission from the government for their brides to come to Canada. After the war, veterans enjoyed preferential treatment, so the Chinese war brides were allowed to enter Canada without paying a head tax. So my mother received a special permission licence numbered 00026. She finally came to Canada in 1946. It was unfair that European women married to Canadian soldiers in Europe were free to enter Canada anytime they wished.

After the war, many veterans went to university under government sponsorship. My father wanted to be a dentist, but the school he wanted to go to already had its enrollment quota full. So he turned to pharmacy instead. He was the first Chinese person in that school. After graduation, in light of the many Chinese residents in Chinatown, he opened a pharmacy there and named it Tom Lock Drugs. At that time there were only two Chinese pharmacies in Canada. The first one was in Vancouver and the second was my

---

† This is a reference to Operation Oblivion. Thomas Lock was one of twelve Chinese soldiers selected for this mission.

father's. My mother was a microbiologist. She used to work in a hospital in Australia. After coming to Canada, she joined a hospital in Toronto.

THE REPEAL OF THE CHINESE EXCLUSION ACT

Towards the end of the Pacific War, efforts by Chinese servicemen and veterans to pursue citizenship rights began to pay off. After the war, the equal rights campaign led by the Chinese Canadian Veterans Association of Canada for Canadian-born Chinese was endorsed by the Army, Navy and Air Force Veterans in Canada. This achievement greatly encouraged the Chinese community to initiate another round of struggle aimed at the repeal of the anti-Chinese legislation.

Postwar immigration law in Canada relaxed from its wartime rigidity and reflected new economic and political trends. Economically, postwar recovery demanded huge inputs of labour supplied by large numbers of immigrants. Politically, discriminatory immigration policy and legislation posed potential embarrassment to Canada, which had become a founding member of the newly organized United Nations. The Chinese Exclusion Act contravened the UN Charter of Human Rights, which stated that all races were entitled to equal rights and that discrimination based on race was forbidden. But deep-seated prejudice against Asian immigrants, especially the Chinese, continued to influence immigration procedures in Canada. To each new injustice, the Chinese community counteracted and renewed its efforts aimed at the repeal of the Chinese Exclusion Act.

The Republic of China, which had close diplomatic ties with Canada, played a role. James Allison Glen, minister of mines and resources, announced on May 29, 1946, that new legislation would allow the entrance of a legal entrant's relatives but would not be applied to Asian immigrants. The Chinese consul immediately lodged a complaint, denounced this act in the *Chinese Times* as "further discrimination against the people who had been loyal to the country in the past difficult years," and questioned the fairness of the Canadian government in its treatment of Chinese immigrants.

By early 1947, the anti-exclusion movement had built up considerable momentum. That year, the Chinese community in Vancouver set up the Movement Committee for the Repeal of the 43 Harsh Regulations to discuss measures for overthrowing the law. This initiative soon spread to other Chinatowns. Meanwhile, responses from the Canadian government indicated serious consideration of abolishment; pro-repeal Westerners unreservedly voiced their support. There was every sign that social trends favoured the Chinese position.

In late January, in a phone call to the minister of citizenship and immigration Canada, the Chinese Freemasons of Calgary requested the termination of the harsh regulations. On January 31, the *Chinese Times* reported that the minister had replied, "I much appreciate your party's efforts in assisting the modification of regulations related to Chinese immigrants." On January 26, at a public assembly held at the hall of the Chinese Consolidated Benevolent Association of Ontario, Member of Parliament Clawra stated: "I will do my best to make this movement a success." The assembly passed a motion requesting Ottawa's repeal of the exclusion law.

On the same day, the Chinese community in Ottawa also convened an assembly that named the day "Justice Petition Day." A third of the 150 participants were white, including two MPs, the deputy mayor of the city, and representatives of some sixteen major local associations. The assembly unanimously passed a resolution requesting the repeal of the Chinese Exclusion Act and appointed two non-Chinese men, Roy Kennedy, a lawyer, and Dr. Woodside, a United Church minister, and a Chinese man, Zhou Rihong, the vice director of the Communication Society of Overseas Chinese, as representatives to meet the minister of citizenship and immigration.

The anti-exclusion law movement found a positive response across Canada. Telegraphed replies from MPs and ministers of the federal Liberal-led government all favoured the repeal of this act. But although it appeared that there was general agreement that the Chinese Exclusion Act should be repealed, in reality there was considerable disagreement on how Chinese immigration should be administered following its repeal.

On May 1, 1947, Prime Minister William Lyon Mackenzie King proposed that the ban on Japanese immigrants continue but that the Chinese Immigration Act, which was harsher than immigration laws applied to other East Asians, should be repealed. He emphasized, though, that most Canadian citizens would not relish a huge wave of immigration from Asia, so the government should control immigration to prevent drastic changes to the country's population structure and avoid potential ethnic, social, and economic problems. The opposition argued in favour of a quota on the number of Asian immigrants and advocated priority treatment for British immigrants. But there were also Members of Parliament who pointed out the inhumanity of the Chinese Exclusion Act and advocated equal treatment for Chinese immigrants. After a vigorous debate, in May 1947, Parliament repealed the Chinese Exclusion Act of 1923.

FAMILY REUNION AND UNFAIR TREATMENT

The repeal of the Exclusion Act, however, did not automatically confer on Chinese immigrants equality with their European counterparts. Although theoretically the Chinese in Canada could now access Order-in-Council PC 2115, which stipulates that a Canadian citizen could vouch for his wife and children under eighteen years old to enter and live in Canada, few were in fact in a legal position to do so, because fewer than 10 per cent of the total Chinese population in Canada were citizens at the time the act was repealed. Chinese Canadians typically had to wait a year and a half for citizenship after they had applied, making it even more difficult for families to reunite. Compounding the dissatisfaction of the Chinese with this situation was the fact that Europeans immigrating to Canada after World War II were not subject to Order-in-Council PC 2115, and the Canadian government implemented many policies that guaranteed a steady flow of white immigrants.

Such unequal treatment diluted the joy the Chinese felt over the repeal of the Chinese Exclusion Act. In Chinatowns, a new wave of protest was launched. After the repeal, the Chinese Equal Rights Movement Committee of Eastern Canada and its sister organization in western Canada held a celebratory meeting. While attributing the progress that had been made in part to support from cabinet members, Members of Parliament, and other sectors in society, as well as media promotion, the committees explicitly pointed out that most Chinese were still unable to bring their families to Canada as immigrants of other ethnicities were able to do. As a result, the committee organized a delegation to lobby for Chinese immigrants' rights, calling upon the Chinese community to support the fight for equal rights.

By this time, the Chinese community in eastern Canada, especially Toronto, had begun to have closer relations with mainstream society and began to assume a leading role in the movement to win equal rights. As a result, the voice of Chinese immigrants no longer emerged mainly from BC. This change owed as much to the stronger Chinese community in Toronto as to the geographical proximity of Toronto to Ottawa, which made it convenient to lobby Parliament.

In 1948, soon after the New Year holiday, Xi Mo, a lawyer, along with other members of the Chinese Equal Rights Movement Committee of Toronto, went to Ottawa to visit the minister in charge of immigration and other government officials. Accompanied by colleagues from the organization's Ottawa branch, the delegation made two requests: first, repeal the Asian Immigration Regulation, typically observed since the repeal of the Chinese Exclusion Act while a new immigration law was still in the making, and which regulated against the principle of equal treatment; second, enact a new law enabling Chinese immigrants to bring their families to Canada more quickly. The immigration director replied that their first request would need to be considered by the government and that, as for the second request, the immigration authorities already planned to set up an office in Hong Kong within sixty days to attend to Chinese immigration issues, for which officers in charge were already appointed.

With endorsement from the Ministry of Citizenship and Immigration, one of the delegates sent another written proposal to Parliament: since nearly nineteen thousand of over twenty-three thousand married Chinese in Canada were separated from their families in China, the right to bring one's family to Canada should be expanded to all Chinese rather than limited to those few with citizenship.

The continuous appeals from Chinese immigrants had nudged the federal government towards making minor adjustments. Walter Edward Harris, the immigration minister, stated in his reply to Foon Sien of the Chinese Benevolent Association that the government would issue an order on January 7, 1950, allowing Chinese who had applied for citizenship prior to the end of December 1949 to bring their families to Canada on the condition that their families had moved to Hong Kong before December 1, 1949; also, children who were under eighteen at the time of application but older when the application was finally processed would be allowed to enter as exceptions. On January 6, 1951, Harris notified the Chinese community of the relaxed regulation. Order-in-Council PC 2115 was amended to allow the wife, husband, or unmarried children under the age of twenty-one of any Canadian citizen who was in a position to receive and care for his or her dependents to enter the country. According to the parliamentary record, the amendment to Order-in-Council PC 2115, Order-in-Council PC 6229, was released on December 28, 1950. In March 1951, due to repeated protests by the Chinese, the Department of Citizenship and Immigration amended its requirement for a minimum of five years of uninterrupted residence in Canada before an immigrant could apply for citizenship. Had the five-year requirement come into effect, many Chinese immigrants who failed to return promptly from a visit to China due to war there—even though they had lived in Canada for decades—would have had to wait several years for citizenship and the right to bring their family to Canada, by which time their children might have long since passed the application age limit.

On June 29, 1951, in a letter to the Vancouver Chinese Benevolent Association, Harris confirmed that the government would approve the entry of Chinese Canadians' children aged between twenty-one and twenty-five. This meant that due to the unrelenting appeals by the Chinese, the Canadian government conceded that it would make substantial allowances for the children of Chinese immigrants. This special permission was effective from 1951 till March 12, 1955.

In 1956, the Department of Citizenship and Immigration issued a cabinet order allowing Chinese Canadians in Central and South America, Europe, and the Middle East the right to bring their relatives in twenty-eight categories to Canada, including spouses, children, brothers and sisters, brothers- and sisters-in-law, sons- and daughters-in-law, grandchildren younger than twenty-one, nephews, nieces, parents, and grandparents.

One practice that contributed to the problems the Chinese faced in trying to enter Canada was the use of X-rays to establish the age of children. In autumn 1950, the Chinese Benevolent Association of Vancouver began receiving reports from across Canada that many Chinese Canadians had their children's applications to immigrate disqualified due to an X-ray test required by the Immigration Office of Canada in Hong Kong. Many of those turned down for entry were judged above the acceptable immigration age of twenty-one. After receiving more than twenty complaints, the Vancouver Chinese Benevolent Association launched a protest in Ottawa. To prove its case, the CBA consulted experts in biology, zoology, physiology, anatomy, and related disciplines to demonstrate that X-ray films of bone cannot accurately determine the age of a person.

On June 10, 1951, the Chinese Benevolent Association of Toronto also held a meeting to discuss this issue. The *Chinese Times* reported that because of the X-ray test, "many young Chinese became unable to come to Canada while their peers from Europe were exempt from such screening. It was nothing but ethnic discrimination." X-ray tests of Chinese immigration applicants soon attracted attention within the Chinese community across Canada. In 1953, Harris, the minister of immigration, responded to the complaints that a margin of three years would be granted to Chinese children, so if the X-ray film of an applicant indicated his or her age to be twenty, the immigration office could take it as seventeen or twenty-three.

After the repeal of the exclusion law, more and more Chinese brought their children to Canada. When those children, mostly male, had reached a marriageable age, their parents, eager to have grandchildren, sent them to Hong Kong to find a woman to marry. To spare these Chinese brides a long wait in the immigration application line, the Chinese community lobbied the government to allow Chinese brides to enter more quickly for weddings to be held in Canada. Persuaded by the Chinese community, the Canadian government agreed to this request.

Aware that the immigration officials had misgivings over the possibility of things going wrong after a bride's entry, the Chinese Benevolent Association of Vancouver proposed that each of these applicants put down a thousand-dollar deposit to guarantee their wedding ceremony, which would be held within thirty days of the bride's entry; the money would be returned if the wedding ceremony went ahead as planned, and otherwise it would be confiscated and the bride sent back to Hong Kong. After considering this proposal, Parliament agreed on August 8, 1956. The immigration minister specified that this rule would be exclusively applied to Chinese immigrants and that the incoming brides must acquire a licence for returning to Hong Kong prior to departing for Canada, in case anything went wrong. This policy was instituted for a trial period that lasted till April 1, 1957.

This regulation proved effective and was welcomed by the Chinese community. The Chinese Benevolent Association of Vancouver appealed to the immigration authorities to make this regulation permanent or at least to extend its term; it also requested that Chinese women of marriageable age be allowed to bring their fiancés to Canada. The ministry replied on March 11, 1957, that the bride regulation would be extended by one year to April 1, 1958, but nothing else would be changed. But in fact, this regulation remained in force when the Conservative Party won the next federal election. On March 27, 1957, the immigration minister notified the Chinese Benevolent Association that Chinese men under twenty-one years of age and without citizenship could apply for their bride's entry to Canada for their wedding, effective from that day.

Despite the convenience of this regulation for many young Chinese people, not all who helped their spouse-to-be enter Canada ended up happily married. Some got caught unprepared in a scam marriage. Chinese Benevolent Associations across Canada received complaints that some brides from Hong Kong, taking advantage of eager Chinese bachelors looking for wives, used a proposed marriage as a front for immigration and defaulted on the engagement once they had entered Canada. Such scam marriages were a disappointment and a financial loss for the sponsoring Chinese Canadian family. In Toronto, a young Chinese man discovered that his fiancée was defaulting when he met her at the airport and she refused outright to go home with him. A week later, this young woman married another man.

Such marriage scams, brought to public attention by the Chinese media and associations, angered the Chinese community since it abused the hard-earned regulation. The Chinese community therefore appealed to the immigration authority to set up additional, stricter conditions for immigrating brides to protect Chinese Canadians from those intending to exploit the situation. However, government officials did not agree, so that regulation remained as it was.

IMMIGRATION DOCUMENTS FRAUD

Thanks to the efforts of the Chinese community, more and more Chinese were reunited with their families in Canada. But family reunion had its less harmonious moments, mainly involving illegal entry. Before World War II, Chinese families that went to China to visit would register at the immigration office to get a re-entry document so they could return to Canada. The re-entry document contained written information about the family, but no photographs. After the war, returning Chinese were required to provide this document to re-enter Canada. But after the turbulent war years, some of those who had left Canada with such documents died in China, some changed their minds and chose not to return, and some wanted to re-enter with more children. Such circumstances stimulated fraud and transformed the re-entry documents into a valuable commodity. Some Chinese families returned with extra children who were, in fact, relatives that they claimed were born into the family while they were outside Canada. Some used the vacancies in their re-entry documents to bring new immigrants into Canada. In this way, many new immigrants entered Canada, some of them using it as a springboard to the United States.

Low Mock, who came to Canada in 1908 from Zhongshan, Guangdong Province, once tried to pass his grandson off as his son so he could immigrate to Canada—but failed. The attempt was, to some extent, fraudulent but perfectly understandable, given the immigration restrictions. Recalling that episode, Low Chun Quon, son of Low Mock, recounted:

> My father came to Canada in 1908 and made a living by selling vegetables. In 1921 or 1922, he went back to China and married my mother. My mother was named Jang Aiping. She later gave birth to four children. I was the only son with three older sisters. After 1923, the Chinese were prohibited from immigrating to Canada, so my mother was unable to join my father in Canada. He had to come back to see us. Every time it was more than a month travelling on the sea—both tiring and costly. In 1947, my father was in China again. He felt reluctant to return to the tough life in Canada and wanted to stay with us. But then the situation in China worsened drastically. So in 1951, he returned to Canada. Later he was growing vegetables with the grandfather of Richard Lee, a provincial MLA, on the Musqueam Reserve. My father could speak some English and drive a truck, so he was in charge of transportation and sales transactions. At that time, my father wanted to bring the younger brother of his daughter-in-law to Canada as one of his sons. I was attending school in China then. In 1954, father started to apply for us. He reported to the immigration authority that he had three sons, but in fact he meant me and the two sons of my oldest sister, both about 9 years old. Father hired a Western lawyer to file the case. In 1957, the Chinese government approved our application to go to Hong Kong. So I quit university and went to Hong Kong for the immigration interview. The immigration officers got suspicious because they thought my mother was too old to have sons as young as my nephews. So after some cross-examination they found out

the truth and turned down our application. I was also turned down as a result. Later my father reapplied and my mother came to Canada through the family reunification program. It was different for me as I had already passed the age limit for children's application. Two years later, I came to Canada as an employee of the family vegetable garden. I was 27 then. I spent the first half-year working in the garden and later I opened a grocery store with my cousin.

In 1958, the *Chinese Times* reported a case where Li Jia, a forty-seven-year-old Chinese man living in Vancouver, was accused of using fraudulent immigration documents to apply for the entry of Chen Bopi. Li Jia was fined two hundred dollars for trying to illegally facilitate another person's entry into Canada. As time passed by, more lawsuits were brought against the use of fraudulent immigration documents, and the penalties increased.

By 1960, the use of fraudulent immigration documents had become an epidemic in the Chinese community. Preliminary investigations by the police led to a shocking announcement in the *Chinese Times* that in the two decades following World War II, about eleven thousand of the twenty-three thousand Chinese who had immigrated to Canada had used falsified documents, and those who had helped them made millions of dollars. This claim turned out to be exaggerated. Minister of Justice Fulton commented in Parliament that although newspaper reports suggested that over eleven thousand Chinese had illegally entered Canada, that figure is not what Department of Justice or RCMP records indicate. Even the immigration authorities had only a vague number. McKinsterly, an immigration official, mentioned in 1964 that he thought there were only a few thousand cases. When the Liberal Party assumed office in the next federal election, it was disclosed that the Conservatives had estimated that there were between six thousand and nine thousand undocumented Chinese immigrants.

Although the total estimate of Chinese who entered with falsified papers thus varied among different sources, it was believed by the Canadian police, the Hong Kong police, and the Chinese community in Canada that such massive fraudulent entry testified to the existence of an immigration falsification pipeline facilitated by international criminal organizations.

To investigate this theory, a large-scale search was jointly launched by the Canadian police and the Hong Kong police in late May 1960. Focussing on Vancouver's Chinatown, the search occupied thirty-eight of BC's sixty special police officers. On one occasion, they looked into thirteen stores and residences and confiscated many Chinese documents. Senior police officers maintained that this was a nationwide search targeting immigration brokers and labour contractors rather than individual undocumented entrants.

At that time, many Chinese immigrants who entered Canada with fraudulent documents ended up labouring for years at vegetable farms or restaurants in order to pay off the fee they had borrowed to buy the documents. Most refrained from complaining to the authorities for fear of repatriation. Aware of such situations, the police emphatically guaranteed exemption and encouraged individuals to provide information.

The massive search had shaken up and horrified the Chinese community. Rumours began to spread that the government was widening the investigation, but the RCMP and the deputy immigration minister denied that there was any plan to examine every Chinese immigrant. In the House of Commons, the minister of justice also denied that individual Chinese people would be inspected and suggested that policy inquiries were simply interviews and the interviewee could decline to answer.

But the investigation stirred up skepticism among Chinese and also among members of the opposition in the House of Commons. A series of announcements were made by the authorities to clarify that the investigation only targeted the offenders responsible for the false immigration documents, not the entire Chinese community. On July 9, 1960, the immigration minister promised that his department would not try to implicate the majority of the Chinese community in this case, since most were only helping their relatives enter Canada. The intention of the government was instead to identify undocumented immigrants who lied about their real identity, age, marriage status, family situations, and so on. Calling upon undocumented immigrants, the immigration minister said, "If these people really want to get help, the only way is to report their true identity so we can legalize their stay."

Despite the government's explanation, the Chinese community was very concerned about potential damage to its reputation and renewed rejection from mainstream society. To salvage the situation, the community staged the largest protest since the repeal of the Chinese Exclusion Act. Representatives of Chinese communities across Canada gathered in Toronto and formed a special committee. The plan was to visit the prime minister, ministers of immigration and justice, and other relevant officials to voice the concerns of the Chinese community. Prime Minister John Diefenbaker expressed in Parliament his willingness to meet those representatives at a proper time.

There were four parties most concerned with this controversial inspection: the Conservative federal government, the Liberal opposition, the Chinese community, and the Royal Canadian Mounted Police. As the object of the inspection, the Chinese community protested loudly and gained the sympathy of many cabinet members and MPs. Although it had vowed ruthless elimination of immigration fraud at the beginning, the government soon shifted from the offensive to the defensive under the double-pronged attack from the Chinese community and the opposition party. While disclosing individual cases to the public to justify its actions, the government noticeably softened its attitude towards the Chinese community as the immigration minister ruled out any potential massive repatriation of undocumented entrants and narrowed the investigation to those who had profited from the fraud. The minister of justice also echoed this reassurance on many occasions, claiming that the government had no intention of persecuting Chinese individuals.

Aware that it was not just a few who had resorted to falsified immigration documents, the Chinese community tactfully concentrated its protests on the root cause of the problem, namely the discriminatory legislation that had victimized Chinese immigrants before and during the war. At the beginning of the police investigation, Foon Sien, the president of the Chinese Benevolent Association of Vancouver, remarked that had the government been less restrictive and allowed the immigration of Chinese children under twenty-one years old, many such fraud cases would have been avoided. At a meeting in Toronto attended by a thousand people, the representative of Winnipeg's Chinese community blamed the discriminatory legislation for forcing Chinese immigrants to use illegal means. While protesting against the investigation, the Chinese community used the situation to require the government to invalidate all legislation that discriminated against the Chinese. Douglas Jung, the only Chinese Member of Parliament, pointed out that as soon as Chinese immigrants could apply for family immigration on equal terms with European immigrants, the market for fraudulent immigration documents would die out.

The investigation continued, but meanwhile, the government published ten thousand leaflets in Chinese calling for co-operation from the Chinese community and guaranteeing amnesty for undocumented entrants, especially those who had only used fraudulent documents to bring their children and relatives to Canada. The investigation tried to obtain information to bring charges against immigration brokers (nicknamed Zhu Zai Tou, meaning traffickers, by Chinese immigrants). To convince the Chinese community that the investigation was well-founded, the police supplied details about how the fraud schemes were operated by the immigration brokers: charging four thousand dollars per applicant, the broker would produce the false documents that indicated that the applicant had a relative in Canada and was therefore qualified for immigration. Those who could not afford this price were given the option of paying it off with income earned after entering Canada.

Even while calling out for co-operation among the Chinese community, the police began to make a large number of arrests beginning in June 1960, especially in Manitoba and Montreal. Bail set for offenders was as high as ten thousand dollars, and the list of the arrested kept growing. Among the arrested were a priest from Montreal, a travel agent from Winnipeg, and a lawyer from Vancouver, accused of manufacturing false immigration documents, lying to immigration authorities plotting to invalidate the immigration act, and other similar offences. Most striking were the arrests by the RCMP of several community celebrities including William Huang, Li Jian, and George Chen. William Huang was the former editor-in-chief of the *Shing Wah News*, president of the Chinese Benevolent Association of Ontario, and an executive committee member of the Kuomintang. Li Jian managed the Chinese Trading House and served as the finance director of the Chinese Benevolent Association of Ontario. George Chen was a notary and travel agent. William Huang was accused of facilitating two brothers' entry with false documents, while the other two were accused of working as accomplices. The arrested were a mix of all sorts of people.

By October, trials of the arrested suspects were under way across Canada.

To co-ordinate the crackdown, courts in Hong Kong also put on trial anyone who falsified their applications. A twenty-five-year-old woman named Li Ruirou, who had come from Taishan, was turned down twice in her application to immigrate to Canada. On the second occasion, she was accused of swearing a false oath and was ordered by a court in Causeway Bay, Hong Kong, to either pay a three-hundred-dollar fine or spend six weeks in jail. The woman's grandparents were in Canada but her father and three brothers were living in Hong Kong. Li Ruirou paid the fine, but it is not known whether she ever managed to enter Canada.

The controversial investigation into fraudulent immigration documents lasted a long time. Trials against offenders did not come to an end until late 1962. According to the reply from the Department of Citizenship and Immigration to a written inquiry from a New Democratic Party MP in BC, a total of fifty-seven people were charged with illegal operation of an immigration broker business. Given that most offenders in such cases received lenient sentences, this number failed to prove that tens of thousands of Chinese immigrants had used false papers to enter Canada, let alone the existence of an underground organization that sent large numbers of immigrants into Canada illegally. In all of Canada's immigration history, few investigations conducted on such a large scale ended with so few convictions.

MODIFICATION OF THE IMMIGRATION LAW IN 1962

In 1962, the Canadian government enacted a new immigration law. By then it had become clear that the Chinese community would continue to protest as long as immigration laws left the Chinese no choice but illegal entry.

The new law initiated the skilled immigration program, and the family reunification provision, with its stringent limits on age and marital status, was no longer the only way for Chinese people to enter Canada. Their skills became a new grounds for entry, ushering in a new, more respectful era for Chinese immigration. The change in Canadian immigration legislation underscored a shift in the social status of the Chinese in Canada. Furthermore, the new law stipulated that as soon as an applicant was deemed by the immigration authorities to be eligible and capable of becoming self-reliant once in Canada, the applicant could bring his wife and children with him. This was unprecedented in the history of Chinese immigration to Canada.

The provision for family reunification also expanded under the new law. Chinese Canadians were allowed to sponsor the entry of their parents with no age limit. Grandparents and fiancées were also added to the list of eligible family members.

The profound significance of the new immigration law lay in the equal status it granted to Asian immigrants compared to immigrants of other ethnicities. It was a long-awaited recognition for overseas Chinese who had overcome a century of discrimination. The new law opened a thoroughfare for new Chinese applicants. Skilled immigration increased slowly before it took off in 1956. From March 1956 to mid-1966, more than five hundred Chinese families immigrated to Canada under this program.

When the Conservative government announced on November 16, 1962, a law allowing people to correct their identity documents with impunity if they had given false information when they entered Canada (similar to an amnesty), many undocumented Chinese immigrants came forward to legalize their status and become landed immigrants who could later apply for citizenship. Four months later, in March 1963, the immigration minister again asked undocumented Chinese immigrants who had entered Canada before 1960 to report to the police and have their identity corrected and legalized. By August 1964, René Tremblay, the minister of citizenship and immigration in the Pearson government, announced that all undocumented Chinese immigrants, including those who had entered Canada between 1960 and 1962, must have their identity legalized by August 31, as the rectification process would terminate on September 1 and any undocumented immigrants identified thereafter would be repatriated. Government strategy aimed, firstly, to eliminate immigration fraud; secondly, to compel undocumented entrants to identify themselves and be legalized as landed immigrants; and thirdly, by establishing a deadline for the legalization process, establish a clean slate for adopting a more even-handed immigration policy thereafter.

In March 1965, John Nicholson, a Vancouver MP and lawyer with over forty years' legal experience, became the immigration minister. According to him, as many as nine thousand Chinese had registered to correct their identification documents and none had been arrested. He stressed that those who had profited from illegal immigration were not eligible for the amnesty.

In December 1965, during a cabinet shuffle, John Nicholson became the minister of labour and Jean Marchand stepped into his position at the immigration office. Ten months later, on October 14, 1966, Marchand read a modified white paper on the Amended Immigration Policy to Parliament. One of the major changes contained in the amendment was to allow all immigrants with Canadian citizenship, regardless of their ethnicity and country of origin, to sponsor the immigration of their family members to Canada, a right previously enjoyed only by immigrants from Europe and America. The draft amendment attracted wide attention across Canada and was, of course, welcomed by the Chinese community. Still to be debated and passed in Parliament before it came into effect, the draft signalled that a new, fairer immigration law was on the horizon.

The growing demand to redefine immigration law became a pressing issue for the Canadian government after World War II. The struggle by the Chinese community provided a major impetus to government to improve the legislation. After the repeal of the Chinese Exclusion Act, the Chinese wielded their unprecedented political rights fully in order to gain status equal to that of their European peers, because discriminatory details embedded in the unmodified immigration regulations continued to hamstring Chinese immigration and reinforce the inferiority felt by Chinese immigrants when compared with their European counterparts. The Chinese community persevered in promoting its cause and was able to nudge the authorities into gradually extending the application range for Chinese immigrants.

Contrary to the previous lonely fight against the Chinese Exclusion Act, in the selective entry era, three forces from the host society supported the Chinese immigrant cause. The first was support from different political parties and MPs. The federal political landscape after World War II was characterized by a constant shift in power between the Conservatives and the Liberals, a situation favourable for Chinese immigrants as both parties, vying for the Chinese vote, responded positively to Chinese requests. Chinese representatives were granted meetings with the prime minister and immigration officials much more frequently than had been the case previously. Such face-to-face appeals proved very effective. Also facilitating the improvements were Douglas Jung and other MPs who felt sympathetic towards the Chinese immigrants. Public opinion in mainstream society also supported the Chinese cause. After World War II, although discrimination against Chinese Canadians and other Asians was still evident, white supporters began to appear, sometimes even in leading roles, at the sites of Chinese protests. Last but not least was the changed attitude of the English media. Fanning the flames of anti-Chinese sentiment prior to and during World War II, the English media took a dramatic turn in its attitude towards Chinese immigrants during the selective entry era. Championing the legitimate rights of Chinese immigrants, the media's newly supportive stand influenced public opinion. In BC, a province known for its negative attitudes towards the Chinese, mainstream media such as the *Vancouver Sun* and other local newspapers published editorials advocating for the Chinese cause and the removal of unfair regulations. The Vancouver *Province* explicitly pointed out that the majority of Chinese immigrants were decent citizens, and that Chinese requests for easier family reunification merited nothing but humane consideration by the government.

While it is a fact that immigration document fraud and dishonest brokers in the Chinese community incurred legal sanctions, such events did not resurrect the anti-Chinese sentiment of white society or derail the improvement of the immigration law. Times had changed. As a founding member of the United Nations, Canada had to honour equality and human rights. And as the proportion of Chinese people in the Canadian population continued to drop as the influx of European immigrants grew after World War II, a modest increase in Chinese immigrants became less likely to unbalance the country's population growth. In general, the increase in Chinese immigrants corresponded to the amendments to Canadian immigration regulations. A new stage of development had dawned for the Chinese community in Canada.

108 East Pender Street and 112? East Pender Street, Chinatown. City of Vancouver Archives, CVA 677-931. Photographer Art Grice (F-11 Photographics).

CHANGES IN CHINATOWNS

In the postwar period, changing immigration patterns, demographic shifts, increasing acceptance in mainstream society, and a new economic landscape all shaped the development of Chinatowns. For the first time, the strength of Chinatowns and the fortunes of the Chinese population in Canada diverged. The makeup and distribution of Chinese communities diversified, bringing new opportunities for business and community development, while also levelling historic buildings and long-standing institutions.

A CHANGING PATTERN OF IMMIGRATION

Even though the Chinese Exclusion Act had been repealed, immigration law and prejudiced public opinion continued to make it difficult for the Chinese to immigrate to Canada, and the Chinese population continued to decline from 34,267 in 1941 to 32,528 by 1951.

Chinese immigrants accounted for only a tiny fraction of the number of immigrants entering Canada in that decade for several reasons. Between 1947 and 1950, Chinese immigrants were still subject to Order-in-Council PC 2115, which required citizenship as a precondition for family reunification; thus most Chinese residents were unable to sponsor their families. White immigrants, once permanent residents in Canada, could always sponsor their families, regardless of their citizenship status. This disparity spoke of the deep-rooted ethnic prejudice that still existed in Canada.

After the People's Republic of China was established in 1949, the new Chinese government did not permit its citizens to emigrate. Chinese families who wished to move to Canada had to apply for special permission, and if this was granted, they had to go to Hong Kong first, where their applications were processed by Canadian immigration officials. During the 1950s and 1960s, many Chinese nationals left China by illegally travelling to Hong Kong. After they established residential status in Hong Kong, those who had relatives in Canada could apply to emigrate there. Between 1956 and 1965, a total of 14,648 individuals left Hong Kong for Canada, many of whom were Chinese who had escaped from China to Hong Kong.

Immigrants to Canada continued to come from Sanyi and Siyi. Since the Chinese already in Canada at this time had come from these counties, many women and children also came from there to reunite with their husbands and fathers in Canada through the family reunification program. Family reunification also meant that many more female immigrants were entering Canada, shifting the demographic balance.

The socioeconomic status of incoming immigrants also began to change. Industrial restructuring in postwar Canada meant that it was no longer necessary to attract large numbers of unskilled labourers through immigration. This allowed more inclusive immigration policies to be established. Emerging human rights movements also had an impact.

Chinese immigration began to increase in the mid-1950s. Although Guangdong remained the major source of new Chinese immigrants in this period, the number of immigrants from Taiwan, Hong Kong, and the rest of the Chinese mainland was rising. The origins of new Chinese immigrants quickly diversified after the mid-1960s, foretelling more extensive and structural changes to the Chinese community. Because emigrants could not legally travel to Canada directly from the Chinese mainland, 66 per cent of the new immigrants came from Hong Kong, almost 22 per cent came from Taiwan, and the few remaining immigrants came from various other countries. This remained the case until the establishment of formal diplomatic ties between China and Canada in 1970 allowed the mainland Chinese to emigrate.

A CHANGING DEMOGRAPHIC STRUCTURE

According to the 1941 census, there were three times more Chinese in BC than there were in Ontario. But ten years later, the number of Chinese had declined in BC and increased in Ontario. A small increase was also seen in Alberta, but the other provinces all showed a declining trend, like BC.

After the mid-1950s, the distribution of the Chinese population began to change. The Chinese population in Ontario grew and, by 1961, accounted for a much bigger proportion of the total. The steep rise in Ontario continued through the 1960s until its Chinese population was almost as large as that of BC. In Alberta, the Chinese population had grown by 1961 to nearly 7,000 individuals, and in Quebec, to 4,800.

In 1961, the Chinese in BC, Ontario, and Quebec accounted for 87.7 per cent of the total Chinese population in Canada. BC still ranked first but the other two provinces were catching up: between 1951 and 1961, the proportion represented by Ontario rose from 22 per cent to 26 per cent; and in Quebec, from 5.9 per cent to 8.2 per cent.

More than half of the Chinese were clustered in the Chinatowns of larger cities. In 1961, 57 per cent of Chinese Canadians lived in the Chinatowns of Vancouver, Toronto, Montreal, Calgary, Victoria, Edmonton, and Winnipeg. In BC, there were also some Chinese communities in smaller cities such as New Westminster, Nanaimo, Kamloops, and Port Alberni. The total

Chinese population in 1951 was not much different from what it had been in 1941, corresponding to the negligible increase in Chinese immigration in that decade. But by 1961, the Chinese populations in most major cities, including Vancouver, Toronto, Montreal, Calgary, Edmonton, and Ottawa, had more than doubled.

Though Chinese populations had begun to trickle into the suburbs in the 1920s, it was not until the mid-1960s, with a substantial increase in population numbers, changes in the demographic structure, and improved economic status, that the Chinese population began to disperse in great numbers to residential areas outside Chinatown and to smaller cities outside the metropolises. The percentage of Chinese living in major cities was declining as a result of improved transportation, spreading urbanization, and rising property prices. It became more and more common for Chinese people to live in satellite towns near the metropolitan areas.

The repeal of the Chinese Exclusion Act brought fundamental changes to the demographic structure of the Chinese population in Canada, and to the gender balance, in particular. Census data show that there were 30,713 Chinese men and 3,914 Chinese women in Canada in 1941, a ratio of 8:1—a much better balance than had prevailed in the early years of the twentieth century, but still heavily skewed towards the male. An improving gender balance in the 1940s owed more to the baby boom among the second and third generations of Chinese immigrants than to an increase in the number of female Chinese immigrants. But after the exclusion era ended, the number of female Chinese immigrants rose steadily. By 1951, the numbers of Chinese men and women in Canada were 25,669 and 6,859 respectively, and 36,075 and 22,122 respectively in 1961.

As more Chinese women entered Canada to reunite with their husbands or to marry single Chinese men, the number of reunited Chinese families exploded. According to census data, in 1941 there were 1,177 married Chinese couples living in Canada and 20,141 individuals whose wives remained in China. By 1951, the number of resident married couples had increased to 2,842, while those living apart from their families was reduced to 12,882. By 1961, the tables had turned, and there were 11,275 married couples and only 5,384 who lived in Canada without their spouses. The steady increase in the number of family households stabilized the Chinese community, and traditional Chinese values, which emphasize family, education, and Confucian principles, were strengthened, helping Chinese communities make the transition from outsiders to full members of Canadian society.

Not only did gradually easing immigration laws bring an influx of Chinese women, but the Chinese community overall became younger. The first

Chinese immigrants had mostly been young males who worked at gold mines and railway construction sites. These men were now very old. After the Chinese Exclusion Act was legislated, only the birth of the second and third generations countered a general aging trend. But in the post-exclusion era, especially after the mid-1950s, Chinese youths and young adults, many younger than nineteen, flocked to Canada through the family reunification program. Where in 1951, 24 per cent of the Chinese population in Canada had been under nineteen, by 1961, that proportion had risen to 33 per cent. Newly immigrated children and youths plus the Canadian-born second and third generations of Chinese Canadians together brought down the average age in Chinatowns.

The younger Chinese community thrived and became better integrated into mainstream society economically, politically, and socially. Their presence in the broader social hierarchy helped the Chinese community expand beyond the borders of Chinatowns and countered the remnants of anti-Chinese sentiment and institutional discrimination in the Canadian system.

Sophia Leung was the first Chinese woman to become a federal MP (1997–2004). Her husband, Dr. So Wah Leung, was an outstanding Chinese scholar who was highly regarded in the West. Sophia Leung recalled the experiences of her husband as part of the younger generation of Chinese immigrants:

> In 1925, at the age of eight, Dr. Leung came to Canada with his mother and eldest brother from Jiangmen, Guangdong Province, China. They joined his father and second-oldest brother in Canada. During the 1920s, Canada had a strong anti-Chinese policy and the Exclusion Act banned the Chinese from entering Canada. However, Dr. Leung's father was a Church pastor who was invited to come to Canada by the Canadian United Church. So he and his family received a special exemption to enter Canada. Dr. Leung graduated from the dental school of McGill University as a top student and received the Gold Medal. After graduation, Leung went to the University of Rochester, New York, to complete his PhD degree in physiology. He became chairman and professor of the physiology department and Director of Graduate Studies at the Dental School of the University of Pittsburgh, where we met and married. He continued his teaching and research work and became a world-renowned scholar. In 1962, Dr. Leung was invited by the University of British Columbia to become the Founding Dean of the Faculty of Dentistry. As the first Chinese Dean to be appointed to a major university in the West, Dr. Leung made

history and faced the challenge of starting a professional school from scratch. There was no office space, so the school used old trailers as temporary office space. Dr. Leung was extremely busy working with the architects who designed dental clinics and classrooms. He searched the world for qualified professors and office staff and set up admission procedures and curriculum for students. Eventually he was able to assemble a fine teaching team of scholars from the United States, Canada, Australia, and New Zealand. Dr. Leung also became the young leader of dental academia in Canada. Meantime, I completed my master's degree in social work at UBC intending to improve the status of Chinese in Canada and to make social change for our community.

In general, the years after 1947 ushered in an unprecedented period of healthier and more balanced development in the Chinese community. In eastern Canada, especially Toronto, the growth of the Chinese population surpassed that in the old Chinese base, British Columbia. This shift changed the power structure of the Chinese community, resulting in a new situation where Vancouver and Toronto constituted two pillars of the Chinese population. Meanwhile, the younger Chinese generation accelerated its integration into mainstream society. What was once a separate enclave was slowly becoming part of the whole.

OCCUPATIONS OF THE CHINESE

During the period of selective entry, Chinese immigrants were no longer confined to the work that their predecessors had done, and they pursued more diversified occupations. Several factors in the broader postwar economy and internally within the Chinese community enabled this shift.

The repeal of the Chinese Exclusion Act, coupled with rising demand in a postwar economic boom, encouraged the Chinese to explore work opportunities in the broader labour market. As the Canadian economy shifted from wartime austerity to postwar consumerism, new white-collar positions appeared in finance, science, service industries, and the public sector. Changes within the Chinese community also led to occupational diversification. Having been born in Canada and educated better than most of their parents had been, including learning fluent English, more and more second- and third-generation Chinese Canadians were able to pursue career paths that took them beyond the boundaries of Chinatown. Highly educated immigrants also accounted for a bigger proportion of the newcomers. Many individuals entered Canada temporarily as professionals, but later became permanent residents. Because the immigration policy amendment of 1962 facilitated the immigration of skilled workers, incoming skilled Chinese were very different from their unskilled predecessors who had come before World War II. With the postwar decline of Chinatowns and the explosion of the Chinese population in Canada, it also became difficult to make a living in traditional jobs. All these factors allowed the Chinese to follow more diversified careers.

When Chinese immigrants entered Canada, they had to indicate their intended occupations. In the post-exclusion period, the list of occupations changed significantly from the jobs indicated by pre-exclusion immigrants. Between 1954 and 1967, about 40 per cent said they would become professionals such as doctors, accountants, chemists, teachers, and nurses, compared to the 6 per cent that listed unskilled labouring jobs. Service industries and sales also were significant job sectors selected by the incoming immigrants.

Information about the careers the immigrants planned does not reveal the actual employment patterns that ensued. But it is true that many more Chinese found white-collar positions at this time, and their career paths collectively traversed almost the full spectrum of skilled work. There were a number of occupational firsts during this period. Harry Fan, who immigrated to Canada in 1948, became the first Chinese member of the Canadian Bar Association in 1958. The same period saw many highly educated young Chinese women find professional careers and jobs in the public sector. Dr. Huang Lizhen, who immigrated to Canada in 1949, worked first at the Toronto Children's Hospital, then moved to the Vancouver General Hospital and St. Paul's Hospital (also in Vancouver). After qualifying as a pediatrician, she opened her own clinic in Moose Jaw, Saskatchewan. In 1952, Vancouver city hall hired Jessie Lee as its first Chinese Canadian employee. And in 1954, Zhu Shuzhen became the first female lawyer in BC.

However, even though it became much more common for Chinese immigrants to work in professional, scientific, and white-collar jobs, the traditional employment of the Chinese as either labourers or small business owners prevailed. It was still the goal of most of the Chinese to own their own businesses. In the postwar period, an improved business environment, a growing Chinese population, and the expansion of the Chinese community outside Chinatowns all provided Chinese businessmen with broader business opportunities.

Restaurants, pancake shops, laundries, grocery stores, herbal shops, and hotels had been the mainstay among Chinese businesses in the past, and such traditional businesses continued to play a key role. One example was the Chinese Company, which opened in Vancouver's Chinatown in 1953. It was a chain that sold Chinese and Western cuisine.

However, advances in technology significantly changed people's lives in the postwar era, and Chinese businessmen kept up with the times. More retail shops offering modern wares emerged in Chinatowns, upgrading the living standards of the community. Many adopted promotional techniques and other commercial skills used by their Western counterparts to attract customers. High-fashion jewellery shops, gramophone shops, and photography studios were among the new trends in retail at this time. Some shops invested large sums in up-to-date equipment to attract new business: Shao Sam Print House in Vancouver acquired newly developed printing presses to support business expansion.

But the most significant achievement of Chinese businesses in this period was the penetration into mainstream society with well-known retail brands. The parent company of London Drugs, the H. Y. Louie Company, was a family business named after its founder and passed down through three generations. Started by a farm worker in 1903 as a Vancouver grocery store, the company passed into the hands of the founder's son in 1930. He shifted its business focus to wholesale and initiated a succession of acquisitions including IGA supermarkets in BC and London Drugs. Now controlled by H. Y. Louie's grandson, Lei Zhenying, this company has grown into the second-largest privately owned corporation in BC (only Jim Pattison's holdings are larger).

Despite improvements for the Chinese in the business environment in the postwar era, manual work continued to employ far more Chinese Canadians than any other sector, for several reasons. First of all, it was difficult for new immigrants, lacking the necessary language skills or educational background, to change their career path. With no opportunity to receive vocational training, those who did not own their own businesses usually ended up working as unskilled labourers. Secondly, most Chinatown businesses, mainly grocery stores, restaurants, and laundries, offered only unskilled jobs to ordinary labourers. Thirdly, as more Chinese business owners explored opportunities outside Chinatowns, including other ethnic communities, they tended to employ their fellow Chinese as low-paid labourers.

Many of the young immigrants who entered through the family reunification program or through marriage to Canadian residents didn't have the required language and technical skills for a white-collar position. These people constituted the main Chinese labour force. Even many well-educated newcomers found labour jobs the easiest choice when they first arrived, since they often lacked knowledge about how to enter the professional world.

In fact, thanks to the economic boom and industrial upgrading in postwar Canada, newly emerging well-paid technical positions absorbed much of the white labour force, thus significantly easing the competition for manual work. In the manual labour market, farmhands, domestic helpers, tailors, and laundry workers even became undersupplied.

The grandfather of Richard Tsan Ming Lee, a member of the legislative assembly of British Columbia, was a typical vegetable farmer. Recalling the early days of his grandfather in Canada, Lee said:

My grandfather, Lee Kwong Quai, came to Canada in 1913 from the Zhongshan county (called Xiangshan county before 1925) of Guangdong province in China. He paid the $500 head tax to enter Canada. He first worked as a farmer on Vancouver Island and then had several different jobs, all basically manual work. In about 1950 or 1951, he and his friend Liu worked at a vegetable farm on the Musqueam Indian Reserve near UBC. Many of his fellow countrymen were in the same trade.

My grandfather didn't make much money from the farm work. He was not a smoker, nor did he gamble. He was a thrifty man who saved all the money he could to send back to his family in China. The family built a house with the money. Grandfather visited the house after it was completed. He worked at the Musqueam Indian Reserve for at least thirteen or fourteen years, seldom contacting the world outside except for some weekend leisure time at the Hing Mee Society near Chinatown. The Hing Mee Society was an association of Chinese from Zhongshan county, where the hometown fellows could socialize and reminisce.

THE DECLINE OF CHINATOWNS

The decline of Chinatowns after World War II was a conundrum. Theoretically, Chinatowns should have entered a time of booming development after the end of the war, but for a long time after the war, a peculiar phenomenon prevailed in that the Chinese community advanced while Chinatowns declined.

The decline had a number of causes. Historically, living in a Chinatown had been the only option for most overseas Chinese, who had to huddle together for self-preservation during the exclusion era. Many found the confined Chinatown life disappointing. Once the Chinese Exclusion Act was repealed, many of the Chinese, especially businessmen and second- or third-generation Chinese Canadians, moved into residential neighbourhoods and to cities and towns outside the metropolises. Stores remained in Chinatowns, but most of their owners no longer lived there. This migration led to the depopulation of Chinatowns.

A hostile business environment in Chinatowns also fanned the exodus. Discouraged by discrimination from exploring beyond Chinatowns, Chinese immigrants as well as businesses were cooped up in a tiny community. Sometimes vicious competition abounded. So when the external environment improved after World War II, Chinese businessmen eagerly branched out into other neighbourhoods. After this exodus, fewer new shops opened in Chinatowns, and the economic situation was increasingly difficult for the remaining ones, due to shrinking populations. With both population and businesses subsiding, Chinatowns faced an inevitable decline.

In the postwar period, large Chinatowns withered into inner-city neighbourhoods where elderly poor Chinese and new immigrants lived. Some small Chinatowns disappeared altogether. The postwar decline of Chinatowns differed in extent due to disparities in population size and the level of development that had occurred in earlier eras. Though Chinatowns continued to be a stronghold for Chinese in many respects, many residents moved out due to the deteriorating security and living environments. Their vitality drained away by depopulation, Chinatowns became visibly degraded, their narrow streets and alleys littered and filthy. Crime, gambling, opium abuse, and prostitution proliferated, and drunkards, sex workers, and opium addicts could be easily spotted in the derelict streets in Chinatowns and nearby neighbourhoods.

Several factors contributed to the decline and eventual extinction of many old Chinatowns during the 1950s and early 1960s. One of these was the destructive force of fire. Nanaimo's Chinatown, for example, continued to decline after World War II. By 1955, there were only a few shops and restaurants serving a population of about 250. Nanaimo's Chinatown retained the characteristics of a frontier town: its wood frame buildings were lined with wooden sidewalks, and tall verandahs stretched from structure to structure along its full length. Like many Chinatowns in the gold rush days, Nanaimo's Chinatown burnt to the ground on September 30, 1960.

Depopulation was a major cause of the extinction of Chinatowns in Barkerville, Cumberland, Hamilton, Lethbridge, Moose Jaw, and other cities. By the late 1950s, for example, Cumberland's Chinatown had only twenty elderly residents. By 1962, many of its ramshackle buildings had collapsed. In the early 1970s, there were only four men, all over eighty years old, living there, and only one of them, Huang Geng, was still alert.

Depopulation was also conspicuous in the Chinatowns of large metropolitan cities. To the third and later generations and postwar immigrants, Chinatown was not home—these people had not taken part in its formation, and they did not feel a sense of connection to the place. To physically distinguish themselves from the neighbourhoods where earlier immigrants had experienced extreme discrimination, they moved out of Chinatowns to the better residential neighbourhoods occupied by white Canadians. In Vancouver in 1961, 1,109 of the 1,622 Chinese households equipped with a telephone lived outside Chinatown; among those without a telephone, 2,146 out of 5,287 lived elsewhere. Among business owners, 675 of 1,113 no longer lived in Chinatown. The local Chinese community had dispersed and become integrated into communities outside Chinatown. By the late 1950s, most remaining residents of Chinatowns were elderly single men who could not afford better accommodation, or newly arrived immigrants with few resources.

The migration of the Chinese to larger cities contributed to the decline of Chinatowns in smaller towns. For example, the Chinese moved from New Westminster to Vancouver and those from Quebec City went to Montreal, causing the demise of the Chinatowns in both New Westminster and Quebec.

Socioeconomic activities in Chinatowns were also greatly reduced. With more and more Chinese families moving away, the businesses that had characterized the old community also moved away. Well-educated young Chinese people had no desire to work long hours like their parents had or to inherit the family businesses, so many old businesses, stores, and cafés closed down after their original proprietors retired or died.

One symptom of the decline was the unfortunate disappearance of old Chinatown architecture. During the postwar drive for urban renewal in Canada, many late nineteenth-century buildings in Chinatowns were demolished to make way for new office buildings or parking lots. Landlords in Chinatown were responsible for buildings falling into decay. Their reluctance to repair or renovate dilapidated old buildings, because the rents were too low to cover renovation costs, had left the buildings rotting away in Chinatowns in cities like Victoria, Vancouver, and Montreal. When those ramshackle buildings failed to meet new municipal fire and building codes, the landlords usually vacated or demolished them, as was the case in Winnipeg and Victoria when city council implemented new building standards.

Slum clearance and urban renewal projects accelerated the decline and destruction of Chinatowns as downtown expansion brought down buildings. Duncan's Chinatown, for example, was levelled during the early 1970s to provide parking space for the new provincial courthouse. Similarly, much of Kamloops's Chinatown was levelled during the construction of the city's Overlander Bridge in 1961. In some cities where Chinatowns were located in the path of major downtown developments, such as Calgary, Montreal, and Toronto, rising land prices enticed speculative developers into purchasing derelict tenement buildings at low prices. With no interest in maintaining these decaying properties, these absentee landlords sold out as soon as an attractive offer was made.

By the late 1940s, with more of the Chinese living in eastern Canada, Victoria's Chinatown gradually lost its prominence and was eclipsed by the Chinatowns in Vancouver and Toronto. As the provincial capital, Victoria launched large-scale urban redevelopment and renovation after World War II. Many old buildings in Chinatown, mostly owner-occupied or rented housing, were deemed dilapidated and unhealthy by the authorities, and were demolished in the 1950s and 1960s. In the process, many people moved out to other communities in the city or further away to Vancouver.

The depopulation of Chinatown harmed the businesses located there. In the 1960s, many shops in Victoria's Chinatown closed down or moved away. In 1961, the Lee Dye Sons Company, for example, sold its property to the city and moved out of Chinatown.

After World War II, the Chinatowns in Victoria and Vancouver managed to retain the appearance and style of the late nineteenth century. In Vancouver's Chinatown, the buildings of association headquarters were mostly located on East Pender Street between Columbia and Main streets. The west side of Gore Avenue was characterized by many two- or three-storey buildings with a mixture of commercial, residential, and institutional uses. However, the rising number of immigrants and the municipal postwar reconstruction began to change the look of Vancouver's Chinatown, most noticeably in Strathcona.

In 1949, Canton Alley was demolished after the tenement buildings on both sides of it were torn down. Strathcona, located just east of Chinatown, was a neighbourhood with about 7,500 residents after the war: 44 per cent Europeans, 33 per cent English Canadians, 11 per cent Chinese, and 12 per cent other ethnic groups. Throughout the 1950s, an increasing number of Chinese people moved into Strathcona as its white residents began relocating to better residential districts. It was attractive to the new Chinese residents because housing was affordable and the area was adjacent to Chinatown. By 1957, nearly half the residents in Strathcona were of Chinese origin, and the neighbourhood began to be thought of as a residential section of Old Chinatown.

About 60 per cent of Strathcona's properties were structurally unsound or noticeably dilapidated. In January 1958, Vancouver's city council identified Strathcona as a development area because 37 per cent of its 274 structures suffered from inadequate original construction, and nearly 24 per cent had poor or very poor interior conditions. In 1961, Redevelopment Project No. 1 was launched. Within a year, over sixty city blocks in Strathcona had been appropriated, and their structures, including the Hing Mee Society building and other historic Chinese tong houses, were demolished to provide sites for new housing projects. About three hundred Chinese residents were forced to move, and some of them were very bitter about the relocation. In March 1965, city council carried out Redevelopment Project No. 2. Within a year and a half, twenty-four properties had been appropriated for demolition, and about a thousand people, more than half of them Chinese, were evicted. In the summer of 1965, the city's planning department started to work on the final Redevelopment Project No. 3 to clear the remaining housing in Strathcona and to relocate its three thousand residents. In 1968, community activism brought an end to the redevelopment of Strathcona and preempted plans for a major freeway. The Strathcona Property Owners' and Tenants' Association (SPOTA) united Chinese and white residents in protecting their neighbourhood. It is fair to say that Strathcona, where Chinese and Western residents lived as neighbours, formed a unique community in postwar Vancouver.

During the late 1950s and early 1960s, Toronto's Chinatown declined. Nearly two-thirds of the buildings, concentrated on Chestnut and Elizabeth streets, were demolished to make room for Nathan Phillips Square and the new municipal government building. The remaining Chinatown area was slowly strangled by the high cost of land. By 1965, many properties in Chinatown had been sold to developers and most of the Chinese businesses and residents had moved further west along Dundas Street beyond University Avenue. After such drastic shrinkage, the future of the Old Chinatown was uncertain: 58 per cent of its land was owned by speculators and only 42 per cent by Chinese people.

After World War II, many Chinatowns in the rest of Canada had also fallen into decline or even extinction. In the lifeless Chinatown of Winnipeg in 1951, 86 per cent of the remaining seven hundred residents were old bachelors. Calgary's Chinatown was hardly any better, with its Chinese population steadily shrinking as its residents died or migrated. By the late 1950s and early 1960s, all it encompassed was about ten city blocks on the south bank of the Bow River.

In Montreal's Chinatown, properties were rising in value due to postwar downtown development and attracted many speculators. Old buildings in Chinatown were bought and then demolished; the vacant sites were sold when the government or developers offered attractive prices. As a result, many Chinese were forced to move out of Chinatown when low-rent housing became a rarity.

After the mid-1950s, Ottawa's Old Chinatown on Albert Street was on its way to extinction. By 1961, only four Chinese restaurants and one grocery store remained in operation. Things were similar for other Chinatowns. A large part of the Chinatown in Lethbridge was demolished by land speculators, forcing most residents to move away. In Edmonton, the only residents in Chinatown were a few old bachelors since most of the Chinese had moved to better residential areas. With their residents moved out, these once-bustling Chinatowns became lonely, desolate places.

THE BIRTH OF NEW CHINATOWNS

It is a law of history that the new replaces the old, and the Chinatowns in Canada were no exception. With the repeal of the Chinese Exclusion Act, it became inevitable that Chinese immigrants would leave the cramped Chinatowns to explore the outside world. The time was ripe for new Chinatowns to emerge.

Unlike the old Chinatowns, the so-called new Chinatowns were not residential areas and rarely had Chinese institutions. Springing up across

Canada in the 1960s, especially in big cities, they could be sections of a street or shopping plazas of varied sizes with a few or a dozen Chinese-operated businesses that catered to Chinese residents or other ethnic groups in nearby neighbourhoods. New Chinatowns in Ottawa, Saskatoon, and Windsor all emerged as a result of the increasing demand for goods and services from the fast-growing Chinese communities that lived nearby. The new China-towns assumed an important role in maintaining Chinese culture, but in cities where traditional Chinatowns still stood, the new towns attracted vis-itors from the old Chinatowns and indirectly contributed to the decline of the latter.

During the era of selective entry, Chinatowns in Canada were faced with the challenge of transformation. The transformation was marked with decline, a sad fate for these places full of history. But the decline of Chinatowns was not a decline of the Chinese community. On the contrary, with more Chinese integrated into mainstream society, the Chinese com-munity enjoyed more power and influence, shown by the emergence of new Chinatowns.

The Chinese Benevolent Association at 108 East Pender Street and the Sun Ah Hotel at 100 East Pender Street. City of Vancouver Archives, CVA 780-473.

VOLUNTARY ASSOCIATIONS AND POLITICAL PARTICIPATION

Many previously thriving voluntary associations and political organizations that had been prominent in Chinatown before and during the Sino-Japanese War and World War II declined or disappeared during the postwar decades, but new types of associations emerged to replace them, and some of the larger original associations continued to thrive. This period also saw the entry of Chinese Canadians into the mainstream political arena.

THE DEVELOPMENT AND DIVERSIFICATION OF ASSOCIATIONS

After World War II ended, several types of voluntary and political associations in Chinatowns faded as a new era started for both Canada and China. Associations that had been dedicated to fighting the Chinese Exclusion Act disappeared after the act was repealed. Although the Chinese Benevolent Associations still acted as the spokesmen for Chinatowns, they were not as active as they had been previously. Many clan and county associations in small Chinatowns were dissolved during this period.

The primary cause of the demise of many associations was a lack of new members. As older members died or returned to China, the lack of interest showed by younger generations caused once-thriving associations to fail. This is best illustrated by the associations in Victoria's Chinatown. Many associations that were still active in 1945—the Ying On Tong, the Yee Fung Toy Tong, the Chow Oylin Tong, the Chan Wing Chun Tong, and the Mar Gim Doo Tong—were on the brink of extinction by the 1960s as a result of declining membership numbers accompanied by falling income. In addition, after gaining political equality with their white peers, the second and third generations of Chinese Canadians founded their own associations or established branches of the major associations of the mainstream society. These newly founded Chinese associations were much more focussed on local affairs than their predecessors had been. Thus, the 1950s and 1960s saw the decline of older associations and the rise of new ones.

During and after World War II, the Chinese Benevolent Associations across Canada were controlled by the Kuomintang and were the undisputed leaders of Chinatowns. They functioned as spokesmen for the Chinese communities and served as a bridge linking the Chinese community to the Canadian government and mainstream society. Chinese people in small Chinatowns did not have a CBA of their own and established their own umbrella associations to represent them. The Chinese in Prince Rupert established the Overseas Chinese Federation of Prince Rupert in May 1953, and the Chinese community in Duncan, BC, founded an Overseas Chinese Association in 1964.

The Canadian government still enforced discriminatory immigration policies even after it had abolished the Chinese Exclusion Act. Immigration authorities continued to X-ray Chinese children to determine their age— even though medical authorities had stated that the age of a person could not be precisely determined in this way. Foon Sien, president of the Vancouver CBA, took up the fight against this and other restrictive regulations applied to Chinese Canadians. In 1949, this CBA changed its name to Quanjia Zhonghua Zhonhuiguan, meaning the Pan-Canadian Chinese Benevolent Association Headquarters; in English, it was called the CBA (National Headquarters). This change of name enabled Foon Sien to claim in Ottawa that the organization represented all the Chinese across Canada. Although the directors of the CBA (National Headquarters) were not elected by CBAs in other cities, and it was not officially a national organization, Chinese people across Canada accepted it as their representative in the fight against discriminatory regulations. On November 30, 1952, an inauguration ceremony was held in the new building's auditorium, and on the front of the new building was mounted a wide new sign reading "Chinese Benevolent Association of Canada"; the Vancouver association was thus renamed.

The umbrella organization in Toronto was officially named the Chinese Community Centre of Ontario Incorporated, but it was usually called the Toronto Chinese Benevolent Association by the Chinese community. In November 1951, the Vancouver CBA suggested to the Toronto CBA that a national meeting be called to protest the X-ray testing of young immigrants. However, the Toronto association felt that a national meeting should discuss all issues of concern to the Chinese rather than just a single issue. After a meeting in May 1952, the Vancouver organization decided not to attend the pan-Canadian meeting, but instead to send its chairman, Foon Sien, to petition the federal government over the X-ray issue.

In May 1960, the Toronto Chinese Benevolent Association sent out a notice inviting its fellow CBAs, branches of the Chinese Trade Association, and branches of the Chinese Canadian Club across Canada to send delegates to Toronto for a meeting to be held on May 28. The purpose of the meeting was to form a delegation to Ottawa to demand equal treatment of the Chinese from the Canadian government. The Vancouver CBA (National Headquarters) was disgruntled by Toronto's assumption of leadership and again refused to attend. In the 1960s, however, most of the Chinese in Canada did not care much about the power struggle between the two CBAs, mainly because many Chinese felt that most of the CBA directors were Kuomintang members who cared more about denouncing Communist China than the welfare of the Chinese in Canada.

CHINESE POLITICAL ORGANIZATIONS

In the decades following World War II, the Kuomintang and the Chinese Freemasons, especially the former, still dominated the political views of other overseas Chinese associations. The Chinese Freemasons had always advocated for peace between the Nationalist Government (KMT) and the Communists, to bring an end to civil war in China. As a result, Chiang Kai-shek called a national assembly of overseas Chinese delegates to be held in Nanjing on December 25, 1947, to enlist their support against the Communists. The CBAs in Canada, under the control of the Kuomintang, selected two delegates from a short list of six candidates from Vancouver, Toronto, and Victoria. The Chinese Freemasons, who had opposed the KMT in Canada, refused to send representatives to the CBAs as potential delegates to the assembly. Had they sent representatives, the CBA would definitely not have selected them as delegates.

After the Korean War (1950–53) and various campaigns against corruption, China set out on a path of peaceful progress. The Canada-China Friendship Association was formed in 1964 and tried to persuade the Canadian government to establish diplomatic relations with the People's Republic of China, but this did not occur till 1970.

The Hongmen Chee Kung Tong was known in English as the Chinese Freemasons. In October 1925, the CKT had been reorganized as a political party, known as Chee Kung Dang (Chee Kung Party). In March 1944, it was renamed China Hongmen Chee Kung Dang, and in November, this name was adopted by Hongmen members throughout Canada. In August 1946, it was again renamed, this time becoming the China Hongmen Minzhidang (China Hongmen People's Rule Party). The party headquarters were established in Shanghai, and the Canadian headquarters were in Vancouver. The party's policy agenda was to stop civil war in China and to peacefully unify the country.

Western Canada had a larger Chinese population than the rest of Canada and therefore more Hongmen members. The Hongmen branches in Victoria and Vancouver had accumulated many properties, which helped maintain their strength. They were financially strong enough to help with the construction of new buildings for branches in Vernon and Port Alberni in British Columbia and in Calgary and Edmonton in Alberta.

As early as 1920, the Hongmen Chee Kung Tong members had already used "Chinese Freemasons" as their English name. Therefore, Chinese

Freemasons has become the term in use for the organization variously called Hongmen Chee Kung Tong, Hongmen Chee Kung Dang, and Hongmen Minzhidang.

Speaking about the history of the Hongmen Society in Toronto, Wu Peifang, a senior member of the Chinese Freemasons of Toronto, recounted:

> The Hongmen Society of Toronto was founded in 1894, its tong located in Chinatown. It was just a branch here in Toronto and the headquarters were in Vancouver. So we used to take orders from Vancouver and turned over part of our membership fees to them. We held many activities during the selective entry era, such as celebrations of the Spring Festival of China and Dominion Day on July 1. Before 1947, we used to have a nursing home for aged members and hired someone to cook for them. There was a doctor named Luo, who was the chairperson of Toronto Hongmen Society. He helped by applying for subsidies from the government. But by 1957, we were bankrupt and all activities were suspended. It was not until 1968 that the Hongmen Society of Toronto recovered its operation.

VOLUNTARY ASSOCIATIONS

Clan associations had emerged early in the history of Chinese immigration to Canada and quickly gained a foothold in the Chinese community. Before large-scale entry of skilled immigrants was allowed, clan associations represented a large proportion of the voluntary associations and were the very bedrock of umbrella associations such as the Chinese Benevolent Associations. This situation lasted throughout the era of selective entry, although many clan associations underwent restructuring to keep abreast of a changing social milieu.

In addition to restructuring, the most prominent change in that period was the emergence of youth branches. During the exclusion era, clan associations had faced shortages of members as old members aged and died while second- and third-generation Chinese Canadians were not interested in joining the organizations of their parents. As more young Chinese came to Canada thanks to relaxed postwar immigration policies, clan associations established youth branches to attract young people. In 1951, the Lee's Benevolent Association of Vancouver established a youth branch for a group of youths recently arrived from China. They held a founding ceremony on March 18, the birthday of the clan's ancestor, to build a bond between the newly arrived and the existing young members. In 1952, Vancouver's Lung Kong Tin Yee Association and Yee Fung Toy Tong also set up youth branches. In 1953, Vancouver's Suoy Yuen Benevolent Association experienced a major expansion thanks to the arrival of new immigrants from this clan. Since its total membership had increased to over a hundred members, with young members accounting for several dozen, a youth branch was founded. Other clan associations in Vancouver and Toronto set up youth branches during the 1950s.

In the postwar era, the greater mobility of both old and new Chinese immigrants led to the restructuring of many clan associations and the establishment of new branches. The Toronto Wong Kung Har Tong, founded in 1912, ceased operations for a period before recovering in early 1951. In 1952, in order to have its own property, it joined with some clan members from the Wong Wun Sun Association and, with a fund of fifty thousand dollars, they bought three buildings on Dundas Street West and moved their offices to one of them. In 1962, with the agreement of most members, the two associations merged into the Wong Kung Har Wun Sun Association. In 1955, Chinese Canadians in Vancouver bearing the surnames Tam, Hui, and Tze joined together to form the Chiu Luen Benevolent Association, and those surnamed Yip, Tang, and Yuen collectively formed the Nan Yang Benevolent Association.

Some clan associations opened new branches during this period. For example, in June 1956, with help from the Vancouver Mah Society, a branch was opened in Prince Albert, Saskatchewan. New clan associations were also founded, including the Lim Jiu Mu Gong Suo Sai Hor Association of Ontario in 1960, the Gee How Oak Tin Association in Vancouver in 1962, and the Chow Oylin Kung Shaw in Toronto that same year. In Calgary, the Gee How Oak Tin Association was set up in 1964.

Despite the disappearance of clan associations in some vanishing or small Chinatowns, new clan associations continued to emerge in cities with a substantial Chinese population. The very existence of such kinship organizations underlined the close bond that the overseas Chinese had always maintained with their places of origin.

Although the origins of Chinese immigrants diversified significantly during the era of selective entry, most new arrivals entered Canada through the family reunification program, so a large proportion of the new immigrants continued to come from the four counties of Guangdong Province that had been the major source of Chinese immigrants in the past. This trend was quite favourable for the development of county associations, although many of the smallest county associations folded due to lack of new members and financial difficulties.

Like the clan associations, county associations also set up youth branches in the 1950s. Vancouver's Kong Chow Benevolent Association and Shon Yee Benevolent Association each set up a youth branch in 1952, and the Yu Shan Zong Gong Suo followed in 1953.

As the immigration pattern changed and became more diversified, new county associations emerged and new headquarters were set up. On June 5, 1955, Zhongshan County Association of Calgary celebrated its foundation; its members had immigrated from Guangxi Province. In 1959, natives from the three counties of Nanhai, Panyu, and Shunde founded the Sam Yap Society in Victoria. It was open to all the Chinese in Victoria who had originally come from these counties. The Yu Shan Zong Gong Suo (head association of Yushan County) in Vancouver assisted their fellow Yushan County natives in Victoria to establish the Yushan Fensuo (Yushan County Branch Association).

Like the clan associations, county associations organized activities for their members such as celebrations of traditional Chinese festivals, ancestor worship, elections of association directors, visits to the sick, and sending the money left by deceased bachelors back to their families in China.

In the postwar era, with the improved status of the Chinese in Canada and the language barrier no longer a problem, the Canadian-born second and third generations of Chinese Canadians founded their own associations, including sports organizations, or established branches of the major associations of the mainstream society. Many of the younger Chinese did not feel the strong clan and county bonds that had held their forebears together and instead embraced the mainstream associations of white society. Wishing to expand into the Chinese community, these associations welcomed their efforts. Representative associations included the Elks–Chinatown Branch and the Lions Club–Chinatown Branch. The Lions Club International is a global charitable organization that welcomes members without regard for race, religion, or political convictions. The Vancouver branch of the Lions Club was founded in 1955 and that of Victoria in 1956.

The Mon Sheong Foundation was founded in 1964, the first Chinese charitable organization to be recognized by the federal government. It established the Mong Sheong Senior Home in downtown Toronto. The foundation held charitable events every year, either independently or together with its Western counterparts. The funds raised through such events were mostly spent on overseas Chinese elders, buying them food, visiting them when they were ill, and funding their leisure life.

In Victoria's Chinatown, Canadian-born Chinese youths established the Chinese Youth Sports Club, the Shengyun Musical Club, and other sports associations in the 1960s, featuring activities that differed from those conducted by the older clan or county associations in that they were more westernized.

Another postwar organization, the Chinese Veterans Association, was formed in May 1946. It consisted of about seventy Chinese veterans from Vancouver. On February 27, 1947, the national All Canada Chinese Veterans Association was officially founded. Besides striving to achieve its own goals, the veterans also championed equal political rights for all Chinese immigrants. Many veterans made remarkable contributions in different fields, prominently represented by Douglas Jung, the first Chinese Member of Parliament. Commemorating the military service of the overseas Chinese, the Chinese Veterans Association actively participated in Remembrance Day ceremonies every year on November 11. Intended to remind Canada of the sacrifices and contributions of overseas Chinese in wartime, the celebration significantly raised the visibility and image of the Chinese community.

There were also some independent youth associations, such as the Vancouver Youth Club of Overseas Chinese founded in 1952; women's associations set up by Canadian-born Chinese women; and associations of newly immigrated young Chinese, such as Montreal's Zhonghua Qingnian-hui. These new associations organized various activities, including educational events, social gatherings and outings, and hospital visits to comfort sick Chinese in order to enhance the quality of life in the Chinese community.

Among all the overseas Chinese associations in the postwar era, sports organizations were perhaps the most visible. Some sports organizations were affiliated with major associations, for example, the Chinese Freemasons Sports Associations of Vancouver and Toronto, and some were formed on their own. The latter group included the Vancouver Chinese Women's Gymnastics Team, the Regina Chinese Youth Sports Association, and the Moose Jaw Chinese Sports Association.

Active in both Chinese and Western communities, these sports associations held various competitions in basketball, volleyball, table tennis, baseball, football, gymnastics, Go (*weigi*, a Chinese board game played with black and white pieces on a board with 361 crosses), and other sports. Those competitions effectively brought closer the Chinese and white communities and contributed to a spirit of equality that had been long lost in the institutionalized discrimination of the past. In March 1962, the Vancouver Hai Feng Sports Team held a table tennis tournament on the field of the Young Women's Christian Association. Players from various table tennis teams in Vancouver participated, including twenty-six Westerners and eleven Chinese. In the end, a Chinese player named Li Wenlu won the competition.

Chinese sports groups also began to appear at sports events held by the host society. In July 1965, Port Alberni's Hongmen Sports Association was invited by the Elks of Canada to take part in the events of Lumbermen's Sports Day, which marked the first participation of a Chinese group in Western activities in Port Alberni. On the afternoon of July 10, members of the association impressed their Western audience with a dazzling performance of Chinese martial arts using fist, stick, sword, spear, and other traditional weapons.

Meanwhile, sports events held in Chinatowns also energized the community. For example, the En Qing Cup Basketball Open Tournament that began in April 1964 in Vancouver included Gong Li, Hongmen, Hai Feng, En Qing, Han Sheng, Britannia, Qing Lian, and Ding Hao teams. Hai Feng eventually won the competition, while En Qing and Hongmen ranked second and third respectively. At a table tennis tournament organized by the Hai Feng Sports Association in April 1966, Li Wenlu again won the first prize in singles. In July the same year, at Hai Feng's Chinese Chess Contest, Ma Ziping was victorious. These games not only exhibited the athleticism of the Chinese, but emphasized the importance of fitness within the community.

During the selective entry era, new associations were founded to address specific business and labour issues. Workers joined together in such organizations as the Chinese Employees' Union, the Chinese Workers' Protection Association, and the Chinese Employees' Federation, each dedicated to safeguarding the rights and interests of Chinese workers. Business owners formed the Chinese Chamber of Commerce to deal with business issues, and the Chinese Agriculture Association, founded in March 1963, dealt with agricultural issues of concern to Chinese market gardeners and farmers, including allowing more Chinese farmers to immigrate and assistance with agricultural development. Although varied in mission, each of these organizations did its part in developing the Chinese economy and community.

THE CHINESE ENTER CANADIAN POLITICS

When the Chinese first arrived in Canada, they had voting rights. However, few took advantage of them. Between 1875 and 1945, most Chinese Canadians were disenfranchised. After World War II, Chinese veterans were granted the vote, and eventually the franchise was extended to all Chinese people. But the path towards political participation was not smooth, and in the decade between 1947 and 1956, not a single Chinese Canadian was elected to municipal, provincial, or federal government.

There were several reasons for this. For one, the prejudice against the Chinese needed time to change. Proficiency in English, education, and economic status were slowly improving in the Chinese community, but they realized that if they did not have elected spokespeople in government, they would have no leverage and their status would remain precarious. Integration into mainstream society would be very slow, and unfair treatment would be difficult to resolve. Thus the appearance of Douglas Jung in federal politics was a tremendous breakthrough, bringing new hope to the Chinese community.

The year 1957 was a milestone in Chinese Canadian history. In that year, Chinese Canadians Harry Poon and Douglas Jung were respectively elected as a city councillor in Stettler, Alberta, and as a federal Member of Parliament. Their success was a prelude to the future participation of

Chinese Canadians in politics. Douglas Jung's election in particular was especially significant.

Jung was born in Victoria in 1924 with no legal status as a Canadian, an issue he addressed on behalf of all Chinese later in his career. During World War II, he enlisted in the Canadian army, serving in the Pacific theatre, and becoming part of Operation Oblivion. After the war ended, he became the first Chinese Canadian to earn a university education through the Veterans Affairs program, receiving two degrees from the University of British Columbia in 1953, a bachelor of arts and a law degree. He was called to the BC Bar in 1954 and opened a law practice in Vancouver. His qualifications to participate in the political arena were comparable to those of his white counterparts.

However, Jung's first foray into politics was unsuccessful. In 1956, he ran for the Progressive Conservative Party in a provincial by-election in Vancouver Centre but lost to the Social Credit candidate. Nevertheless, he was the first Chinese Canadian candidate ever to run in a provincial election, and he came in a respectable second behind the winner. His campaign reached out to Chinese voters, stating his political views and urging them to make good use of their right to vote. In spite of his loss, this campaign greatly improved his reputation and laid the foundation for his future election.

In the federal election of 1957, Douglas Jung once again represented the Progressive Conservatives in Vancouver Centre. His previous failure led him and his team to carefully craft his election platform. He would demand changes in immigration policy, allowing the Chinese to be treated equitably. He criticized the federal Liberals for giving preferential treatment to refugees from Europe, while treating the Chinese differently. He proposed that once elected he would reform the Old Age Pension Plan so that all who qualified could receive their pension while living anywhere in the world. His demands were intended to attract all voters, not just Chinese and other ethnic minority voters. He was well aware that he needed the support of white voters to win the election, since the recent enfranchisement of the Chinese and the small number of qualified Chinese Canadian voters made it unrealistic for him to rely on support from the Chinese community alone.

Jung's chief rival in the election was Ralph Campney, the sitting Liberal minister of defence, making the competition even more challenging. But Jung campaigned vigorously. He was active and vocal in the Western and Chinese communities, and his efforts were welcomed with a positive response. To avoid any spoiled ballots from Chinese Canadians who were less proficient in English, the Chinese Benevolent Association issued a notice with instructions for Chinese voters.

June 10, 1957, was a milestone in the history of the Chinese in Canada. Douglas Jung, the first Chinese candidate ever in a federal election, won with 8,954 votes, becoming a Member of Parliament in the Canadian House of Commons, while his rival, defence minister Ralph Campney, fell almost 4,000 votes behind with 5,141 votes. It was a great victory for Jung, one that was shared with the Chinese community in a series of celebratory banquets hosted by the Chinese Benevolent Association of Canada and the Chinese Association of Canadian Armed Forces, among others. Jung's breakthrough win also received wide coverage in the English-language press, putting him in the spotlight. What made the victory even sweeter was that it occurred in Vancouver, once the site of the worst discrimination against the Chinese—and now the home of the first Chinese MP. Becoming a highly regarded member within the Progressive Conservative Party, he was also the youngest MP and was later elected chairman of the Canadian Youth Association of the Progressive Conservatives.

The Liberals had been in power for more than twenty-two years and there was a movement to replace them. It was a perfect time for the Progressive Conservative Party to regain power. Jung's personal efforts aside, it was undoubtedly true that the overall situation worked in favour of his party. Leading the Liberals by only seven seats in this election, the Conservatives had an unstable minority government. So on March 31, 1958, Canada held another national election only nine months after the last. This time the Conservatives gained a large majority, winning more than two hundred seats in Parliament. Jung was re-elected with a record 13,830 votes, his Liberal rival receiving only 3,848 votes. The Liberals were reduced to fewer than fifty seats. The Progressive Conservative Party, now with a solid majority government, could begin to govern effectively, and Douglas Jung was entrusted with considerable responsibility.

In June 1960, Douglas Jung was elected the first Chinese chairman of a cross-party committee in parliamentary history. In Parliament, Jung was active in his unique role as the very first Chinese MP. Besides pushing for pension reform, he contributed to the improvement of immigration-related legislation, such as the amnesty proposal that granted legal citizenship to thousands of undocumented immigrants. He also lobbied for a more lenient legal environment that would enable Chinese immigrants to bring family members from a wider range of categories than just immediate family to Canada for family reunification.

Jung served with Canada's national interests at heart. This was especially true when he proposed a controversial yet visionary diplomatic approach towards the newly founded China. As a member of the Conservative party, Jung was reluctant to criticize the policies on China that his party held, but he openly talked about his plan for a private visit to mainland China in 1958. He and other MPs supportive of diplomatic ties with China believed that diplomatic recognition of China would be beneficial for Canadian foreign trade. But Prime Minister John Diefenbaker made it clear that Jung's plan to visit mainland China was not endorsed by the government and in no way reflected official policy. And Liu Youtang, the consul general of the Republic of China (Taiwan) to Canada, also expressed concern over Douglas Jung's comments on "Red China" in a press interview. Jung's proactiveness on this topic was not even appreciated by the Chinese community, which had a deep misunderstanding of mainland China at that time. What was made obvious by this issue, however, was that Douglas Jung was neither a puppet nor an opportunist, but a conscientious statesman upholding his own principles—an approach that brought criticism from some quarters and admiration from others.

Douglas Jung also led the Canadian delegation to the Model NATO Youth Summit. On that trip he was called a "Chinaman" by a Liberal MP from BC who questioned the government's appointment of a Chinese Canadian to head the Canadian delegation. Such insulting words ignited criticism from both inside and outside the Chinese community.

Jung had always put the pursuit of the legitimate interests and rights of Chinese Canadians in a broader legal context, thus maintaining a consistent stand towards both the Chinese and non-Chinese communities. He urged the government to apply the same standards for both European and Chinese refugees. Thanks to his appeal, on May 22, 1962, Prime Minister John Diefenbaker announced that Canada would open its doors to one hundred Chinese refugee families. On May 30 of the same year, in Vancouver's Chinatown, Diefenbaker affirmed a half-million-dollar in-kind donation to Hong Kong refugees. On June 9, on behalf of the prime minister, Jung announced the principles enshrined in a new refugee law that stipulated that refugees with both a spouse and children under the age of twenty-one in Hong Kong would be given preferential acceptance. Such unprecedented concessions attracted enormous attention from the Chinese community, especially when immigration had been plagued by the problem of false documents used by many Chinese immigrants to enter Canada. In principle, Douglas Jung sympathized with undocumented Chinese immigrants and blamed the Canadian immigration law that discriminated against the Chinese, hindering families from reunion for as long as two or three decades and thus disqualifying many immigrant offspring who had passed the twenty-one-year-old application ceiling. The amnesty he proposed would allow undocumented Chinese immigrants to report themselves and obtain citizenship aimed to remedy this situation, yet he also cautioned his fellow Chinese, "If one fails to seize the opportunity in time, the government will not indefinitely extend the availability of such opportunity but implement stringent laws." In the end, Jung concluded that the amnesty period had been sufficient and should be terminated. His agreement to end the amnesty cost him the favour of many in the

Chinese community. Discontent with him lingered till the federal election of 1963, in which he lost his seat to the popular Liberal lawyer John Nicholson, but only by five hundred votes. Regardless of his loss, Douglas Jung had done an impressive job as the first Chinese Canadian MP, and his election was a prelude to more Chinese participation in Canadian politics.

Although Douglas Jung failed to win unanimous acclaim from the Chinese community and did irritate a few nerves during his tenure in Parliament, it is undeniable that his performance and political capabilities as an MP influenced the impression of the Chinese community held by mainstream parties in Canada. In fact, when a new federal election was called in 1962, all the party leaders campaigned in Chinatowns, now eager to attract the Chinese voters.

Although the 1963 election ended the only Chinese MP's career in Parliament prematurely, it changed Chinese participation in federal politics in two ways. First, over the four decades that followed this election, Chinese Canadians would support the federal Liberals over the Progressive Conservatives or any other party, a preference unchanged until the beginning of the twenty-first century. And second, despite the sentiment that "Chinese support Chinese," Chinese voters more often followed current political trends rather than ethnic allegiances in elections.

Despite losing his seat in Parliament and encountering some dissatisfaction with his policies among his Chinese compatriots, Jung went on to have an extremely distinguished career. He was appointed by Diefenbaker to serve as the chair of Canada's legal delegation to the United Nations and was appointed a judge on the Immigration Appeal Board in Ottawa. In addition, he was inducted into the Order of Canada and the Order of BC and received numerous other lifetime achievement awards from Chinese community organizations.

Although he served in Parliament for only five years, Jung's political contribution left an indelible mark on the history of Chinese Canadians. Not every Chinese Canadian had cast a ballot in his favour, but everyone in the Chinese community agreed that he was a pioneer in enhancing the political status and encouraging the political participation of Chinese Canadians.

Chinese Canadians had no representative in the federal government for a few years after Douglas Jung left office. But his success encouraged many Chinese Canadians, incuding some women, to engage in politics at the municipal level. In Vancouver's 1962 municipal election, for example, Lady Zhang Ji ran for the Vancouver Parks Board, marking the beginning of Chinese women's political participation. Though not elected in the end, Zhang set a model for other Chinese women in the future.

During this period, a number of other outstanding Chinese Canadians won local elections: George Ho Lem was voted city councillor in Calgary in

1959; Ed Lum was elected to city council in Saanich, BC, in 1965; and Peter Wing became the first Chinese Canadian mayor of Kamloops in 1966. All in all, once enfranchised, Chinese Canadians began to actively wield their voting power and to participate in mainstream politics, taking difficult but rewarding first steps into a new era of active political participation.

Chinese Public School, 499 East Pender. City of Vancouver Archives, CVA 1135-22. Photographer William E. Graham.

EDUCATION AND CULTURE IN CHINESE COMMUNITIES

During the postwar period and into the 1960s, there were changes in the education of Chinese children as more of them attended the provincial public schools and the Chinese schools became more closely focussed on transmitting Chinese language and important cultural traditions. Also in these postwar decades, the cultural activities in the Chinese community broadened to include movies and a variety of musical forms beyond Cantonese opera.

CHINESE EDUCATION

In the first decade of the selective entry era, there were few new Chinese schools, and the number of teachers and students at existing schools declined. Many schools simply shut down. However, as immigration regulations gradually relaxed during the two decades following World War II, more children entered Canada, and new Chinese schools were needed to accommodate them. The postwar environment demanded that Chinese schools adapt, just as it did for the Chinese community as a whole. But despite a temporary setback during the transition period, both the Chinese community and mainstream society later began to appreciate Chinese education.

Few new Chinese schools were built in the postwar years, although some opened in Vancouver, Victoria, Edmonton, and Toronto, and Christian night schools offered occasional Chinese language and writing classes. The older, larger schools in major cities continued to function as the cornerstones of Chinese education, including the Mon Keang School sponsored by the Wongs' Benevolent Association and the CBA's Chinese Public School in Vancouver, the Victoria Chinese Public School, and Chinese public schools in Calgary, Regina, Toronto, and Montreal. Chinese schools in a number of smaller towns also continued to operate in the decade following the war.

Many schools, big and small, were financially pinched and had to constantly raise money from the Chinese community to cover their operating expenses. To make things worse, many of the aging Chinese schools needed new buildings, partly due to more stringent municipal building codes, partly to the large numbers of new students crowding into the existing buildings—even the Chinese who had moved out of Chinatown sent their children to

254 — Great Fortune Dream

Chinese schools there, contributing to overcrowding. The Mon Keang School, the Vancouver Chinese Public School, and the Calgary Chinese Public School all found themselves in need of new buildings.

On some occasions, fundraising efforts failed to raise enough money to complete a building. Even schools with such strong community resources as the Vancouver Chinese Public School, for example, had difficulty financing a new building, and drained its funds on the interior, leaving little money to finish the exterior work. The school appealed for a second time to donors in 1953 in the *Chinese Times*: "This enormous project has exhausted all the donations received so far, yet is far from being finished. We are forced to seek the generosity of our fellow Chinese once again." Other schools used donated facilities for some of its activities. The Winnipeg Chinese Public School, for example, used a donated auditorium for classes and student performances, with free electricity and water supplied by the Kuomintang.

In addition to raising funds through benefit performances and campaigns soliciting direct donations, some schools collected money by selling traditional Chinese foods made from donated ingredients. On one occasion in 1964, local Chinese grocers donated to the Duncan Chinese School bean sprouts, fermented black bean oil, noodles, turkey and goose meat, salt, and other foods, which were sold to the public. The varied forms of donations demonstrated the severe financial strain experienced by the Chinese schools.

For small schools, the economic conditions were even more grim. Victoria's Yu Shan School, a decade-old school sponsored by the Yu Shan Chong How Benevolent Association, ran into budgetary problems after the war and relied on the Zong association to raise operating money so it could continue to function.

A few new Chinese schools opened during the 1960s. The Vancouver United Church Chinese School opened in early 1961 and expanded quickly. Another new school, the Hamilton Chinese School, opened in 1965. There continued to be a strong demand for Chinese education within the Chinese community in the selective entry period era, and although many Chinese children attended provincially funded schools, they continued to learn Chinese language and literature, calligraphy, and other cultural traditions at the Chinese schools.

Before the war, Chinese schools organized student trips in the spring. During April's Qingming festival—a three-day festival honouring the dead—students would tour British Columbia, a tradition from China that was carried over to Canada. Schools often collaborated with each other to organize these tours, and as many as a thousand people participated, including students, teachers, parents, and prominent citizens or volunteers from the Chinese community. After the war, with fewer donations coming in, many retained this tradition but on a much smaller scale, with a few hundred participants—another indication of the stretched finances of Chinese schools and the negative effect on the schools' development. But that didn't necessarily mean that the Chinese had become tight-fisted towards education; the fact was, with improving social status, Chinese children began to have greater access to mainstream Canadian schools. The generosity of the Chinese community receded with their lessening dependence on Chinese schools.

Despite dwindling numbers and the constant challenge of raising money to stay open, three new features emerged in Chinese education.

First was the use of Mandarin Chinese. As a result of the changed political landscape in Asia, Chinese schools in Canada began to use Mandarin as a teaching language alongside the Cantonese and Taishan dialects. Though the Kuomintang government retreated to Taiwan when the Communist Party established the People's Republic of China in 1949, the two parties' antagonism did not extend to education. Language was one of the commonalities that crossed the Taiwan Strait, since the Communist Party of China promoted Putonghua (the Mandarin language of China's mainland) in the public education system on the mainland while the Kuomintang promoted Mandarin (Taiwan) on the island.

It was natural for Chinese schools overseas to follow this trend. For example, the Mon Keang School in Vancouver began offering a Mandarin course in 1951. Huang Xiongshen, one of its teachers, taught an optional one-hour Mandarin course every Saturday. By 1953, the school had hired Huang Yuekui to teach Mandarin; she also taught classes on general knowledge, singing, and other subjects. In July 1963, the Vancouver Chinese Christian Church began offering a Mandarin class Tuesday and Thursday nights. It was clear that more and more of the Chinese in Canada wished to speak Mandarin, and even though Mandarin classes were relatively rare among Chinese schools, their emergence in Canada during this period began to respond to this need.

The second new feature of Chinese education was its intensified contact with and recognition by the mainstream culture. Although Chinese schools continued to educate students in the traditional Chinese way, in the 1960s they also began to incorporate some of the features of the provincial school system. For example, in addition to celebrating Confucius's birthday, they also began celebrating Christmas.

Chinese schools were established in the beginning because of the segregation imposed on Chinese students, as well as the Chinese community's desire to maintain its traditional culture. After World War II ended, the larger society gradually came to recognize Chinese schools and invited them to participate in various activities. In 1954, for example, when the United Nations held a summer camp for middle school students in western Canada at the University of British Columbia, Chinese students were invited to attend.

The CBA loaned its auditorium to the UN for the opening ceremony of the camp and hosted a dinner for participants at a Chinese restaurant. The National Film Board shot an episode of its 1950s television series *Perspectives* in Vancouver's Chinatown to introduce Chinese culture to the rest of Canada. As part of the show, the camera crew paid a visit to the Tai Kung Charity School. The contents and approach of Chinese education had clearly caught the attention of the mainstream media.

The third new feature of Chinese schools was that they became communication hubs for Chinese culture. As Chinatowns declined after World War II, with many of the more wealthy Chinese leaving Chinatowns to live elsewhere, they became marginal, desolate places, in which the schools assumed the role of preserving Chinese culture. Although there were fewer of them overall, Chinese schools, especially those with a long history, became the new custodians of culture in Chinatowns. Three prestigious schools in Vancouver were recognized by the Canadian government through awards presented by the immigration minister—the Chinese Public School, the Mon Keang School, and the Tai Kung Charity School. These schools were highly respected in both the Chinese community and mainstream society. It thus became natural that cultural resources, whether from private Chinese households or from libraries in mainland China, flowed to those schools and contributed to the formation of first-class cultural programs such as the Culture Room and regular special lectures offered by the Mon Keang School.

Planning for the Mon Keang School's Culture Room began in 1953. According to the *Chinese Times*, it aimed to "exhibit cultural items from ancient and present-day China to teach the younger generation about their motherland, foster patriotism, and enhance morality." During a lengthy preparation period, donations of exhibit items came from all sectors of the Chinese community to fill the room with calligraphy and paintings by celebrated artists, porcelain, carvings, pottery, lacquerware, poetry, photographs, books, and other objects. Among all the items, the most precious was a handwritten memorial to the emperor that had been created by Kang Yuwei. The school received a large number of books, including Chinese and English journals, world atlases, and textbooks from the Overseas Chinese Affairs Commission of the Taiwan government. The Culture Room of the Mon Keang School was a miniature museum that exhibited Chinese culture to the world—1,100 non-Chinese people visited the room the first year after it opened.

Besides the Culture Room, the special lectures organized by the Mon Keang School were also widely acclaimed. The first three lectures were "Chinese Society through History," by Ma Ruochuan, a teacher visiting from the Portland Chinese Language School in Oregon; "From Prehistory to the Present Day: Chinese Nationalities and Their Environment," by Seto Ying Shek; and "China's New Culture Movement and Its Ideas," by Peter Chow, an expert on Roman law sent by the Vatican. These informative lectures were welcomed by the Chinese community as well as students, and the program enhanced the intellectual life of the Chinese community.

After 1947, Canadian universities opened their doors to Chinese students. Dr. Vivienne Poy, the first Canadian of Asian descent to become a Canadian senator, recalled her time at McGill:[†]

> I went to St. Paul's Co-educational School. After graduation from middle school, I came to Canada in 1959 and started as a sophomore in the history department at McGill University. Back then there were few overseas Chinese students in Canada, let alone females. There were only twelve Chinese female students at the whole university. I entered with a British passport, so after marrying my husband, Dr. Neville Poy, a Chinese Canadian citizen, I only needed to change to a Canadian passport and didn't have to go through the usual immigration procedures.

Most of the twelve female students mentioned by Dr. Poy came from Hong Kong.

Long-established Chinese schools had by now graduated several generations of students and had many outstanding alumni. These schools began to set up alumni associations to encourage members to donate directly to their former school or to assist with fundraising in the community. Such associations also aimed to build contact between current students and graduates so that these successful graduates could encourage students to study hard and find similar success.

The first alumni event was held by Victoria's Chinese Public School, part of the school's fortieth anniversary celebrations held in June 1947. The school's location in the oldest Chinatown in Canada attracted attention to this event. In 1951, a group of alumni from Vancouver's Mon Keang School founded an association to establish contact among alumni and promote aid for the development of the school and Chinese education in general. The association's office was located inside the school, and membership was open to all graduates. Similar associations were established at the Toronto True Light School and at other Chinese schools.

Overall, between the end of World War II and the mid-1960s, more Chinese schools closed than opened. Despite this, the Chinese community continued to emphasize traditional education and promote Chinese cultural

---

† While serving in the Senate from 1998 to 2012, Dr. Poy focussed on immigration issues and multiculturalism and helped establish May as Asian Heritage Month across Canada. In her distinguished career, she also served as the chancellor of the University of Toronto from 2003 to 2006.

heritage to students. With the support of Chinese associations and individuals, many schools made substantial improvements in their buildings and their curriculum design.† More importantly, schools in this period began to interact with the mainstream society, and cross-cultural communication began to emerge. They helped change the prejudiced and uninformed opinions of the West towards Chinese culture, introduced the fine traditions of China, and, to some extent, laid a foundation for the future cultural diversity of Canada.

CHINESE ARTS AND MEDIA

In the era of selective entry, Chinese newspapers played a more crucial role than they had before the war. There were three reasons for this. First, Chinese newspapers became the best platform for communication among the Chinese, because immigrants from mainland China, Taiwan, and other regions increasingly diversified the population's dialects and customs. Secondly, with the repeal of the Chinese Exclusion Act and the continual adjustments to immigration policy, Chinese newspapers were needed by both the Chinese community and the Canadian government to understand each other's concerns. Newspapers became a channel through which the Chinese community communicated with the government. Governments monitored the Chinese newspapers and then reacted by discussing issues of concern with Chinese community leaders; these discussions influenced policy making. Lastly, the major political parties paid much more attention to Chinese immigrants who were now able to vote. Newspapers became a forum in which political opinions were expressed.

In the early postwar period, the Chinese newspaper landscape was dominated by a few publications affiliated with political associations like the Hongmen Society and the Kuomintang, including the *Chinese Times*, the *New Republic Chinese Daily News*, and the *Shing Wah News*. After the Communists came to power in China in 1949, Chiang Kai-shek and the Kuomintang retreated to Taiwan. The conflict between the Communist Party and the Kuomintang led to a parallel ideological division within the Chinese community in Canada. Some newly founded newspapers openly advertised their political allegiances.

In 1950, the East Wind Club in Montreal started a journal named *East Wind Monthly*. This free publication advocated communism and was able to publish for seven or eight years until financial problems caused it to fold.

---

† The Chinese government in Taiwan changed the curriculum of the overseas Chinese schools to match the curriculum in Taiwan. This did not affect all schools—just those strongly influenced by Taiwan. The People's Republic of China also revised curriculum, and changes were made in the overseas schools aligned with mainland China. Most of the Chinese schools in Canada were Taiwanese influenced.

In Vancouver, left-wing youths founded a bi-weekly named *Da Zhong Bao* in 1960 expressing their support for mainland China's government. In Montreal, the Kuomintang founded the *Guang Zhi Ye Kan* in 1961, a journal dedicated to reporting news from the Chinese community with a strong pro-Kuomintang bias.

However, being an ocean away from China, the major newspapers in Canada's Chinatowns gradually reduced their coverage of Chinese politics and instead focussed on the needs of the local Chinese community. Several new publications demonstrated this trend. In 1953, a World War II veteran named Ma Guoguan founded the *Chinese News*, a biweekly magazine in Vancouver. It was a non-political journal that reported on events in the Chinese community and promoted Chinese culture. In 1954, Wu Limin, who had immigrated from Anhui Province in China, and several leaders from the Chinese communities in Victoria and Vancouver founded the *Chinese Voice* in Vancouver. This newspaper aimed to introduce Chinese culture, advocate reforms and progress made by the Chinese community, and promote nationalism. Enjoyed by readers for its lively contents and wide coverage of topics, this paper had impressive sales records. Another newspaper, *Chong Shing Yit Pao*, was founded in the spring of 1955 in Vancouver by a Chinese businessman, Li Shaosen. It only circulated for a few months before it suspended publication due to poor management. The *Chinese-Canadian Bulletin* of the China-Canada Publishing Company was a bilingual Chinese-English newspaper that maintained a neutral political stance, promoted peace and trade between China and Canada, and sought benefits and equal treatment for overseas Chinese. Collectively, these publications functioned as the voice of Canada's overseas Chinese community.

Besides the news media, there were also magazines solely devoted to entertainment, without political content. These were also very effective at disseminating information. In 1953, the *Chinese Businessmen's Biweekly* published its first issue in Edmonton. It included news about China's mainland, but also fiction by writers from Hong Kong, Macao and Taiwan, illustrated with cartoons. *Feng Yue Tan*, first published in Vancouver in 1955, contained tips for daily life, information about physical health, local news, recipes, fiction, and so on. The *Life Mirror*, founded by the Chinese Cultural Company in 1955, was printed in Hong Kong and circulated in Vancouver. Its contents focussed on stories of swordsmen and legends, and the journal boasted extensive readership.

Wenxin Press in Montreal also published a few Chinese novels, poems, and essays to cater to the Chinese readers. Also worth mentioning was *Chinese Youth Monthly*, founded by the Young Chinese Recreational Press in Edmonton, which focussed on issues confronting Chinese youths and real-life issues in the Chinese community.

Some clan associations published periodicals, like the *Monthly*, published by the Lee's Association. Clan and other associations also issued special publications to introduce themselves or celebrate their accomplishments. In July 1950, the Kai Ping Benevolent Association in Vancouver issued a publication that included a profile of the association. In 1953, the youth branch of the Vancouver Lung Kong Tin Yee Association published a special issue to encourage mutual support among members. In May 1954, the art department of the Jin Wah Sing Musical Association published *Hua Feng* to promote itself. To celebrate its first anniversary, the Saskatoon Chinese Youth Association issued a publication in March 1964 that included short stories, features, the association's annual report, news of arts and sports activities, charitable work records, and local news. And in 1966, Vancouver's Chinese Guide Press published the *Overseas Chinese Special Issue on Economics* to promote local businesses. It included information on Canada's immigration and economic policies, profiles of local industry leaders, investment opportunities, and so on. Many of these informative magazines were very helpful to new and recent immigrants.

In addition to local publications, magazines from China's mainland, Taiwan, and Hong Kong were available to the Chinese community in Canada. These periodicals helped keep the overseas Chinese informed about developments in their distant homeland.

The still sizable population base in Chinatowns, eager for information about Chinese communities at home and abroad, kept existing bookstores and newsstands in business and encouraged the opening of new ones. Chinese associations also developed reading clubs for their members, maintaining collections of Chinese-language books in their association buildings. For example, the Wongs' Reading Club was established in Calgary in May 1959 to provide a quiet and relaxing reading space for members of the Wong association. Other popular reading clubs included the Gao Yang Reading Club, the San De Book Club, the Min Xing Reading Room, the Yu Ying Book Club, and the Hongmen Chee Kung Tong Reading Club. Political organizations' reading clubs supplied information to advance party policy.

New bookstores opened in response to rising market demand. In November 1962, for example, the Hua Min Bookstore opened on Main Street in Vancouver. It carried novels, magazines, art books, travel literature, and other books, most of them imported from China. Other new bookstores opened in major cities such as Vancouver, Victoria, and Toronto. Some companies, including the Chinese Company, the Jian Li Corporation, and the Overseas Chinese Federation Books, published and marketed a few Chinese books. Those bookstores and companies provided readers with a wide variety of Chinese reading materials: contemporary and classic fiction, poetry, essays, history, maps, general non-fiction, medical and scientific books, the works of

Mao Zedong, Chinese-English dictionaries, and newspapers and magazines. Books from China's mainland were usually available to the overseas community as soon as they were published, keeping the overseas Chinese current with literature and events in China.

The development of Chinese newspapers and magazines in the 1950s and 1960s helped stimulate the later development of Chinese Canadian literature, which gradually grew into an important branch of overseas Chinese literature.[†]

Before and during World War II, the Chinese in Canada had little opportunity to develop their literary talents. After the war, though, as their social and economic status improved, they began to seek the satisfaction of artistic expression. Access to publications from Hong Kong and other regions greatly enriched the reading experience of the overseas Chinese and inspired a creative atmosphere in the community.

Many of the Chinese newspapers and magazines mentioned above published literary supplements, providing an outlet for emerging writers. They also sponsored writing contests, as did churches and associations. To celebrate its fiftieth anniversary, the *Chinese Times* organized an essay contest; the winning essay celebrated the eleventh anniversary of the founding of the People's Republic of China. Similarly, the Vancouver branch of the Chinese Freemasons held a writing contest in 1964, the entries describing the achievements of the society. Although these events were of small scale and little literary significance, they helped nourish the development of Chinese Canadian literature.

For Chinese Canadian writers, there was never a lack of subject matter. The complex and difficult history of the overseas Chinese, the vagaries of their political and economic status, the relationship with the host society, and divided political stands within the Chinese communities all provided fertile themes for Canadian-born writers to explore.

From the late 1940s to the early 1950s, depopulation in Chinatowns began to take a toll on traditional Cantonese opera as the elderly audience died out while new immigrants and the growing group of second-generation Chinese Canadians showed much less interest in the form. Losing the new generation to modern movies and music, Cantonese opera fell into a temporary slump.

[†] Important Chinese Canadian writers include Sky Lee, Wayson Choy, and Paul Yee, among others. In 1995, three of the five books shortlisted for the Books in Canada Best First Novel Award were written by Chinese Canadians. Chinese Canadian literature has also attracted the attention of scholars, and writings on and courses in Chinese Canadian literature are now commonplace at Canadian universities.

By the mid-1950s, though, as more and more immigrants had their aging parents come to Canada, traditional opera enjoyed a renaissance, although in no way comparable to its previous popularity.

In the postwar era, the younger Chinese community enjoyed movies, modern music, and modern drama in addition to Cantonese opera. Beijing opera, dance, and other art forms gained in popularity, so in addition to the existing Cantonese opera troupes and music clubs, new arts groups emerged. In the increasingly diversified art scene in Chinatowns, the Jin Wah Sing Cantonese Opera Troupe was the most prominent because it expanded widely across Canada.

Responding to the growing interest in movies among members of the Chinese community, the Jin Wah Sing Opera Study Association of Vancouver established the Jin Wah Sing Movie Association. It held its first movie festival showing Chinese comedies and detective stories from Hong Kong at the Majestic Theatre on January 3, 1960, and it was enthusiastically received.

The 1950s saw the founding of new opera troupes in several cities. In 1951, a group of young Chinese immigrants from different provinces of China founded the Vancouver White Cloud Drama Troupe. Similarly, Calgary witnessed a revival of Cantonese opera thanks to a growing number of Chinese immigrants. On December 8, 1952, a group of enthusiastic youths and opera lovers founded the Jin Wah Sing Opera Study Association to explore the intellectual aspects of Cantonese opera, promote Chinese culture, and establish connections among amateurs. The group was supported by the Chinese community and associations in Calgary. In 1953, two members of Montreal's Chinese Freemasons, Huang Youxuan and Chen Gongxia, founded the Han Yuen Club. Headquartered in the auditorium of the Chinese Freemasons, it attracted many newly immigrated young people. In 1957, another branch of the Jin Wah Sing Musical Association was founded, this one in Edmonton.

Other music clubs continued to appear in the 1960s. The Yi Lin Music Club was founded in Vancouver in 1960 by some Chinese music lovers, and the Overseas Chinese Music Club was founded in Calgary the same year. In 1963, a group of opera stars and Chinese businessmen founded the Chinese Movie & Opera Association, and the Cantonese Music Association was established in Toronto. Many arts and entertainment groups were active in this period and played an important role in enriching the leisure life of overseas Chinese.

Traditional Cantonese opera troupes and individual performers suffered in the postwar era. As mentioned above, the troupes' business declined severely in the late 1940s; even the opera-infatuated city of Vancouver was no exception. The audiences of the Jin Wah Sing Troupe dwindled. Many of its performers had to seek a livelihood in other cities like Toronto or New

York. With a reduced staff and its former building demolished and transformed into a parking lot, the troupe was forced to move into a basement on Pender Street, a place just big enough to store its stage property. The troupe gradually became virtually dormant.

But by the mid-1950s, the growing number of immigrants breathed renewed life into the organization. In 1954, the Jin Wah Sing Troupe was re-launched, restructured, and renamed the Jin Wah Sing Musical Association. On April 23, 1954, the new troupe performed *Western Chamber under the Moon* at the Hastings Theatre as its inaugural performance. In December 1957, it moved to more spacious offices, holding a "housewarming" performance that month. In 1961, the association hired Huang Tao, a famous Cantonese opera artist from Hong Kong and the former secretary of the Bach Musical Opera Troupe there, as its musical coach. Under his guidance, the troupe quickly expanded, recruiting a dozen young performers and purchasing new costumes and musical instruments. It received a gift that year from the Hong Kong White Flower Oil Medicine Limited for its apron stage: a yellow curtain set embroidered with the four Chinese characters "*Chong Zhen Hua Sheng*" (Revive the Chinese Opera).

Recalling his performing experiences in the 1960s, Huang Tao, now a centenarian, was full of emotion:

> When the Jin Wah Sing Troupe was founded, it was joined by many opera lovers such as Songshao, Dingguo, Jian Guo'an, and Zheng Jiongguang, who contributed both their money and energy and brought a revival to the troupe. In 1960, Zhenhua invited me to teach the Cantonese music team of the troupe. So I came to Canada alone from Hong Kong in 1961. I taught at Jin Wah Sing for a year and a half. The salary then was $125 per month. At that time, the troupe hired a few top-notch opera stars from Hong Kong as well as some local actors. The performance was usually staged at the Royal Theatre or some Chinese school. Tickets to the performance only cost a few dozen cents. Most of the audience were older Chinese from the community. My family joined me in Canada in 1963. To feed the family, I had to work at some five jobs one after the other—in the fishery, at a wood factory, and other places. But all the while I insisted on teaching at the troupe every Saturday and Monday for as long as thirty-seven years. Many of my students became Cantonese opera performers.
>
> In the 1940s and 1950s, many steamships from the United States or Hong Kong had their own on-board opera troupes. The Jin Wah Sing Troupe used to invite experienced performers from such troupes to perform on land. Sometimes the performers

chose to stay after performing, and some illegally entered the United States. It was impossible for the stowaways to take all the costumes with them, so they only picked the most expensive pieces and left the rest at Jin Wah Sing. Many were old costumes from the 1920s with delicate embroidery. I was then assigned to take care of those costumes. There were a few hundred pieces. We wanted to sell them to antique shops but were discouraged by the extremely low offers. Later the costumes were collected by the UBC Museum of Anthropology.[†]

As is evident in Huang's words, it was impossible to support a family by performing or teaching operas in those days. Pure interest and a sense of responsibility towards traditional Cantonese opera was what kept these opera champions motivated.

Traditional operas about imperial life continued to dominate the stage for most troupes during the era of selective entry, although contemporary plays were occasionally produced. In 1956, Vancouver's Jin Wah Sing Musical Association staged *Mu Guiying Goes into Battle* and *The New Stern-faced Husband of the Empress*. On February 11, 1962, the association performed the *Ten-Year Dream of Yangzhou*, *Sworn Brothers*, and other classic operas at the Majestic Theatre. The association had purchased a large number of fine costumes from Hong Kong and hired celebrated opera artists to perform, impressing the audience with these shows. In July 1962, Vancouver's Hongyun Troupe enthralled audiences with *Flower Princess*, *Legend of the White Snake*, *Su Wu the Shepherd*, and other classic operas.

Cantonese opera troupes often performed at associations' celebrations or fundraising events. When Calgary's Dart Coon Club celebrated its thirty-sixth anniversary, the local Jin Wah Sing branch was invited to perform the opera *Talent and Beauty*. The celebration happened to take place on a snowy day, but the chilly weather didn't prevent people from coming out to enjoy the performance.

The repeal of the Chinese Exclusion Act had made it easier for international performers to enter Canada, which facilitated communication between Canadian troupes and their international peers. Such communication greatly promoted the renaissance of Cantonese opera in the Chinese community in Canada and also enhanced the quality of the local troupes. In 1956,

---

[†] The Museum of Anthropology added these Cantonese opera costumes to its collection in the 1970s and maintains them still. It is the world's largest collection of old Cantonese opera costumes. In 1993, the museum curated a special travelling exhibition of the costumes called A Rare Flower: A Century of Cantonese Opera in Canada. Members of the Chinese community assisted the curator to develop the exhibition.

Chu Qiao, Huang Jinlong, and Liang Shaoping led a performance group to Vancouver. In April 1958, Liang Minshi, a famous guzheng performer—a guzheng is an ancient Chinese musical instrument—stopped in Vancouver while on tour, and a special welcome reception for her was held by the Ching Won Musical Society. At the reception, Ms. Liang shared her experiences as an artist and then enchanted her audience with well-known guzheng pieces such as "A Phoenix Worshipped." In October 1965, the Jin Wah Sing Musical Association offered a series of performances that starred four distinguished opera actresses from the United States; their performances included plays such as *Fortune Comes With Blooming Flowers* and *Birthday Greetings by Eight Deities*. The superb vocal performance and vivid theatrical scenes captivated the audience.

To promote Cantonese opera to non-Chinese audiences, Chinese opera troupes also actively participated in Westerners' activities. On May 1, 1958, the Jin Wah Sing Troupe performed at the International Trade Fair in BC. Their performance was warmly received by the Western audience.

Opera troupes were greatly affected by the development of movies and struggled to stay in business. Many were forced to raise funds periodically to survive and received support from the Chinese community and associations. To raise money to fund business growth, Vancouver's Jin Wah Sing Troupe sponsored a screening of the movie *Opera Fans' Sweetheart* in August 1953. In 1958, the troupe held another fundraising event, for which generous support flowed in as usual.

Apart from professional troupes, amateur troupes also had their moment in the spotlight. On January 4, 1953, the Youth Federation Troupe of Vancouver's Han Sheng Youth Branch performed a three-act play that was warmly received by the audience. In 1955, the Wenhua Movie Society, an affiliate of Ontario's Chinese Benevolent Association, showed a filmed version of the Cantonese opera *Legend of the White Snake*.

Despite all the ups and downs during the era of selective entry, Cantonese opera troupes continued to provide traditional entertainment and culture to the overseas Chinese.

Although Cantonese opera remained the most popular art form in the Chinese community after the war, the expansion of art exchanges between Canada and the world spurred the diversification of art forms in Chinatown too. One new opera genre that began to appear was Beijing opera, then known as Peking opera. Although it took a long time before Beijing opera was successful in the postwar Chinese community, seeds were sown for its future popularity among the ever more diversified Chinese population. At first it was enjoyed only by a minority, and the few Beijing opera performers actually made a living teaching Kung Fu to the actors playing martial arts roles in Cantonese opera. In August 1960, a ninety-five-person touring company of the Peking Opera Troupe of Beijing visited Vancouver for their first stop in North America. Their first show at the Queen Elizabeth Theatre was a phenomenal success. Tickets were sold out, and at the request of audiences, the troupe added an extra performance to its schedule, the *Legend of the White Snake*. Tickets were just as quickly bought up by the enthusiastic audience for this performance. The troupe's performance was highly praised in the Western media. After their stop in Vancouver, the troupe performed in Calgary and other cities, with great success along the way. In October 1962, the Taiwanese Fuxing Troupe was invited to perform in Seattle and stopped in Victoria and Vancouver on the way. On the evening of October 18, it performed *The Drunken Beauty* at Vancouver's Dayun Theatre. Performances by these Beijing opera troupes promoted the culture of China and unlocked an enormous potential market for Beijing opera in Canada.

The case was similar for Chinese dance and music, which were sometimes performed at mainstream social events to interest Western audiences in Chinese art forms. Vancouver's Weiyun Song and Dance Troupe performed to great applause at Winnipeg's sixtieth anniversary celebration in 1952. In Calgary, an amateur Chinese song and dance troupe was often invited to perform for both Chinese and Western associations. Their dance program typically included *Song of the Fishermen*, *Dance of Friendship*, and *Dance of Youth*, which were routinely acclaimed in both Chinese and Western media.

However, it was not until professional dancers began to visit Canada that Chinese Canadians realized that song and dance, like traditional Cantonese operas, could be first-class art on their own. On October 25, 1964, Zhang Zhongwen, who starred in the movie *Calendar Girl*, gave a concert at the Majestic Theatre in Vancouver. Singing songs such as "Embroidery," among others, Zhang graced her stage with the dancer Huang Meifang, who performed exotic dances from various ethnic groups. The audience was fascinated by this superb performance.

Intensified international art exchanges had broadened the vision of the Chinese in Canada and inspired their interest and confidence in seeking the development of various new forms of art, which helped lay the foundation for the community's future artistic diversity.

After the war, going to the movies became an important way the Chinese spent their leisure hours. Alongside an increasing number of cinemas, many traditional opera theatres began to show movies or simply played short movies before opera performances to attract a larger audience.

In the 1950s and 1960s, the Chinese watched dramas, opera films, musicals, and cartoons. Some were Western, including those from Hollywood (some of these had Chinese subtitles) and some were Chinese. Vancouver boasted a large group of cinemas and theatres that attracted Chinese audiences with advertisements in Chinese media. A *Chinese Times* ad from May 1963 said, "Da Yun Theatre will play the movies *Princess Miu Sin* and *New Year Celebration by the Blundering But Lucky* on May 12 and anyone with this advertisement clipped from the newspaper need only pay 50 cents to enter the theatre."

Some theatres invited movie stars to perform on their stage and interact with the audiences to promote ticket sales. On August 2, 1964, at a screening of the movie *Dancing Snake-girl*, the Majestic Theatre invited the leading actress from the movie, Xue Yanmei, to perform and meet the audience. It also invited the Han Sheng Musical Association to perform Chinese music. Their performance, including a Xinjiang dance and classic musical pieces, enchanted the audience.

Chinese art lovers used films as a means to promote the community's appreciation of traditional Chinese culture and operas. Art societies and associations that had an opera study group would often rent a theatre for a performance or to show a film. Such organizations included the Le Guan Association, Vancouver's Hua Sheng Recording Club Preparation Office, and Victoria's Le Guan Association, among others. The Vancouver Culture Movie Society leased the Queen Theatre to screen movies from Hong Kong. In October 1955, the Vancouver Youth Club showed the movie *The White-haired Girl* at its auditorium, and the audience welcomed it and requested a repeat show. To let the Chinese in Canada learn more about China, the Victoria Branch of the Canada-China Friendship Association screened documentary films about contemporary China. In short, movies had become an important channel for the Chinese community to learn about traditional Cantonese opera, the new China, and the world.

Unidentified Chinese man in traditional clothing. City of Vancouver Archives, CVA 371-1912. Photographer P. L. Okamura. Circa 1898.

EPILOGUE

❧

The migration of the Chinese to Canada began in 1858, and over 50 per cent of Chinese Canadians lived in British Columbia until 1951. For over a century, the Chinese in Canada were segregated physically, socially, and culturally from mainstream Canadian society. Their entry to Canada was restricted from 1885 to 1923 by the requirement to pay a heavy head tax, and from 1923 to 1947, the Chinese Exclusion Act prohibited the Chinese from entering Canada as immigrants. On May 14, 1947, the federal government repealed the Chinese Exclusion Act, but various inequitably applied regulations and policies continued to discriminate against the Chinese, despite Canada's membership in the newly formed United Nations, which prohibited discrimination on the basis of race.

But in 1960, things began to change. The Conservative Diefenbaker government passed the Canadian Bill of Rights, which explicitly forbid discrimination based on race. In 1962, this government passed a new immigration law to reflect the Bill of Rights. Although immigration policy opened the door to the Chinese at this time, there were still restrictions applied to Asians that were not applied to white immigrants. The 1962 act introduced the points system, in which applicants were evaluated according to points awarded for such things as education, the ability to speak Canada's official languages, and work experience.

In 1967, the Liberal Pearson government again revised the immigration law to eliminate remaining inequities and barriers, and from this time forward, immigration policy treated the Chinese in the same way as any other immigrant group.

Portrait of an unidentified woman. City of Vancouver Archives, CVA 287-7. Photographer Hannah H. Maynard. Circa 1905.

BIBLIOGRAPHY

GOVERNMENT DOCUMENTS

British Columbia. Land Registry Office. Absolute Fees Book vol. 2, fol. 619; vol. 8, fol. 895; vol. 22, fol. 229, DD pocket 987 (April 3, 1903); certificate no. 12864-N.

British Columbia. Minister of Mines. Annual Reports, 1893.

British Columbia. *Thirty-ninth Annual Report of the Public Schools of the Province of British Columbia, 1910–1911. Sessional Papers of the Province of British Columbia 1911.* Victoria: Richard Wolfenden, 1911.

British Columbia. *Report of Oriental Activities within the Province.* Victoria: Charles F. Banfield, 1927.

Statutes of the Province of British Columbia 1872.

Statutes of the Province of British Columbia 1876.

Statutes of the Province of British Columbia 1878.

Statutes of the Province of British Columbia 1919.

Canada/Dominion Bureau of Statistics. Censuses of Canada, 1881–1961.

Canada. Department of Immigration and Colonization. Annual Reports, 1931–32, 1934–35.

Canada. Department of Mines and Resources. Annual Report, 1947.

Canada. House of Commons. *Debates.* May 8, 1922.

Canada. *Report on Losses Sustained by the Chinese Population of Vancouver B.C. on the Occasion of the Riots in that City in September, 1907* (Royal Commission: W.L. Mackenzie King). *Sessional Papers,* No. 74f, 1908.

Canada. *Royal Commission on Chinese Immigration: Report and Evidence.* Ottawa: Printed by Order of the Commission, 1885.

Canada. *Royal Commission on Chinese and Japanese Immigration. Sessional Papers 1902* vol. 13, no. 54.

Canada. *Royal Commission on Alleged Chinese Frauds and Opium Smuggling on the Pacific Coast, 1910–11.* Ottawa: Government Printing Bureau, 1913.

Canada. An Act to Restrict and Regulate Chinese Immigration into Canada. *Statutes of Canada 1885.* Ottawa. Ch. 71, 207–12.

Canada. An Act Respecting and Restricting Chinese Immigration. *Statutes of Canada 1900.* Ottawa. Ch. 32, 215–21.

Canada. An Act Respecting and Restricting Chinese Immigration. *Statutes of Canada 1903*. Ottawa. Ch. 8, 105–11.

Canada. An Act to Amend the Immigration Act and to Repeal the Chinese Immigration Act. *Statutes of Canada 1947*. Ottawa. Ch. 19, 107–9.

Canada. An Act to Prohibit the Importation, Manufacture and Sale of Opium for Other than Medical Purposes. *Statutes of Canada 1908*. Ch. 50.

City of Edmonton. Planning Department. "Downtown Plan Working Paper No. 1: The Future of Chinatown." 1978.

City of Vancouver. Planning Department for the Housing Research Committee. "Vancouver Redevelopment Study." December 1957.

City of Vancouver. Planning Department. "Urban Renewal Program: Proposed Study under Part V of the National Housing Act." August 1966.

City of Vancouver. Planning Department. "Urban Renewal in Vancouver: Progress Report no. 7." 1966.

CITY DIRECTORIES AND YEAR BOOKS

British Columbia Directory. Victoria: Williams, 1882–99.

British Columbia Directory. Victoria: Wrigley's, 1918–32.

Canada Year Book: 1906, 1912, 1916–17, 1921, 1922–23, 1924, 1951.

Lethbridge City Directory. Lethbridge: Henderson, 1909.

Montreal City Directory. Montreal: Lovell, 1910–11, 1931–33.

Ottawa City Directory. Ottawa: Might, 1931, 1941, 1961.

Victoria City Directory and Vancouver Island Gazetteer. Victoria: Henderson, 1912–14.

NEWSPAPERS

[British] Colonist (Victoria)
Cariboo Sentinel
Chinese Daily News (Taiwan) (Chinese text)
Comox District Free Press
Daily Times (Victoria)
Globe and Mail (Toronto)
Hung Chung She Bo (Toronto) (in Chinese text)
Kamloops Daily Sentinel
Ledge (New Denver)
Lethbridge News
Nanaimo Free Press
Province (British Columbia)
Shing Wah Daily News (Toronto) (Chinese text)
Similkameen Star
Sing Tao Jih Pao (Vancouver) (Chinese text)

Tai Hen Kong Bo [*Chinese Times*] (Vancouver) (Chinese text)
Daily Globe (San Francisco)
Toronto Star
Vancouver Daily World
Vancouver Sun
Victoria Gazette
Victoria Times
Winnipeg Tribune

UNPUBLISHED DOCUMENTS

Acts and Proceedings of the Presbyterian Church in Canada. 1901, 1902, 1915, 1922.

Annual report of the Missionary Society, Methodist Church of Canada, 1888–89, 1892–93.

Archival materials of Chinese Consolidated Benevolent Association in Victoria, stored in the Archival Library, University of Victoria.

Archival materials of Hongmen Chee Kung Tong, Vancouver Hongmen Headquarters.

Archival materials of Chee Kung Tong, Barkerville Provincial Park.

Baureiss, Gunter, and Julia Swong. "The History of the Chinese Community of Winnipeg." Unpublished report, Chinese Community Committee, 1979.

Burial records, Ross Bay Cemetery, Victoria.

Chan, Y. L. "Planning for Change: The Winnipeg Chinese Community and Its Responsiveness to Government Services." Master's thesis, University of Manitoba, 1962.

Cheung, Helen Kwan Yee. "The Social Functions of Cantonese Opera in the Edmonton Chinese Community, 1890–2009: From Sojourners to Settlers." Master's thesis, University of Alberta, 2013.

City of Vancouver. Chinatown HA-1A Design Guidelines. Land Use and Development Policies and Guidelines. April 2011.

Constitution of the Workingmen's Protective Association.

Friesen, Darren. "Canada's Other Newcomers: Aboriginal Interactions with People from the Pacific." Master's thesis, University of Saskatchewan, 2006.

Guibord, Maurice Conrad. "The Evolution of Chinese Graves at Burnaby's Ocean View Cemetery: From Stigmatized Purlieu to Political Adaptations and Cultural Identity." Master's thesis, Simon Fraser University, 2013.

Hong, Jane, et al., "Chinese Community in Newfoundland" Unpublished manuscript, Chinese Student Society of Memorial University of Newfoundland, 1976.

Joyer, J. B. "Lethbridge Chinatown: An Analysis of the Kwong On Lung Co. Building, the Bow On Tong Co. Building, and the Chinese Free Masons Building, 1985." Unpublished manuscript submitted to Historic Sites Service, Edmonton, Alberta.

Mah, Vallerie A. "The 'Bachelor' Society: A Look at Toronto's Early Chinese Community from 1878 to 1924." Unpublished bachelor of arts essay, University of Toronto, 1978.

Marie, Gillian. "Attitudes toward Chinese Immigrants to British Columbia 1858–1885." Master's thesis, Simon Fraser University, 1976.

Maxwell, Judy. "A Cause Worth Fighting For: Chinese Canadian Debate Their Participation in the Second World War." Master's thesis, University of British Columbia, 2002.

Meares, John. "Voyages Made in the Years 1788 and 1789, from China to the North West Coast of America." Unpublished journal, London, 1790 (presented to the House of Commons, May 13, 1790).

Pasacreta, Laura J. "White Tigers and Azure Dragons: Overseas Chinese Burial Practices in the Canadian and American West (1850s–1910s)." Master's thesis, Simon Fraser University, 2005.

Siewsan, Lily Chow. "The Forgotten Ties: Relationships between First Nations People and Early Chinese Immigrants in British Columbia, Canada (1858–1947)." Paper presented at the 5th WCILCOS International Conference of Institutes and Libraries for Chinese Overseas Studies on Chinese through the Americas, May 16–19, 2012, University of British Columbia.

Wong, May, et al. "A Report on the Development of the Chinese Community in Hamilton." Unpublished manuscript, Chinese Cultural Association of Hamilton, 1984.

Yee, Tim, et al. "An Ethnic Study of the Chinese Community of Moose Jaw, Moose Jaw, 1973." Unpublished report on Opportunities for Youth Project, May–August 1973.

BOOKS AND ARTICLES

Agrawal, Sandeep Kumar, and Abdulhamis Hathiyani. "Funeral and Burial Sites, Rites and Rights in Multicultural Ontario." In *Our Diverse Cities* 4, edited by Katherine Graham, 134–138. Ottawa: Metropolis, 2007.

Anderson, Kay J. "The Idea of Chinatown: The Power of Place and Institutional Practice in the Making of a Racial Category." *Annals of the Association of American Geographers* 77 (4): 580–598.

Balf, Mary. *Kamloops: A History of the District up to 1914*. Kamloops: History Community, Kamloops Museum, 1969.

Balf, Ruth. *Kamloops: 1914–1945*. Kamloops: History Community, Kamloops Museum, 1975.

Ban Seng Hoe. "Chinese Community and Cultural Traditions in Quebec City." *Chinese Consolidated Benevolent Association 1985 Tri-Celebration Special Issue*. Victoria: Chinese Consolidated Benevolent Association, 1986.

Barman, Jean. "Beyond Chinatown: Chinese Men and Indigenous Women in Early British Columbia." *BC Studies* 177 (spring 2013): 39–64.

Baureiss, Gunter. "The Chinese Community of Calgary." *Canadian Ethnic Studies* (1971): 51-2.

Baureiss, Gunter, and L. Driedger. "Winnipeg Chinatown Demographic, Ecological and Organizational Change, 1900–1980." *Urban History Review* 10 (1982): 11–24.

Belshaw, John Douglas. "The British Collier in British Columbia: Another Archetype Reconsidered." *Labour/Le Travail* 34 (autumn 1994): 11–36.

Berton, Pierre. *The Last Spike*. Toronto: McClelland & Stewart, 1971.

Bowen, Lynne. *Boss Whistle: The Coal Miners of Vancouver Island Remember*. Lantzville: Oolichan Books, 1982.

"Brief introduction of the CBA of Regina, Saskatchewan." *Special Issue of the Annual Meeting of Pan-American CBAs*. Vancouver: Chinese Benevolent Association of Canada, June 1994, pages unnumbered (in Chinese text).

Cao Jianwu. "History of CKT Movement for Revival of the Nation." *The 140th Anniversary Issue of Hongmen Contributions to Canada*. Vancouver: Lammar Offset Printing (Overseas), 2003 (in Chinese text).

Chan, Anthony B. *Gold Mountain: The Chinese in the New World*. Vancouver: New Star Books, 1983.

Chan, Claudia. *A Thematic Guide to the Early Records of Chinese Canadians in Richmond*. City of Richmond Archives, August 2011.

Chan, K. B., and D. Helly, eds. *Tossing Off the Shackles of Racism: One Hundred Years of the Chinese Experience in Canada*. Beijing: China Social Sciences Publishing House, 1977.

Cheadle, Walter B. *Cheadle's Journal of Trip Across Canada, 1862–1863*. Victoria: TouchWood Editions, 2010.

Chen Chi. "Visit to the Exhibition of a Century of Canton Opera in Canada." *Chinatown Newsletter* 2, no. 47 (June 1995): 12.

Chen Guoben. *Smoke and Fire: The Chinese in Montreal*. Translated by Wang Yelong, Wang Yi and Yang Liwen. Beijing: Peking University Press, 1996 (in Chinese text).

Chen Hansheng, Lu Wendi, et al., eds. "Chinese Labourers in the U.S. and Canada." In *Collection of Historical Documents Concerning Emigration of Chinese Laborers* no. 7. Beijing: Zhonghua Book Company, March 1981 (in Chinese text).

Chinese Canadian Historical Society. *Historic Study of the Society Buildings in Chinatown*. Report, July 2005.

Chinese Presbyterian Church, Victoria, B.C. 1892–1983. Victoria: Chinese Presbyterian Church 90th Anniversary Celebration Committee, 1983.

Da Rosa, Gustavo. *A Feasibility Study for the Development of Chinatown in Winnipeg.* Winnipeg : Winnipeg Chinese Development, 1974.

Dyck, Lillian Eva. "Invited Speeches." Website for Senator Lillian Eva (Quan) Dyck, Ph.D., D.Litt., for Saskatchewan. http://www.sen.parl.gc.ca/ldyck/html/eng/06speeches.html.

Elections British Columbia. *Electoral History of British Columbia: 1871–1986.* Prepared by Elections British Columbia and the Legislative Library, n.d.

Feng Ziyou. *Overseas Chinese Revolution History for Foundation of the Republic of China.* Shanghai: The Commercial Press, 1947.

Fung, James. "On the Same Boat, First Nations People Proud of Having Chinese Blood." *Metropolitan Vancouver, Edition of World of Immigrants,* September 2, 2011.

Gao, Wenxiong. "Hamilton: The Chinatown that Died." *The Assianadian* 1 (1978): 15.

George, Peter James. *Government Subsidies and the Construction of the Canadian Pacific Railway.* Toronto: Armo Press, 1981.

Hibben, T. N., et al., eds. *Guide to the Province of British Columbia, 1877–78.* Whitefish, Montana: Kessinger Publishing, 2007.

Hong, W. M. *And so That's How It Happened: Recollections of Stanley Barkerville, 1900–1975.* Spartan Printing, 1978.

Howay, F. W. *British Columbia from the Earliest Times to the Present.* Vancouver: S. J. Clark, 1914.

Huang Jinpei and Alan R. Thrasher. "Cantonese Music Societies of Vancouver: A Social and Historical Survey." *Canadian Folk Music Journal* 21: 31–39.

Huang Kuizhang and Wu Jinping. *The History of Chinese Canadians.* Guangzhou: Guangdong Higher Education Press, 2001 (in Chinese text).

Ji Shan. *Concerted Nation-Saving Efforts and Eight-Year Party Ban,* Issue 5. New York: Huanghuagang Press, April 2003 (in Chinese text).

Jian Guo'an. "The Development Record of Jin Wah Sing." *Special Issue of the 60 Year Anniversary of Jin Wah Sing Musical Association, 1934–1994.* Vancouver.

Jian Jianping. *Chinese Freemasons in Canada.* Chinese Freemasons of Canada, September 1989.

Johnson, Elizabeth Lominska. "Cantonese Opera in Its Canadian Context: The Contemporary Vitality of an Old Tradition." *Theatre Research in Canada* 17, no. 1 (spring 1966).

———. "Evidence of an Ephemeral Art: Cantonese Opera in Vancouver's Chinatown." *BC Studies* 148 (winter 2005/06): 55–91.

Johnson, R. Byron. *Very Far West Indeed: A Few Rough Experiences on the North-West Pacific Coast.* London: Sampson Low, Marston, Low, & Searle, 1872.

Johnstone, Bill. *Coal Dust in My Blood: Autobiography of a Coal Miner.* Heritage Record no. 9. Victoria: Royal British Columbia Museum, 1980.

Lai, David Chuenyan. "The Chinese Consolidated Benevolent Association in Victoria: Its Origins and Functions." *BC Studies* no. 15 (autumn 1972): 53–57.

———. "A Feng Shui Model as a Location Index." *Annals of Association of American Geographers* 64, no. 4 (December 1974): 506–513.

———. "Home County and Clan Origins of Overseas Chinese in Canada in the Early 1880s." *BC Studies* 27 (autumn 1975): 3–29.

———. "An Analysis of Data on Home Journeys by Chinese Immigrants in Canada, 1892–1915." *The Professional Geographer* 29 (November 1977): 359–65.

———. "Chinese Imprints in British Columbia." *BC Studies* 39 (autumn 1978): 20–29.

———. *The Gate of Harmonious Interest: From Concept to Reality.* Victoria: City of Victoria, 1981.

———. *Arches in British Columbia.* Victoria: Sono Nis Press, 1982.

———. "The Issue of Discrimination in Education in Victoria, 1901–1923." *Canadian Ethnic Studies* 19, no. 3 (1987): 48–54.

———. "The Chinese Cemetery in Victoria." *BC Studies* 75 (autumn 1987): 24–42.

———. *Chinatowns: Towns Within Cities in Canada.* Vancouver: UBC Press, 1988.

———. "From Self-segregation to Integration: The Vicissitudes of Victoria's Chinese Hospital." *BC Studies* 80 (winter 1988–89): 52–68.

———. "Zhujiang Delta Emigrants to Canada and Their Contributions to Homeland." In *The Environment and Space Development in the Pearl River Delta,* edited by Xu Xueqiang, Antony Yeh and Wen Changen. Beijing: Academic Press, 1989, 276–285.

———. "Cityscape of Old Chinatowns in North America." In *Vision, Culture and Landscape: Working Papers from the Berkeley Symposium on Cultural Landscape Interpretation,* edited by Paul Groth. Berkeley: Department of Landscape Architecture, University of California, 1990, 77–97.

———. "Shipment of Bones to China." *Likely Cemetery Society's Annual Newsletter.* July 1991 (unfolioed).

———. *The Forbidden City Within Victoria.* Victoria: Orca Book Publishers, 1991.

———. "Anti-Japanese War Hero: Fang Shenwu." *Chinatown Newsletter* no. 25 (April 1997): 12–13 (in Chinese text).

———. "The History of Hongmen Minzhidang in Victoria." *Chinatown Newsletter* no. 30 (February 1998): 28–29 (in Chinese text).

———. *Canadian Steel, Chinese Grit: No Chinese Labour, No Railway.* Vancouver: National Executive Council of the Canadian Steel, Chinese Grit Heritage Documentary, 1998.

———. "A Brief History of Chinese Migration to Canada, 1858–2000." *Special Issue on the 10th Anniversary of the National Congress of Chinese Canadians.* September 2001, 40–42 (in English and Chinese text).

———. "Chinese Opium Trade and Manufacture in British Columbia, 1858–1908." *Journal of the West* 38, no.3 (July 1999):, 23.

———. "History and Beautification Proposals of Victoria Chinese Cemetery," *Chinatown Newsletter* no. 49 (April 2001): 31–32 (in Chinese text).

———. "Chinese: The Changing Geography of the Largest Visible Minority." In *British Columbia, the Pacific Province: Geographical Essays,* edited by Colin J. B. Wood. Western Geographical Series, 2001, 147–74.

———. "The Root of Guangdong's Overseas Chinese in Victoria." In *A Collection of Papers presented at the International Symposium on the Literature of Hainan and Guangdong Provinces,* edited by Zhou Weimin. Haikou: Hainan Publishers, March 2002 (in Chinese text), 338–46.

———. "An Analysis of Chinese Politicians, 1957–2002." *Chinatown Newsletter* no. 59 (December 2002): 20–22 (in Chinese text).

———. "Education of Overseas Chinese in Victoria." *Chinatown Newsletter* no. 67 (April/May 2004): 23 (in Chinese text).

———. "Origin of Head Tax." National Congress of Chinese Canadians 15th Annual General Meeting, September 9–10, 2006, Calgary, 86–87.

———. "Dates of Establishment of Vancouver Chinese Benevolent Assn. and Chinese Benevolent Assn. (National Headquarters)." *Chinatown Newsletter* no. 83 (December 2006/January 2007): 21–23 (in Chinese text).

———. "The Four Anniversary Chinese History Events in 2007." *Chinatown Newsletter* no. 86 (June/July 2007): 21(in Chinese text).

———. "A Concise History of Victoria's Hongmen." *The 34th National Convention of the Chinese Freemasons of Canada Special Issue,* October 2008, 60–64 (in Chinese text).

———. "Chinatowns: From Slums to Tourist Destinations." Paper #89, LEWI Working Paper Series. David C. Lam Institute for East-West Studies (LEWI). July 2009, 1-21.

———. "Reminiscences of Overseas Chinese Education in Canada." *Toronto Season* no. 51 (July 2010): 8–9 (in Chinese text).

———. *Chinese Community Leadership.* Singapore: World Scientific Publishing, 2010.

————. "A Brief Chronology of Chinese Canadian History: From Segregation to Integration." Canada Chinatown Series. Simon Fraser University, 2012. http://www.sfu.ca/chinese-canadian-history/chart_en.html.

————. "Vancouver Chinatown." Canada Chinatown Series. Simon Fraser University, 2012. http://www.sfu.ca/chinese-canadian-history/vancouver_chinatown.html.

————. "History of Hongmen and Hongmen in Canada" (in Chinese text). Hong Kong: Commercial Press, 2015.

Lee, David T. H. *A History of Chinese in Canada.* Vancouver: Canada Free Publishing, 1967 (in Chinese text).

Leung, Matthew. *Canada 1863–2003: The Chinese Freemasons Contribution for 140 Years.* Vancouver: Overseas Press, 2003.

Li Chunhui et al., eds. *History of Chinese in Americas/History of Huaqiao and Huaren in Americas.* Beijing: Oriental Publishing House, 2009.

Li, Peter S. "Chinese Immigrants on the Canadian Prairie, 1910–1947." *Canadian Review of Sociology and Anthropology* 9 (1982): 527–40.

————. *The Chinese in Canada.* 2nd edition. Toronto: Oxford University Press, 1998.

Liang Qichao. *New World Travels (Xindalu Youji).* Hunan People's Publishing House, 1981.

Liu Jintao. "Stories of WWII Narrated by Chinese Veterans of the Guangdong Air Force." In *Historical Accounts of Guangzhou: Selection*, vol. 2. Guangzhou: Guangdong People's Publishing House, 1983.

Luo Jialun. *Research on the Historic Documents of Kidnap of Sun Yat-sen in London.* Shanghai: The Commercial Book Company/Nanking, Jinghua Yinshu Ju, 1930.

————. *Chronicle of Sun Yat-sen's Life.* Taipei: Historic Document Compilation Committee of Party History under KMT Central Committee, 1969.

Mar, Lisa Rose. "Beyond Being Others: Chinese Canadians as National History." *BC Studies* 156 (winter 2007/08): 13–34.

————. *Brokering Belonging: Chinese in Canada's Exclusion Era, 1885–1945.* Oxford: Oxford University Press, 2010.

March, Leonard. *Rebuilding a Neighborhood: Report on a Demonstration Slum Clearance and Urban Rehabilitation Project in a Key Central Area in Vancouver.* Research Publication no. 1. Vancouver: University of British Columbia, 1950.

Marshall, Alison R. "Winnipeg Chinese Organizations from 1910 to 1949." In *Celebrating 100 Years, Winnipeg's Chinatown Centennial: A Remarkable Achievement 1909–2009*, edited by Philip Chang and Patrick Choy. Winnipeg: Chinese Cultural and Community Centre, 2010.

Mayse, Susan. "Coal Town, Boomtown, Ghost Town?" *Canadian Heritage*, October/November 1985, 18.

McCormack, Gavan. "1930s Japan: Fascist?" "Japanese Society: Reappraisals and New Directions," special issue of *Social Analysis: The International Journal of Social and Cultural Practice* no. 5/6 (December 1980): 125–143.

McLaughlin, Dennis, and Leslie McLaughlin. *Fighting for Canada.* Ottawa: Minister of National Defence, 2003.

Morley, Alan. *Vancouver: From Milltown to Metropolis.* Vancouver: Mitchell Press, 1961.

Morton, James. *In the Sea of Sterile Mountains.* Vancouver: J. J. Douglas, 1974.

Mouat, Jeremy. "The Politics of Coal: A Study of the Wellington Miners' Strike of 1890–91." *BC Studies* 77 (Spring 1988): 3–29.

Ng, Wing Chung. "Chinatown Theatre as Transnational Business: New Evidence from Vancouver during the Exclusion Era." *BC Studies* 148 (winter 2005/06): 25–54.

Ningyu Li. *Canadian Steel, Chinese Grit.* Shenzhen: Shenzhen Baofeng Printing, 2000.

Ormsby, M. A. *British Columbia: A History.* Vancouver: Macmillan, 1971.

Osterhout, S. S. *Orientals in Canada.* Toronto: United Church of Canada, 1929.

Paterson, T. W. *Ghost Town Trails of Vancouver Island.* Langley: Stage Coach Pub., 1975.

Ramsey, Bruce. *Ghost Towns of British Columbia.* Vancouver: Mitchell Press, 1970.

Roy, Patricia E. "The Preservation of the Peace in Vancouver: The Aftermath of the Anti-Chinese Riot of 1887." *BC Studies* 31 (autumn 1976): 44–59.

———. *A White Man's Province: British Columbia Politicians and Chinese and Japanese Immigrants, 1858–1914.* Vancouver: UBC Press, 1989.

———. *The Triumph of Citizenship: The Japanese and Chinese in Canada, 1941–67.* Vancouver: UBC Press, 2007.

Ruan, Xihu:. *Canadian Ethnography.* Beijing: Ethnic Publishing House, 2004.

Schofield, Peggy. *The Story of Dunbar.* Vancouver: Dunbar Residents' Association, 2007.

Scholefield, E. O. S., and F. W. Howay. *British Columbia from the Earliest Times to the Present.* Vancouver: S. J. Clark, 1914.

Shen, I-Yao. *Century of Chinese Exclusion Abroad.* Beijing: China Social Sciences Publishing House, 1985 (in Chinese text).

Sun Yat-sen Research Institute of Sun Yat-sen University, History Institute of Guangdong Academy of Social Sciences, and Department of Republican Chinese History under Institute of Modern History of Chinese Academy of Social Sciences. *Sun Yat-sen.* Beijing: Zhonghua Book Company, 1985 (in Chinese text).

Tan, Jin, and Patricia E. Roy. *The Chinese in Canada*. Ottawa: Canadian Historical Association, 1985.

Wang Bing. *Cultural Mosaic: Canadian Immigration History*. Beijing: Ethnic Publishing House, 2002 (in Chinese text).

Wang, Jiwu. *His Dominion and the Yellow Peril*. Waterloo, ON: Wilfrid Laurier University Press, 2006.

Warburton, Rennie. "The Workingmen's Protective Association, Victoria, BC, 1878: Racism, Intersectionality and Status Politics." *Labour/Le Travail* 43 (Spring 1999): 105–120.

Ward, W. Peter. *White Canada Forever*. Montreal: McGill-Queen's University Press, 1978.

Wickberg, Edgar, et al. "Chinese and Canadian Influences on Chinese Politics in Vancouver, 1900–1947." *BC Studies* 45 (Spring 1980): 37–55.

———. *From China to Canada*. Toronto: McClelland & Stewart, 1982.

Willoughby, W. W. *Opium as an International Problem*. Baltimore, MD: Johns Hopkins University Press, 1925.

Wong, Marjorie. *The Dragon and the Maple Leaf: Chinese Canadians in World War II*. London, ON: Pirie Publishing, 1994.

Woodland, A. *New Westminster: The Early Years, 1858–1898*. New Westminster: Nunage Publishing, 1973.

Wu Ziyun and Robert Amos. "Lee's Benevolent Association (Lishi Gongsuo)." *Chinatown Newsletter* 10, no. 4 (December 2008): 32 (in Chinese text).

Yan Qinghuang. *Overseas Labourers and Mandarins (Overseas Chinese Labourers and Qing Government Officials: Protection of Overseas Subjects in Late Qing Dynasty, 1851–1911)*. Translated by Su Mingxian and He Yuefu. Beijing: China Friendship Publishing House, 1990 (in Chinese text).

Yee, Paul. *A Walking Tour of Vancouver's Chinatown*. Vancouver: Weller Cartographic Services, 1983.

———. *Chinatown: An Illustrated History of the Chinese Communities of Victoria, Vancouver, Calgary, Winnipeg, Toronto, Ottawa, Montreal, and Halifax*. Toronto : James Lorimer & Company, 2005.

———. *Saltwater City*. Vancouver: Douglas & McIntyre, 2006.

Zhuang Goutu. Relationship between Overseas Chinese and China. Guangzhou: Guangdong Higher-Education Publishing House, 2001 (in Chinese text).

INDEX

288 — GREAT FORTUNE DREAM